Robert J. Pellegrini, PhD
Theodore R. Sarbin, PhD
Editors

Between Fathers and Sons
Critical Incident Narratives
in the Development
of Men's Lives

Pre-publication
REVIEWS,
COMMENTARIES,
EVALUATIONS . . .

"**W**ith *Between Fathers and Sons*, diverse communities of readers are beckoned toward a shared reading of self, memory, and cultural conventions. This edited volume houses two significant desired projects, inviting to both scholars interested in narrative psychology and those engaged in contemporary projects to understand the form and meaning of men's lives. The book prepares an ingenious recipe: ask a selective group of American psychologists to produce a personal account of father-son relations. That recipe is at once theoretical and textual, experimental and experiential, autobiographical and analytic, and the contributors individually excel in generating rich—sometimes sweet, sometimes savory, and occasionally bitter—stories. Composed by men undeniably skilled in analyzing the commonalities as well as particularities of everyday life, the narratives offer readers remarkable and critically meaningful if, at times, apparently mundane moments of father-son relations. The enactments of fathers and sons pristinely recounted in the chapters often yield an understanding of masculine psychology as at once what it appears to be and much more than it appears to be. The memories and remembrances can be seen as actions, performative and redescribed across time, that inform the lives not only of those who witness the original events, but also others distant in time and space from the originating moment."

Jill Morawski, PhD
Professor of Psychology,
Wesleyan University,
Middletown, CT

More pre-publication
REVIEWS, COMMENTARIES, EVALUATIONS . . .

"This is a book of stories about fathers by their sons—all prominent psychologists. Each unearths critical incidents from his store of memories to gain an understanding of his father and of how his own way of being in the world was shaped by their relationship to each other. The significance of this relationship is not in question but the specific ways in which a father's character, values, and styles may be replicated or resisted—and often both—turn out to be complex and diverse. And it becomes clear in these stories that this process does not end in childhood or in the resolution to a teenager's identity crisis, but continues into adulthood. The strength of this collective effort is that it opens up issues of male identity development for further theoretical and empirical study. There is no special pleading here for one 'best' type of fathering, but rather a sensitivity to the complexity of such deep relationships and an alertness to the social, cultural, and historical contexts in which they are embedded."

Dr. Elliot G. Mishler
Professor of Social Psychology,
Department of Psychiatry,
Harvard Medical School

"As an empirically oriented social psychologist, with interests in emotion and psychophysiology, I approached this edited volume of personal narratives about fathers and sons with some reservation and a good deal of curiosity. It proved to be fascinating, and I will recommend it heartily to both my students and colleagues. It will serve well in seminars on emotion, personality, development, and social psychology, and as supplemental reading in undergraduate classes on those topics. Active investigators in these fields will find themselves stimulated by the content of the narratives, by the challenge they pose to our more conventional investigative approaches to understanding, and by the metatheoretical implications of the narrative strategy."

G. P. Ginsburg, PhD
Professor Emeritus,
University of Nevada, Reno

"This is a warm, intriguing book that lures readers to look at their own fathers. Seventeen men recount episodes that capture the essence of their fathers and allow readers to see how their relationships with their fathers affect not only the present but also the future with their own children and grandchildren. The fathers of these men were important. No father was perfect, yet each was crucial in passing the torch of the future to his son. This book will warm the heart and stir the memories of male and female readers alike."

Margaret Thaler Singer, PhD
Professor Emerita,
Department of Psychology,
University of California, Berkeley

Between Fathers and Sons
*Critical Incident Narratives
in the Development
of Men's Lives*

HAWORTH Marriage and the Family
Terry S. Trepper, PhD
Executive Editor

Parents, Children, and Adolescents: Interactive Relationships and Development in Context by Anne-Marie Ambert

Women Survivors of Childhood Sexual Abuse: Healing Through Group Work: Beyond Survival by Judy Chew

Tales from Family Therapy: Life-Changing Clinical Experiences edited by Frank N. Thomas and Thorana S. Nelson

The Therapist's Notebook: Homework, Handouts, and Activities for Use in Psychotherapy edited by Lorna L. Hecker and Sharon A. Deacon

The Web of Poverty: Psychosocial Perspectives by Anne-Marie Ambert

Stepfamilies: A Multi-Dimensional Perspective by Roni Berger

Clinical Applications of Bowen Family Systems Theory by Peter Titelman

Treating Children in Out-of-Home Placements by Marvin Rosen

Your Family, Inc.: Practical Tips for Building a Healthy Family Business by Ellen Frankenberg

Therapeutic Intervention with Poor, Unorganized Families: From Distress to Hope by Shlomo A. Sharlin and Michal Shamai

The Residential Youth Care Worker in Action: A Collaborative, Competency-Based Approach by Robert Bertolino and Kevin Thompson

Chinese Americans and Their Immigrant Parents: Conflict, Identity, and Values by May Paomay Tung

Together Through Thick and Thin: A Multinational Picture of Long-Term Marriages by Shlomo A. Sharlin, Florence W. Kaslow, and Helga Hammerschmidt

Developmental-Systemic Family Therapy with Adolescents by Ronald Jay Werner-Wilson

The Effect of Children on Parents, Second Edition by Anne-Marie Ambert

Clinical and Educational Interventions with Fathers by Jay Fagan and Alan J. Hawkins

Couples Therapy, Second Edition by Linda Berg-Cross

Family Therapy and Mental Health: Innovations in Theory and Practice by Malcolm M. MacFarlane

How to Work with Sex Offenders: A Handbook for Criminal Justice, Human Service, and Mental Health Professionals by Rudy Flora

Marital and Sexual Lifestyles in the United States: Attitudes, Behaviors, and Relationships in Social Context by Linda P. Rouse

Psychotherapy with People in the Arts: Nurturing Creativity by Gerald Schoenewolf

Critical Incidents in Marital and Family Therapy: A Practitioner's Guide by David A. Baptiste Jr.

Family Solutions for Substance Abuse: Clinical and Counseling Approaches by Eric E. McCollum and Terry S. Trepper

Between Fathers and Sons: Critical Incident Narratives in the Development of Men's Lives by Robert J. Pellegrini and Theodore R. Sarbin

Women's Stories of Divorce at Childbirth: When the Baby Rocks the Cradle by Hilary Hoge

Between Fathers and Sons
Critical Incident Narratives in the Development of Men's Lives

Robert J. Pellegrini, PhD
Theodore R. Sarbin, PhD
Editors

THCPP

The Haworth Clinical Practice Press
An Imprint of The Haworth Press, Inc.
New York • London • Oxford

Published by

The Haworth Clinical Practice Press, an imprint of The Haworth Press, Inc., 10 Alice Street, Binghamton, NY 13904-1580.

Cover design by Anastasia Litwak.

Library of Congress Cataloging-in-Publication Data

Pellegrini, Robert J.
   Between fathers and sons: critical incident narratives in the development of men's lives / Robert J. Pellegrini, Theodore R. Sarbin.
      p. cm.
   Includes bibliographical references and index.
   ISBN 0-7890-1511-0 (alk. paper)—ISBN 0-7890-1512-9 (alk. paper)
   1. Fathers and sons. I. Sarbin, Theodore R. II. Title.

HQ756 .P45 2002
306.874'2—dc21

                                                                              2001039109

This book is dedicated to Bob Pellegrini Jr., Ted Sarbin Jr., Jim Allen, and Ron Allen, the sons who have enriched the narratives of *our* lives beyond measure, and to the loving memory of Genevieve Sarbin, whose humor and nurturant vitality will live forever in the hearts of all of us who had the extraordinary good fortune to share any part of our lives with her.

CONTENTS

ABOUT THE EDITORS

Robert J. Pellegrini, PhD, is Professor of Psychology and Chairman of the Psychology Department at San Jose State University. He has served as a National Institute of Mental Health Research Fellow in clinical methods at the University of Colorado School of Medicine. He has also taught extensively in alternative educational outreach programs for maximum-security prisoners.

Dr. Pellegrini has published widely in the study of personality and social psychology. His book Psychology for Correctional Education is the standard reference for its field. His current research is inspired by his time as a Research Associate at the University of California at Santa Cruz, under the mentorship of Dr. Theodore Sarbin, and is focused on holistic-organismic studies of personal identity development and adjustment.

Bob Pellegrini and his son Bob Jr. made history together on August 19, 2000, when both won finalist awards in competitive bodybuilding in the same nationally sanctioned bodybuilding contest.

Theodore R. Sarbin, PhD, is Professor Emeritus of Psychology and Criminology at the University of California at Santa Cruz. Before coming to the Santa Cruz campus in 1969, he taught for twenty years at the Berkeley campus. He has held a number of fellowships, including a Fulbright and a Guggenheim.

Dr. Sarbin has been the recipient of a number of awards, including the Henry A. Murray Award (1994) from Division 8 American Psychological Association. His bibliography contains more than 250 entries, including Believed-in Imaginings: The Narrative Construction of Reality; Constructing the Social; Narrative Psychology: The Storied Nature of Human Conduct; Studies in Social Identity; and Schizophrenia: Medical Diagnosis or Moral Verdict? He is currently working on projects directed toward clarifying the narrative quality of emotional life.

CONTRIBUTORS

Frank J. Barrett, PhD, is Associate Professor of Systems Management at the Naval Postgraduate School, Monterey, California, and a faculty member in the Human and Organizational Development Program at The Fielding Institute. He has written and lectured widely on social constructionism, appreciative inquiry, organizational change, jazz improvisation, and organizational learning. He has published articles on metaphor, masculinity, improvisation, organizational change, and organizational development as well as numerous book chapters.

Ki-Taek Chun, PhD, has served in various management positions at the U.S. Commission on Civil Rights, including deputy director of the Office of Research and director of the Eastern Regional Office. His research interests range over epistemology of psychological theorizing, racial/ethnic and national identity, democracy building, assimilation and cultural pluralism, and cross-cultural methodology. He maintains a practice as a licensed psychologist and has published two books and over forty articles and reports.

Alan C. Elms teaches at the University of California–Davis. His research concentrates on whole-life psychobiography. He has published one book and more are in progress.

Mark Freeman is Professor of Psychology at the College of the Holy Cross, Worcester, Massachusetts, and is the author of two books and numerous articles on the self, autobiographical narrative, and the psychology of art.

John Stanford "Stan" Gergen is a graduate of Duke University. He is a human resources professional in the telecommunications industry. He rejoined Nortel Networks in 2000 in a leadership development and compensation initiatives role.

Kenneth J. Gergen is the Mustin Professor of Psychology, Swarthmore College, Swarthmore, Pennsylvania, and the founder of the

Swarthmore College program in Interpretation Theory. He is Associate Editor of *Theory and Psychology* and *The American Psychologist*.

Genaro Gonzalez, PhD, is Professor of Psychology, University of Texas–Pan American, Edinburg, Texas. His research interests include issues of acculturation and ethnic identity. He has published two novels and a collection of short stories.

George S. Howard's research spans topics in clinical/counseling psychology, consultation, program evaluation, prevention, narrative psychology, environmental psychology, and sport psychology. His specialty is in developing alternate methodologies for probing research questions that are resistant to traditional methodologies.

Joseph B. Juhasz, PhD, is Professor of Architecture and Environmental Design at the University of Colorado. He is the author of well over 200 professional publications.

Ernest Keen, PhD, retired in 2000 after thirty-six years of teaching at Bucknell University, Lewisburg, Pennsylvania. He has published six books, earlier in existential-phenomenological psychology and psychotherapy, and most recently focusing on psychopharmacology and its accompanying philosophical problems.

James C. Mancuso, PhD, is Professor Emeritus at the University of Albany–State University of New York. He has published five books exploring the process of developing a theory of personality, in addition to about sixty journal articles and book chapters. He has investigated and written about parenting practices, particularly reprimand processes, the processes of motivation and emotion, and the use of narrative in framing personal anticipatory role constructions.

Chase Martini is an eighth grader at the Davis Drive Middle School, Cary, North Carolina.

Julian Rappaport, PhD, is Professor of Psychology and a member of the Clinical/Community and Personality and Social Ecology Programs at the University of Illinois at Urbana-Champaign. His research has been concerned with empowerment theory and alternatives to professional services for people who are typically labeled as dependent or disordered. His current interests are in the relationship between community narrative and personal stories in the construction of identity.

George C. Rosenwald, PhD, is Professor of Psychology at the University of Michigan and a psychotherapist in private practice in Ann Arbor, Michigan. For more than twenty years he has been involved in research using life history materials, narratives, interviews, and the multiple case study format.

William McKinley Runyan, PhD, teaches in the School of Social Welfare at the University of California at Berkeley, formerly on human development and abnormal psychology, and more recently on personality theory life histories and case studies. Since 1994, he has been working on the biographical side of the history of psychology.

Karl E. Scheibe, PhD, is Professor of Psychology at Wesleyan University, Middletown, Connecticut and Professor at DUXX, Graduate School of Business Leadership, Monterrey, Mexico, and a psychotherapist in private practice. He is the author of four books and the co-editor of two more.

Donald P. Spence, PhD, is Clinical Professor of Psychiatry at the Robert Wood Johnson Medical School, University of Medicine and Dentistry of New Jersey, Piscataway. He is the author of three books.

Mark B. Tappan, EdD, is Associate Professor and Chair of the Education and Human Development Program at Colby College in Waterville, Maine. He is the co-editor of two books and has published numerous articles and book chapters in the areas of moral development, moral education, narratives, hermeneutics, gender differences, and adult development.

Richard E. Tappan, EdD, spends time in community volunteer work and genealogical research in his retirement. His life work has included ministry on the college campus, denominational administration, junior college teaching and administration, and retirement center administration.

Chapter 1

General Introduction

Robert J. Pellegrini

FROM A STORY TO A BOOK

This collection of stories about critical incidents in men's father-son experience developed out of a flashback memory scene that occurred to me while on a high desert wilderness trip with my own son. I was absolutely taken by the moving clarity of that spontaneous obtrusion into consciousness of an otherwise very long-lost childhood event. I'm not sure whether it was more for professional or purely personal reasons, but I recorded this reminiscence in a few lines scrawled hastily on the back of a paper placemat that Bob Jr. and I had used to wrap some leftover bread from the last indoor place at which we would eat for a week or so.

Upon our return home, I relegated those placemat notes to my "I'll Get Back to This Eventually" file. Operationally, the latter file is nothing more than a pile of wastepaper stored indefinitely in a drawer, insofar as I haven't retrieved anything from it in the thirty-two years of its existence. There those notes remained for several weeks, until I related the story to Sam Maio, an award-winning writer and literary critic who teaches English here at San Jose State University. When he asked to see what I had written, I told him that all I'd produced looked like a sketchy, fragmented diary entry by someone who doesn't keep a diary. He urged me to elaborate those musings into an organized form and submit the finished product for publication.

In short, thanks to the persistent encouragement of Dr. Sam Maio and Dr. Dona De Sanctis, Communications Director of the National Italian American Foundation in Washington, DC, an adapted version of the essay which is my contribution to this anthology, and which ultimately inspired this book, was published as a featured article in *Ambassador* magazine (Pellegrini, 1998).

My friend and mentor Ted Sarbin has taught me a lot of things, not the least of which is an appreciation of the narrative as root metaphor for the study of psychology. From the perspective of a narrative psychologist, and not just a guy writing down observations about his boyhood, it was clear to me that in constructing the story described previously, I had touched upon some very fundamental stuff in my life. Almost simultaneously, it occurred to me that the kind of autobiographical exercise in which I had engaged here might serve as a useful paradigm for exploring the development of men's consciousness in general, and the development of their identity in particular. Thus, I prevailed upon Ted, who, at the age of ninety, has more professional deadlines and project commitments than anyone else I know, to help me produce this book.

In asking for Ted's help, I confess to feeling more than a little bit guilty about how strongly I emphasized the centrality of his influence on the thinking out of which the idea evolved, and the fact that without his contribution, the book would never be. His career-long pattern of inability to refuse such invitations from students, friends, and colleagues persisted. He agreed, and our partnership in this project was established.

RATIONALE, OBJECTIVES, AND METHOD

As discussed in more detail below, the emotional life of men and boys has only quite recently come to the forefront of systematic attention from a number of professional perspectives. Clearly, the previous scarcity of such formal scrutiny reflects a traditional pattern of gender role definition observed in cultures throughout the world, whereby males are encouraged to minimize their public expression of sentimental acts and to maximize their expression of instrumental ones. Given this legacy, along with its homophobic component, it's not at all surprising that the issue of men's emotional relationships to one another has been so widely ignored.

The work presented here involves a narrative approach to exploring the same-sex relationship that occurs, in one way or another, in every man's life. This unique collection of essays is offered as a novel inquiry into the nature of father-son relationships, and how the power and meaning of those relationships may be revealed in autobiographical essays about critical incidents in men's lives.

The purpose of this project was *not* to produce a comprehensive, analytic review of literature relevant to the topic at hand. Nor was the intent to assemble a compendium of scholarly referenced dos and don'ts about such matters, packaged as a mechanistically structured, behavioral cookbook for fathering (or "soning" for that matter). Rather, the book was designed to speak to the heart and soul of what it means to be a father or a son, through a series of autobiographical, critical incident glimpses into men's personal experiences in these roles. Thus, each contributor was asked to write a story about an experience in his life as either father or son, where the event had an especially meaningful, longevous, perhaps even turning-point-like influence on one, both, or perhaps even other individuals involved in the episode.

Format

The contributors' task was to write a good story rather than scholarly text. So as to encourage rather than just permit a creative diversity of style and content representations, few restrictions were imposed on the construction of these essays. In fact, the only structural guidelines prescribed as parameters were for the authors to tell (a) when the incident happened, (b) where it happened, and (c) who were the people involved. Otherwise, the assignment was left completely to the writers' own freestyle, artistic-expressive devices.

Orientation

Since personal experience was the subject matter here, the autobiographical essay was chosen as content vehicle. In accord with the concepts of narrative psychology (Sarbin, 1986), the primary working assumption here is that the meaning of interpersonal relationships, between fathers and sons or otherwise, is encoded in personal constructs of the individual, which are organized cognitively in the form of stories. A corollary to the latter view is that, like scenes in a theatrical production, the discrete events of our lives are identified, integrated, differentiated, and remembered in terms of one or more themes and subthemes of the stories in which they are encoded. This book is all about stories that the writers offer as representing critical incidents or aspects of their own lives as fathers or sons.

Essay Contributors

Authors of the essays presented here are all men who have devoted their professional lives to the study and guidance of human development as social scientists, educators, and/or clinical practitioners. Congruent with the orientation described above, these invited contributors are all part of a growing cadre of professionals whose work qualifies them as narrative psychologists. These selection criteria were premised on the assumption that the contributors so chosen would all have the skills, experience, and inclination to communicate articulately about critical father-son incidents in their own lives. Commentary on the narratives is provided by Ted Sarbin, whose own work is widely identified with the definition, advancement, and assimilation of narratological approaches in the social sciences. Sarbin's commentary is offered in Chapter 2. The contributed essays have been grouped thematically according to a three-perspective schema. This grouping reflects the extent to which the stories have been judged to emphasize one or another of three overlapping dimensions of psychological development: (a) identity, (b) emotional life, and (c) self-understanding.

Target Audience

In academic settings, it is hoped that this book will find its place as a supplementary text for a wide variety of courses in psychology (e.g., social psychology, personality, human development, maturity and aging) as well as other courses dealing with human relationships in anthropology, communication studies, and sociology (e.g., marriage and the family). Beyond formal academic readership, it is hoped that the book will have a more widespread appeal to people interested in thoughtfully produced pieces that talk to *both* men and women about core relationships in their lives.

CONTEMPORARY SOCIOCULTURAL CONTEXT

Across a broad spectrum of ideological orientations today, there is an apparently deepening concern about the American family. In a particularly trenchant sociological analysis, Dana Mack (1997) has argued that we are living in an increasingly family-hating culture, wherein the various institutions of our society are undermining the family in what she characterizes as an "assault on parenthood." Mack's scholarly critique is representative of a diversely constituted genre of contemporary thought, focusing on what is seen as an erosion in American family values and structure since the end of World War II. From this perspective, parental roles, parents' quality and intensity of sincere involvement with and commitment to their children, and children's sense of trust in and connectedness to their own loving, caring parents, are all seen as having deteriorated in the post–World War II period. The resulting devolution in the nuclear family attributed to this process is regarded as presenting enormous challenges to every institution in our society at best, and as an imminent threat to the viability of our democracy at worst.

To many contemporary social scientists, public officials, religious community and civic leaders, as well as members of the population in general, changes that have occurred in the American family over the past fifty years or so signal an unraveling of the fiber out of which the very best of life in our society is woven. And statistics indicative of all sorts of social pathology, from the alarming numbers of children bringing guns and other weapons to school every day to the plummeting of SAT scores, are invoked (Bennett, 1994) as empirical testimony to the measurable consequences of such unraveling. As Mack has put it, the statistical data represent "only the peak of a slow-growing iceberg of childhood misery in our country" (1997, p. 14).

If there was a crucial event impelling the recent wave of concern about the American family, it was probably the 1992 presidential campaign speech by then Vice President Dan Quayle, in which he suggested that the plight of America's inner-city children could be traced to a crisis in family values. He focused on single-parent lifestyles as central to this crisis, and on the apparent approval and acceptance, and maybe even glorification, of the one-parent family in popular culture. The often acrimonious public debate and controversy that followed was doubtlessly intensified by Quayle's specific reference to the TV show *Murphy Brown*. Quayle observed that despite the image conveyed in that show, children *need* fathers, and that in economically impoverished neighborhoods where father absence has become the norm, gang leaders are the only real-life role models of manhood available to boys.

Criticizing one of America's favorite situation comedy characters proved to be politically injudicious for Quayle's campaign effort. In so doing, he not only ignited a firestorm of heightened consciousness about American family values, but also provided the catalyst for serious reappraisal of *fathering* as a potentially critical variable mediating many of America's most serious problems. Murphy Brown had become something of a heroic icon of the strong, independent, professional woman raising her born-out-of-wedlock child quite on her own, in a society in which sexual equality and tolerance had evolved to the point where such things are taken as pretty much OK. Media advocates and personalities quickly responded with highly critical, often derisive counterargument to Quayle's comments. But as the debate on this issue unfolded, Quayle's critics were confronted with a substantive volume of social scientifically established evidence indicating a greater incidence of emotional problems, failure in school, and criminal delinquency among children raised in single-parent, female-headed families.

As it turns out, Quayle's point of view is supported by the results of a number of well-respected studies (Dawson, 1991; Ensminger, Kellam, and Rubin, 1983; Kellam, Ensminger, and Turner, 1977; Wadsworth, 1979). As such data became ever more widely cited in the ongoing exchange, a discernible transformation occurred in media coverage of the "family values" issue. Thus, in a 1992 article titled "The Murphy Brown Policy," Quayle's position was ridiculed in *Newsweek* as representing an obsolete way of thinking that was a ". . . '50's fantasy of mom and dad and 2.2 kids [that] went the way of phonograph records and circle pins" (Clift, 1992, p. 46). A little over a year later, *Newsweek* featured a cover story titled "Endangered Family," in which the authors proclaimed that "Fatherless homes boost crime rates, lower educational attainment and add dramatically to the welfare rolls" (Chideya et al., 1993, p. 17). Representative of the shift in both content and tone of media attitudes regarding this controversy was a widely quoted *Atlantic Monthly* article titled "Dan Quayle Was Right," in which Barbara Dafoe Whitehead (1993) decried the trends toward illegitimacy and divorce in America as reflecting an adult mentality of self-involved individualism, expressed in a preoccupation with personal fulfillment that overrides parents' concern for their children's developmental needs. According to Whitehead's logic, this kind of self-involvement is indulged at the expense of our children, who are thereby deprived of the opportunity to grow to adulthood in the comfort, security, and stability of an intact family.

Public sentiment still seems to lean quite decidedly toward acknowledging the functional significance of the traditional, intact family for the raising of children. In accord with such attitudes, a number of organizations have been formed with the goal of putting absent fathers back into their children's lives. Among the most influential of these is the National Fatherhood Initiative in Pennsylvania, whose advocacy efforts are directed toward the establishment of public policies aimed at putting an end to fathers' emotional and financial abandonment of their children. The National Center for Fathering in Kansas has established a database for fathering statistics, as well as information on fathering, community resources to facilitate fathering, etc. Popular books continue to emerge, addressed to all sorts of practical issues relevant to the operational aspects of fathering (Golant, 1992; Levine, 1998).

Thematically, this book interfaces with heightened consciousness concerning the critical role of fathering in children's lives as described above, and a concomitant trend toward systematic inquiry into the nature of *men's* lives, apparently inspired by intensified attention to women's issues over the past thirty years. The institutionalized legitimacy of men's studies as an area of professional specialization is indicated by the establishment of corresponding divisions and subdivisions within professional organizations (e.g., the American Psychological Association's Society for the Psychological Study of Men and Masculinity).

Historically, with some noteworthy exceptions (e.g., Parke, 1981), fathering has been relegated to a status of relatively benign neglect in the field of developmental psychology. At least in part, it seems likely that the comparatively greater attention to mothering follows from a long-established view of the mother-infant bond as the most critical interpersonal emotional attachment in a child's life (Ainsworth, 1982, 1989; Bowlby, 1969, 1973, 1979). However, the father's role in parenting has become an increasingly active area of research by developmental psychologists over the last decade or so (Parke, 1996; Phares, 1992).

The provocative bestseller *Iron John,* in which Robert Bly (1990) addresses a number of problems including the effects of remote fathers and the disappearance of male initiation rites in our culture, provided an engaging literary contribution to the modern study of men's psychosocial development. More recently, McLean, Carey, and White (1996) have examined contextual relativity of the multiple and often contradictory meanings of masculinity, in a collection of essays written from a social constructionist point of view. McLean et al. consider problems such as structured power, inequality, and oppression within a framework that simultaneously acknowledges women's ongoing struggle for gender justice. William Pollack's (1998) book, subtitled *Rescuing Our Sons from the Myths of Boyhood,* deals with outdated gender stereotypes that compel conformity to an inhibiting "Boy Code," with its profoundly dysfunctional impact on the lives of the individuals so pressured, as well as the whole society in which they grow to manhood. Even more recently, Susan Faludi (1999) has argued eloquently in her book titled *Stiffed: The Betrayal of the American Man,* that understanding the "male crisis" in America today requires serious consideration of father-son relationships.

To this growing body of work concerned with the social/cognitive complexities that operate to give structure and meaning to men's experiences of their own reality, thus impacting on the way they think, feel, and act in all sorts of situations, we now offer our book. Here, the father-son relationship is examined through the unique quality of personal depth that is achieved through autobiographical narrative reconstructions of experiences that may be described as focal, central, salient, or critical incidents in the writers' lives.

THE ESSAYS

The prompt to invited contributors was planned to encourage a variety of styles and content representation. Contributors' responses fulfilled the latter plan at a level of success beyond our wildest expectations. I guess that's what happens when you give a novel, ego-involving task to superb writers who are also experienced social scientists, educators, and practitioners. On balance, if structural uniformity was compromised somewhat for an enlivened richness of meaning here, the resulting benefits of this trade-off are seen by the co-editors as having greatly outweighed the costs. In any case, as noted above, the essays are presented in three sections organized according to judged emphasis on the development of identity (Section I), emotional life (Section II), and self-understanding (Section III).

Clearly, the freedom to write with minimal constraints about a very personal aspect of the writer's own life facilitated just the kind of creatively articulate expression we hoped to elicit. Just as clearly, this was a task in which each of the contributors became very deeply involved, which engaged their considerable technical-cognitive skills, and also aroused their passion. Each of these narratives has an elegance of its own. The co-editors take this opportunity to thank all of those whose work is represented here for the collective contribution of their time, energy, exquisite skill, and abundantly apparent pride-of-craft that allowed this finished product to happen.

AND JUST ONE MORE THING

From the outset, the only agenda for this book was to promote further understanding of personality and social development in men, using a critical incident narrative approach focused exclusively on the father-son relationship. This project was not structured in terms of constraints imposed by any a priori theoretical, empirical, social, or political formulations regarding the ontogenesis of male gender roles or alternative expressions of "male identity." Thus, any reliable insights of the latter sort that may be derived from these essays or their deconstruction are accepted as serendipitously coincidental to our primary objective. It is hoped, however, that at least some of the experiential observations and conceptual interpretations offered here will contribute not just to more dialogue, formal theory, and empirical inquiry, but to substantive humanistic social changes in thought, feeling, and action that effectively enhance the relationships between all fathers and sons, as well as their relationships with all of the mothers and daughters in their lives.

REFERENCES

Ainsworth, M. D. S. (1982). Attachment: Retrospect and prospect. In C. M. Parkes and J. Stevenson-Hinde (Eds.), *The place of attachment in human behavior* (pp. 3-30). New York: Basic Books.

Ainsworth, M. D. S. (1989). Attachments beyond infancy. *American Psychologist 44*, 709-716.

Bennett, W. J. (1994). *The index of leading cultural indicators.* New York: Touchstone.

Bly, R. (1990). *Iron John: A book about men.* Reading, MA: Addison-Wesley.

Bowlby, J. (1969). *Attachment and loss: Vol. 1. Attachment.* New York: Basic Books.

Bowlby, J. (1973). *Attachment and loss: Vol. 2. Separation: Anxiety and anger.* New York: Basic Books.

Bowlby, J. (1979). *Attachment and loss: Vol. 3. Loss.* New York: Basic Books.

Chideya, F. (1993). Endangered family. *Newsweek* August 30, p. 17.

Clift, E. (1992). The Murphy Brown policy. *Newsweek* June 1, p. 46.

Dawson, D. A. (1991). Family structure and children's health: United States, 1988. U. S. Department of Health and Human Services, *Vital and Health Statistics* Series 10, No. 178, June.

Ensminger, M. E., Kellam, S. G., and Rubin, B. R. (1983). School and family origins of delinquency: Comparisons by sex. In K. T. Van Dusen and S. A. Mednick (Eds.), *Prospective studies of crime and delinquency* (pp. 73-97). Boston: Kluwer-Nijhof.

Faludi, S. (1999). *Stiffed: The betrayal of the American man.* New York: Morrow-Williams.

Golant, M. (1992). *Finding time for fathering.* Westminster, MD: Fawcett Books.

Kellam, S. G., Ensminger, M. E., and Turner, R. J. (1977). Family structure and the mental health of children: Concurrent and longitudinal community-wide studies. *Archives of General Psychiatry 34,* 1012-22.

Levine, J. A. (1998). *Working fathers.* Orlando, FL: Harvest Books.

Mack, D. (1997). *The assault on parenthood: How our culture undermines the family.* New York: Simon and Schuster.

McLean, C., Carey, M., and White, C. (Eds.) (1996). *Men's ways of being.* Boulder, CO: Westview Press, Inc.

Parke, R. D. (1981). *Fathers.* Cambridge, MA: Harvard University Press.

Parke, R. D. (1996). *Fathering.* Cambridge, MA: Harvard University Press.

Pellegrini, R. J. (1998). Reality: Who Needs it! *Ambassador 38,* 28-31.

Phares, V. (1992). Where's Poppa? The relative lack of attention to the role of fathers in child and adolescent psychopathology. *American Psychologist 47,* 656-664.

Pollack, W. S. (1998). *Real boys: Rescuing our sons from the myths of boyhood.* New York: Random House.

Sarbin, T. R. (Ed.) (1986). *Narrative psychology: The storied nature of human conduct.* New York: Praeger.

Wadsworth, M. E. (1979). *Roots of delinquency.* New York: Barnes and Noble.

Whitehead, B. D. (1993). Dan Quayle was right. *Atlantic Monthly 271,* April, 47-50.

Chapter 2

Sons and Fathers: The Storied Nature of Human Relationships

Theodore R. Sarbin

When Bob Pellegrini and I began this project, we intended it to be a contribution to the field of contemporary discourse that has come to be known as narrative psychology (Sarbin, 1986; Bruner, 1986; McAdams, 1993). Central to narrative psychology is the premise that we live in a story-shaped world. Stories may be said to have an ontological status as well as being a mode for representing reality. Before their telling, stories are lived in the myriad relationships between persons and things in multidimensioned contexts (Carr, 1986).

The seventeen stories eloquently speak for themselves. In this commentary, I point to some highlights, some commonalities, and some ambiguities. It is important to underscore that these rememberings, like all stories, are *rendered*. No different from other storytellers, the contributors to this volume have engaged in a poetic reconstruction of biographical events. They have taken bits and pieces of rememberings (random text) and rendered them into an emplotted narrative. Whether the stories would satisfy the truth criteria of a cliometric historian is not at issue. They do satisfy the primary criterion of narrative truth—verisimilitude. Each narrative has a coherence, not only a beginning, a middle, and an ending, but also a point. As in any well-told story, the point is the outcome of an explicitly or implicitly recognized moral issue—in some cases resolved, in other cases held in abeyance.

I am grateful to my colleague, Ralph M. Carney, for discussions that were most helpful in rounding out this chapter.

The narrative as a means of understanding human action is put forth as a contrast to traditional scientific methodology. Bruner (1986) supplied specifications and names for the two nonoverlapping ways of doing psychology. To the traditional hypothesis-testing model, he attached the label "paradigmatic"; to the model favored by historians, biographers, and other representatives of the humanities, he applied the "narrative" label. The usual research programs on close relationships follow the paradigmatic, hypothesis-testing format. Life history data are coded and reduced via statistical operations. To make the findings intelligible, the researcher recasts the findings into one or more storied accounts, sometimes using psychological categories such as traits, conditioned responses, cathexes, or complexes to connote the multifaceted efforts of people as agents trying to make their way in an imperfect, unpredictable world.

On the basis of recent work in developmental psychology, the counterintuitive argument has been advanced that parental variables have little, if any, effect on the personality development of offspring (Harris, 1998; Lewis, 1997). The conclusion follows from a methodology that had its origins in mechanistic worldviews, a methodology that sought correlation coefficients for many variables about faceless and nameless parents and offspring. Underlying the methodology was the premise that prediction is the primary goal of science. The low correlations between parental variables and measurements taken in adolescence or adulthood do not generate useful predictions. The failure to find correlations that would allow for prediction is now attributed to the impossibility of taking into account the variety of social, cultural, and even chance happenings that make up the context for living a life (Lewis, 1997). Traditional research methodology is simply not suited to the task of studying close relationships.

In contrast, the present work leans heavily on the worldview of contextualism, the root metaphor of which is the historical act in all its complexities. The narrative format allows for identifying the contexts that may influence or give meaning to any particular action. Adopting a narrative approach, our study of fathers and sons begins and ends with stories about men with proper names. The advantage of storytelling is that contexts can be identified and elaborated. Storytelling avoids the tyranny of laboratory-like methods that are used to pursue the goal of prediction.

GENRES

All the contributors were given the same open-ended instructions—to write of critical incidents involving father and son interactions. Half the contributors adopted a genre other than straight autobiographical reporting. Kenneth Gergen, for example, employed the saga, a story of four generations. His chapter includes contributions written by his son and grandson. In addition to the stories, he offered a penetrating commentary on the transformative effects of participation in emotional life. George Rosenwald chose the epistolary form, writing a letter in reply to the invitation tendered by Pellegrini. His letter included a portrayal of the historical context in which a critical incident occurred. Ernest Keen also made use of the epistolary form by including a letter to his wife that attempted to clarify gender-related issues. Joseph Juhasz adopted the soliloquy, interspersed with stream-of-consciousness renderings in which he compared his self-narrative with that of Hamlet. James Mancuso wrote his contribution as a dialogue, reminiscent of Diderot's *Rameau's Nephew,* in which the writer records a conversation between two voices. Mark Tappan's rendering of a pivotal childhood event was followed by a somewhat different account rendered by his father, which was in a *Rashomon* genre. Alan Elms wrote in the narrative present—a strategy that might influence the reader to adopt an unconventional temporal frame of reference. Stories told to him about his father influenced Elms' development of his adherence to the virtue of responsibility.

STYLE AND CONTENT

Not only is there variation in the genre chosen, the writing style of each contribution has unique qualities and the content of each memoir differs from author to author. George Howard, for example, wrote his memoir in a style favored by sportswriters, a style appropriate to the central theme of his story—the personal gratification resulting from his role as coach to preadolescent basketball players. The remaining contributions are rendered as literary autobiographical sketches. Donald Spence revealed the influence on his own identity development of his father's preference for silence—for "doing" rather than talking. Frank Barrett told of his father's ineptitude in the verbal expression of love and of clumsy strategies of communication that were substitute expressions for love and caring. Ki-Taek Chun wrote in a formal style of conflicts with his son that centered on different role expectations, reflecting the difficulties in acculturation to the host culture. Chun introduced the metaphor of father-son role scripts, ". . . but our role scripts came from different plays authored by different playwrights" (p. 182). Mark Freeman described the persisting narrative force of his father's death on the significance he assigned to what might have been an unremarkable car ride together. Genaro Gonzalez narrated his growing up in Texas among Mexican-American farm workers, of rejection by his father and indifference by his stepfather, and in the end, easing into an "avuncular" relationship with his aging father. Robert Pellegrini's story centers on his relationships with his father and uncle, immigrants who resolved to become Americans, and the power of silence in resolving moral conflicts between father and son. Julian Rappaport's memoir is about a traumatic boyhood incident that influenced him to construct a set of storied imaginings about his father, who had died some years before, and how he used these imaginings as a model for his own identity development. William Runyan's contribution is a tribute to his father and reveals how the positive attributes of the father influenced Runyan's moral and social identity. Karl Scheibe's story contains a theme that is repeated in most of the other narratives—despite living together for twenty or more years, and despite many occasions of mutual caring, the father remained a mystery.

Some authors focused on a single incident that influenced the course of their lives (e.g., Tappan, Rosenwald, Freeman). Others (e.g., Juhasz and Elms) identified a series of interactions. Runyan's memoir also depicted a series of events and augmented the picture of his father with trait descriptors of his personal style.

SACRED STORIES

A close reading of the memoirs reflects the power of stories to guide one's life choices. On examining each memoir, it becomes clear that the stories sons tell about their fathers are not merely entertaining accounts of father and son interactions. These stories have a special sacred quality bordering on the mythic. I am not using "sacred" in its religious sense. Sacred stories are highly valued, not unlike treasured possessions. Also, they are durable and persistent. They are consulted in times of stress. In reflecting about the seventeen contributions, it becomes apparent that every author's telling of critical or focal incidents is the telling of a sacred story. Julian Rappaport's story may be taken as an example of the sacred. After the traumatic boyhood incident in which his stepfather failed to act on his behalf, Rappaport transformed disconnected scraps of information about his deceased father into a story. With very little in the way of concrete facts, he poetically constructed a portrait of his father as a lover of books. In addition, from knowledge that his father as a young man had shoveled coal in the boiler room of a merchant marine vessel, Rappaport fashioned a fantasy of strength and stamina, replete with bulging muscles. Both of these constructions became part of a sacred story, a story that tacitly guided his decisions in critical life situations. Although the portrait of his father was based on imagined extrapolations from minimal bits of information, Rappaport assigned credibility and fidelity to the portrait. The centrality and the long-term influence of this poetic construction qualifies the story as sacred.

THREE PERSPECTIVES

The stories in this anthology may be viewed from at least three overlapping perspectives: (1) as accounts of the function of close relationships in the construction of identity, (2) as identifying significant features in the development of emotional life, and (3) as a means of achieving some degree of understanding of self or other. None of the stories is a pure exemplar of each perspective. It is a matter of emphasis. Some of the authors emphasize the identity perspective. James Mancuso, for example, tells stories of childhood experiences that had a direct bearing on his intellectual development and ultimate professional identity. As noted above, Rappaport's identity development flowered under the guidance of imaginings about his dead father. Other authors emphasize aspects of self-understanding. Juhasz, for example, in the telling of his story, comes to a degree of self-understanding through recounting the identity changes necessitated by his father's religious conversion and name change.

Identity Features

Identity is forged out of relationships, reciprocal actions, and self and other valuations. Each of the stories contains critical father and son incidents that were instrumental in forging a *social identity.* These narratives explicitly or implicitly center on events serving to answer the ever present identity question that takes the form, *who am I?* In addition, some of the stories focus on rememberings of father-son interactions that served to answer questions of the form, *what am I in relation to the Good?* The latter may be called *moral identity* and includes self descriptions of one's connection to the virtues, to socially or individually developed codes of conduct. In practice the two forms of identity overlap. Moral identity questions are always asked and answered in the context of social identity and vice versa. Nevertheless, the separation of social and moral identity is useful for our analytic purposes.

Through the medium of storytelling, the authors fashioned focal narratives that reflected lasting effects on their social and moral identities. All the father-son stories in this anthology reflect the poetics of identity, some more explicitly than others. The poetics of identity involves the framing of one's efforts to locate oneself intelligibly in some storied context. Such framings are influenced by the stock of stories in one's culture, the individual putting idiosyncratic touches on any particular formulaic cultural story.

As I mentioned before, Mancuso's account is a clear exemplar of interactions that influenced the forming of a social identity. The teasing "wet hair" experience laid the groundwork for Mancuso's interest in the construction of meaning, an interest that guided his studies and ultimately his identity as a theorist and practitioner of constructivist psychology.

Donald Spence's memoir is another instance of social identity linked to stories about father. The introductory account of his father being a man of action and of few words has the mythic properties of a sacred story. His father's setting out on foot from a snowbound dwelling in the dead of winter, expecting to hitchhike to a railroad station with no assurances that the trains were running, to attend a committee meeting two hundred miles away, exemplified the father's personal style: a preference for *doing.* Talk allowed for ambiguities; actions were more trustworthy. Spence connects his social identity—as a life saver in the literal sense and also in the figurative sense as a psycho-analyst—to lessons learned from his father, lessons taught by example rather than didactically.

George Howard's contribution shows the impact of stories in which his father served as a model for his social identity. He links his intellectual and moral development to his mother's guidance and example. It is apparent that Howard's current commitment and enjoyment in his role as basketball coach to preteenagers has direct antecedents in his father's devotion as coach to the boys in Little League baseball teams. The second part of the memoir reflects storied accounts of the father's efforts at nurturance and Howard's growing appreciation of his father's moral qualities, despite the wide gulf in their lifestyles and intellectual interests.

Alan Elms' memoir reflects a direct connection between the stories told about his father and his own moral identity. The connection between father's and son's moral postures was mediated primarily by stories told, not by observation of events. One story had to do with his father's protecting his pregnant wife against an impending car crash. At the time, Elms was in utero. The other story was about his father's declining to consider an attractive opportunity to accompany a friend to distant parts to capitalize on his musical gifts. This event occurred when Elms was an infant. These stories were kept alive in the family, always implying the moral category of paternal responsibility. Like so many other stories told in this anthology, the stories told about Elms' father have the elements of the sacred. The stories are treated as valued possessions; they endure, and they provide the background for Elms' continued attachment to the virtue of responsibility.

Another example of the influence of stories about fathers on social and moral identity is provided in Runyan's contribution. It is primarily a tribute to his father, who appeared to be an exemplar of all the virtues. Runyan took the opportunity to pay tribute to the man who took naturally to the nurturing aspects of fatherhood. The account shows a direct connection between his father's interest and achievements in sports and Runyan's long-time participation in various athletic activities. To the extent that social identity includes placing oneself in a social category such as captain of the soccer team, it is clear that a connection can be made between father and son. From the time he was a young child, his father taught him how to throw and catch a ball and other athletic skills. Runyan struggled with the task of trying to connect the legacy of his father with his own academic interests and achievements. He does entertain the hypothesis that his social identity as a professor and researcher interested in the subjective side of lives may have an indirect connection with the storied portrait of his father that centered on nurturance. Growing up in a paternal environment characterized by warmth and nurturance may have made it easier and safer to inquire and talk about personal experiences.

Emotional Life

All the stories in this anthology reflect features of emotional life, some more clearly than others. As some of the stories are representative of concern with social or moral identity, others recount events that reflect the failures and successes of emotional life. For example, Kenneth Gergen's four-generation saga tells of attempts at love, indifference, disappointment, pride, anger, and guilt. Parenthetically, the reader, now immersed in narratives, will note how effortless it is to interpret these emotion terms as names for narrative plots rather than psychophysiological events.

Mark Tappan wrote his memoir in a unique way. The focus of the story was an event that took place when he was six years old. He wrote of the event and the effect on his life and then invited his father to write his recollection. Each engaged in writing without knowing of the other's rememberings. After they had concluded their writing tasks, they recorded a discussion, which is included in the contribution. The event in question had to do with the son hooking a fish at a campground attended by fathers and sons. The son remembers his father taking the hook out of the fish. In the process, the wriggling fish slipped back into the pond. Without hesitation, the father leaped into the pond, clothes and all, and tried to recapture the fish. But the fish got away.

The father's story covered much the same ground with a major exception: he recaptured the fish. The *Rashomon*-like story has become part of the mythology of the family. Both father and son write of the emotional effects of the event. The son drew the conclusion that his father must have loved him intensely to leap into the pond to retrieve the much-prized catch. It was a turning point in his emotional development in that the concept of paternal love now entered his consciousness. The father interpreted his spontaneous act against the background of the uncertainties in national and international life in the 1960s, among them the resistance to desegregation and the perils of nuclear warfare. Leaping into the pond to catch the fish was an act from a "father who wanted to protect his son from all of the future uncertainties of life" (p. 97). The story of the fish that got away has become a sacred story—it has provided both father and son with a durable emblem of love and caring.

The Tappan memoir shares some features with the story written by Frank Barrett. The remembered story has served as a vehicle for the son's recognition of paternal love. The story is about the gift of a baseball presumably autographed by Barrett's baseball idol. After proudly displaying the ball to his peers, an older boy declared that the name of the hero was misspelled. Barrett reluctantly came to the conclusion that the autograph had been forged by his father. Instead of being disappointed, he was happy that his father cared so much about him that he would go to the trouble of getting the ball and writing the name of the hero on it. The context for this adventure in emotional life is that Barrett's father was inarticulate in expressing his love and nurturant feelings toward his son. Barrett's subsequent discussion places the story of the forged autograph into the category of sacred stories.

Ernest Keen introduces an element of emotional life not explicitly considered by other contributors—the influence of the feminist movement on what have been traditional masculine virtues. Following a contretemps with his wife that centered on his "not reading the directions," he wrote her a letter (reproduced in his memoir) in which he recognized that he had been schooled in self-reliance by his father and by economic necessities. In his explanation of the practice of "not reading the directions," he awakened to remembering his father in actions that bespoke self-reliance as a necessary condition of self-preservation. In the letter he suggested that it is necessary to separate self-reliance as a Good from masculine domination, which is bad. The virtue of self-reliance was handed down to Keen by his father who as a youth had been schooled by his father, who suffered through the rigors of homesteading in the early years of the twentieth century.

Keen discusses the changes in emotional life centering on gender relations as being anchored in generations. He identifies such changes by comparing his sons' constructions of the world with those of his own generation and of his father's. One conclusion is that being a father and being a son are historically situated, a point developed in some detail in Rosenwald's essay.

Silence

To deconstruct the details of emotional life as represented in the seventeen memoirs would be tangential to our purposes. However, a comment seems appropriate about aspects of emotional life that are not usually discussed. In these stories, a critical encounter is met with silence. Traditional theorists of "emotion," involved as they are with psychophysiology, have little to say about the meanings of silence in episodes of emotional life. Silences are an integral feature of communication and are not to be interpreted as absence of communication. Ordinarily, silence is perceived as the ground against which talk or action is the figure. In the examples below, figure and ground are reversed—silence becomes the figure, talk and action the ground. Multiple and sometimes ambiguous interpretations of silences are possible, the interpretation being guided by attention to the total context. Among common interpretations of silence in discourse are the following: anger, disappointment, embarrassment, a pause to gather one's wits, a preference reflecting distrust of talk, attending to an "inner voice," a rhetorical tactic, symbolic withdrawal from confrontation, and a gendered notion about "strong, silent men."

Silences are central to Kenneth Gergen's narrative. "The theme is that of silence—not action but inaction, or rather, action far more consequential by virtue of its very impenetrability as action" (p. 126). He told of several encounters with his father, who characteristically responded to his son's carelessness or rule bending with a heavy silence—a response that led Gergen to interpret the silence as part of a disapproval narrative. His father sat in judgment, as it were, and the silence was the punishment. " . . . those silences seemed to bespeak a disgust the depths of which I could not fathom" (p. 126). In the current telling of the story, Gergen offers a possible reinterpretation of the silence, namely, that his father was hurt and disappointed. The silence was his nonverbal communication of disappointment, a way of communicating that his son's irresponsible conduct had wounded him. Gergen's reflections contain a note of sadness that his father and he were unable or unwilling to hold an intimate conversation that might have clarified the meaning of the silences.

In discussing his relationship with his son, Stan, Gergen tells of intentionally presenting a self to his children that was the opposite of his father who had distanced himself from spontaneous, playful, joyful activity. During his childhood, Stan saw a father who was warm, playful, stimulating, and nonjudgmental. Stan as a rebellious teenager violated the explicit rule not to use the house for a teenage party while the parents were away for the weekend. On his return Gergen found the house had been trashed during a rock and roll party where alcohol was consumed. His response was one of silence—a withholding of communication that lasted six weeks. Gergen recognized that his actions were identical with those of his father for dealing with demonstrations of irresponsibility. Different from the anger script that was almost reflex-like, Gergen recognized that the silence was the only response to having been symbolically wounded by Stan's betrayal of trust. In Stan's contribution to the narrative, silences play a part in several different ways, one of which is silence by absence. His father's frequent travels to foreign lands made him an absentee father. It is noteworthy that Stan metaphorically translated absence as silence.

A moment of silence is central to Bob Pellegrini's narrative. In awakening to the realization that the baseball-shattered window not only brought to an end his own dreams of glory, it also disrupted the fantasies of his father and uncle. The shattering impact of the ball on the glass not only stopped their cutting and stitching, but abruptly ended their involved imaginings in the fanciful and glorious world of grand opera emanating from the radio. In the telling of this boyhood recollection, Pellegrini recognized that the controlled silence of father and uncle not only concealed multiple voices—startlement, anger, hurt, frustration—but, perhaps more importantly, reflected in a refractory moment the adaptation to the abrupt shift from their vicarious participation in the soaring drama of *Otello* or *Rigoletto* to the demanding nuisances of everyday life.

A different kind of silence played a part in Barrett's memoir. He noted that his father would never call just to talk or to learn of his activities. "In those days a large part of our relationship was built upon platitudes and long silences. It kept us going" (p. 112). Barrett notes that his father had no resistance to talking about his son to anyone who would listen. In this context, Barrett plaintively asks, "But why were there so many awkward silences, instances of small talk, and clichés between him and me?" (p. 113).

Another function of silence is noted by Spence. He learned early in life that silence was the best strategy when he made mistakes. His father, whose style of action was "doing" rather than talking, did not believe in explanations. In writing of the influence of his father on his own social and moral identity, Spence noted that talk was less privileged than action and by implication less privileged than silence, " . . . words of any kind always came second to actions; not only did these speak louder but they contained more of a moral presence" (p. 58).

Silences can be a strategy to communicate rejection. Gonzalez created a prolonged silence in his refusal to see or talk to his father. The lengthy silence was intended as a counterrejection for the father's earlier rejection. Just as the father's early rejection had demoted Gonzales to a category of nonperson, the imposed silence carried the same kind of meaning—that the father was not worthy of sharing communication.

Understanding of Self and Other

In this category are those stories that indicate in one way or another that the telling of the story had an effect on understanding one's self or understanding the other (usually the father in these essays). Chun, for example, wrote about persisting unpleasantness with what he perceived as his quarrelsome son. The elder Chun expected the younger to show the deference characteristic of Asian cultures. Chun spent most of his developmental years in Korea and Japan; his son was born and raised in the United States. As the younger Chun adopted the values of his peers in suburban America, the gulf between the two widened. The unpleasantness surrounding the frequent confrontations led the elder to a sharp awareness that the sources of difference were not personal, so to speak, but rather a conflict of cultures. Chun modified his role expectations for his son upon constructing and applying the analogy of two actors reading from different pages in different dramas written by different authors. The interactive nature of the accommodations are reflected in the subtle humor associated with recognition that the father had been "tamed."

George Rosenwald's response to our invitation is in the form of a letter. Not only does he tell a story about an event that happened a half century ago, but he offers the historical and cultural contexts that made the event so meaningful. Some of the other essays make the point about the historical situatedness of social institutions but none so thoroughly as Rosenwald's.

To provide historical background for the focal narrative, Rosenwald discussed observations advanced by Horkheimer and others that during the early years of the twentieth century political and economic factors brought about the decline of parental authority and the concomitant erosion of the moral role of the father. The argument is made that fathers who have little input for decisions about their place in the economic and social worlds are not moral exemplars for their sons. Rosenwald notes his agreement with the general thesis that the particular historical form of society is the background for individual development and family structure. However, to make more intelligible such constructions as authority, family, and individual development, he consulted his personal history for relevant stories. In this connection, he noted that "nothing beats personal narratives when it comes to filling gaps in theory" (p. 218).

Besides the theoretical context, Rosenwald provides the immediate context for the event that became the focus of a story—a sacred story. His parents and he escaped from Vienna to Switzerland during the Nazi terror. Refugees were not allowed employment and were dependent on the charity of Swiss Jews. His father had been a respected lawyer in Vienna. According to the Horkheimer thesis, without employment, his father was supposed to become demoralized and without moral authority for his son. Such was not the case, however. His moral status was maintained in part by the telling of stories of his professional, musical, and social successes in Vienna. In addition, he spent his time learning new skills and languages, and participating in the cultural life of the refugee community. The portrait of his father was that of a man who successfully resisted the degradation of identity that is associated with unemployment and whose social and moral identities were flawless. What a model for an eleven-year-old boy!

Rosenwald's presentation of the theoretical and the social context for the focal event is justified—for without this discussion, the event would have little meaning. In playing the piano accompaniment for a choreographed entertainment for the Jewish community, his father began by playing the wrong overture. Rosenwald was in the wings, not as a participant, but as the son of the pianist, and experienced acute embarrassment. Upon being told by the stage director that he was playing the wrong piece, the father played the correct composition flawlessly. Rosenwald's remembered response to the incident was that his father was not perfect, that he was like others who under pressure make mistakes. More importantly, the event sensitized him to other imperfections that perhaps he had recognized only at the margin of consciousness. Rosenwald regarded the story as a turning point—the beginning of exploring the world from a more realistic perspective.

What of the Horkheimer thesis? Rosenwald does not see the deviation from the theoretical prediction as a falsification of the theory. Rather the theory needs to be augmented with a provision that allows for individual differences in how one responds to the potential demoralization of unemployment.

It is noteworthy that Rosenwald does not remember telling the story to anyone before. One can entertain hypotheses about why the story remained private and only now is released from the vaults of memory. Would the telling of the story to friends or family have put the father in a disapproving light? Would he want to keep intact for others the portrait of the father as a paragon of virtue?

Mark Freeman's essay poignantly reveals the influence of a significant story on his self-development. As a youth, he participated in the counterculture and had no idea of a future time perspective. His relations with his father were cordial but superficial. Like so many other contributors, he is aware that that he did not really know his father.

The significant event in his life was a car ride from college at the end of his sophomore year. Father and son *talked* for four hours, "making up for the strains and silences of a lifetime" (p. 170). The specific content of the conversation is lost to memory, but the subtext remained with the son—that despite his counterculture emblems (such as long hair) he would amount to something; he would find his place in the world. A few weeks after the ride home, noted by Freeman as being in many respects unremarkable, his father died. Freeman delves deeply into the forces at work that rendered the car ride such a significant event. To be sure, the death so soon after was a factor in reconstructing the remembering. He entertains various interpretations and settles on the poetics of memory. He took his point of departure from narrative psychology and contemporary memory research that remembering is reconstructive and dependent on skill in imagining.

Freeman regards his memory as formed through poesis. This conclusion takes him into the function of poetry in one's life; in his case, experiencing his father's absence as a presence. With this construction, the task of understanding the self in relation to rememberings of his father and "what might have been" remains an ongoing and unfinished narrative.

The discussion of the poetic function is consistent with my earlier comments about the fashioning of sacred stories. The poetic function brought together the car ride, the death of the father, and his own search for identity into a sacred story. The memoir contributed by Juhasz brings together the plot of *Hamlet*, early childhood rememberings, family dynamics, living through the Nazi terror, and present-day observations—all in the interest of self-understanding. The currents and cross-currents in his personal narrative, symbolized by stream-of-consciousness renderings, make for conflict, doubt, suppressed anger, thoughts of revenge, and reconciliation. In this commentary, I address features of his narrative that seem central to the status of his self-understanding. Juhasz' father came from German-Jewish stock with the name Haas. Before his son, Joseph, was born, he became a Catholic. At the same time, he took another name, Juhasz. The confusions in the son's identity arising from knowledge of name changes and from religion changes enter into the formidable task of self-understanding. In addition, the father would mysteriously disappear for months at a time.

In employing the "prison-house" metaphor from the speech of the ghost of Hamlet's father, Juhasz implies that the answers to questions about self are constricted by historical events in the family and in the wider society. The father's religious conversion had remote effects into the third generation. The son's three daughters by his first marriage were all baptized in the Catholic faith, although their mother was Jewish. (According to Jewish law and custom, the daughters remained Jewish.) The middle daughter married a Jew and later had a daughter, Juhasz' first grandchild. The naming ceremony for the grandchild followed Jewish traditions, including a service performed by a rabbi. It was at this service that Juhasz was able to reconcile his stories about his father with the innocence of the baby and her entry into the faith of her ancestors.

The denouement of the narrative makes explicit the "longing for continuity," a feature of many other contributions to this anthology.

The form and the content of the Gergen saga reflect this longing. Freeman's narrative invokes such a construction. In the subtexts of the memoirs of Keen, Barrett, and Rappaport, the reader can detect this motivational feature that appears to be central to self-understanding.

REFERENCES

Bruner, J. (1986). *Acts of meaning.* Cambridge, MA: Harvard University Press.

Carr, D. (1986). *Time, narrative and history.* Chicago: University of Chicago Press.

Harris, J. R. (1998). *The nurture hypothesis: Why children turn out the way they do.* New York: Free Press.

McAdams, D. P. (1993). *The stories we live by: Personal myths and the making of the self.* New York: Morrow.

Lewis, M. (1997). *Altering fate: Why the past does not predict the future.* New York: Guilford Press.

Sarbin, T. R. (Ed.) (1986). *Narrative psychology: The storied nature of human conduct.* Westport, CT: Praeger Publishers.

SECTION I:
IDENTITY STORIES

Chapter 3

I Am Older Than My Father

Julian Rappaport

On November 5, 1947, I opened my eyes and ran to the bathroom mirror. If I stood on the toilet seat and opened the medicine cabinet door to just the right angle I could see my whole body, head to toe. I had been certain that on my birthday I would grow taller. I knew I would look different than I had yesterday, when I was only four. Now I wondered, "What does it mean to be 'older'? Does it mean something other than bigger?" If it did I had no idea what; but I *did* know that I could never be older than my father.

For a long time now I have been older than my father. But when I was ten I still did not think that was possible. I did not know anyone older than their father. Actually, I was only guessing about this because I did not know many fathers. But the ones I did know seemed old, a lot older than their kids, and they were either very quiet or very mean. Yet I noticed they seemed to take care of their own children. Sometimes I would see them, father and son, talking together at the ice cream stand down the block. Sometimes I'd see them in school explaining something important to a teacher.

When I was ten I got the first glimmer of a possibility that I could be older than my father and what that might mean. That was when I realized that I might be able to take care of myself. When I grasped that possibility my whole world began to change. I am certain I was ten because I never spoke to Barry again, even though we lived right next door to each other. And that was the last year we walked to school together, or played in the breezeway. That was the year I gave up collecting baseball cards.

Barry and I lived in adjoining Philadelphia row houses. They were two of perhaps twenty-five stuck to one another for half a city block until the breezeway separated them from another twenty-five houses on our side of the street. The breezeway was a remarkable thing. It was like a pond in a wilderness. Right there in the middle of every block in my neighborhood was a green lawn between two houses! Whoever lived there had all the advantages of living on a corner with neighbors only on one side, plus enough open space so you could play with pinkies or pimple rubber balls and not worry about cars running over you, or worse, running over the ball. And there was a wall where you could flip baseball cards with other kids "for keeps." My mother said that the richest people were the ones who lived at the corners (often doctors or dentists who used the ground level as their neighborhood office) or owned a breezeway house. When my mother talked about the neighborhood she always said we lived in a "sixteen-foot-airlite-that-cost-ten-two-ninety," for which we paid $77 a month. I had no idea what she was talking about. But she said the breezeway cost a lot more.

The breezeway house on my block was owned by a pharmacist, but I don't think I ever saw him or his wife. Barry, Alan, and I used to play there and nobody bothered us. The year we moved to the new neighborhood was 1952. We were leaving the public housing project where my father had died five years before and where I first met Ben. Ben was my stepfather. He was a salesman who had never married before. My mother said we were lucky because "who would want to marry a woman with two children?" My sister was thirteen months old when my father died. My mother worried a lot about money and, as it turns out, Ben was a pretty poor salesman. She reminded him of that fairly regularly. Years later when I read *Death of a Salesman* I thought Arthur Miller must have interviewed Ben. I imagined that Ben must have experienced the world exactly the way Willy Loman had.

Although Ben was a "poor provider," I knew that my mother got "veteran's benefits" for me and my sister every month, and would until we were eighteen. I was sure that veteran's benefits meant money because she told us how she paid for our school clothes. She also told us about the life insurance policy that paid her $37 a month for the rest of her life. She said we could get our hero father's GI Bill benefits to pay for college even after we were eighteen. These were things I only faintly grasped, but they were repeated often enough so I "knew" that my father had been a smart, sensitive, caring man who "put his wife first," loved his children, and even though he was dead, continued to provide for us somehow magically through the powers of the "VA," who had declared his death due to a "service connected disability," even though he died at home on our green couch. I remember my father on that couch, his head on a pillow, people gathered around him, someone calling the ambulance. I never saw him again.

The VA said we'd only get the money if we were not adopted by our stepfather, so I never understood why my mother seemed to panic when Ben threatened to leave us, a threat he screamed frequently in their daily arguments. I would have been happy if he had left; but I sometimes had to beg him to stay because my mother seemed very upset when he said he was leaving. Ben was a tall man, much taller than me. His voice was high pitched and shrill. He frightened me because he yelled at me regularly. It was very loud. I do not recall a moment of comfort, fondness, or pleasure that passed between us. Ben could string together graphic profanity in sing-song fashion that reminded me of the burly huckster who drove down the alley-way behind our row of houses, chanting "tomatoesweetcornwatamellon." Ben's favorite was "sonofabitchbastardcocksucker," directed at my mother or me. He never hit me, although once he kicked in the door to my bedroom. I was afraid of him in some way that I did not understand. Now I think perhaps it was more anxiety than fear. He always came into the house from the basement entrance behind it, having driven his car down the same alleyway as the huckster, both singing about what they were selling, I thought. I can still hear the methodical thump, thump, thump as he climbed his way up the thirteen steps of the stairway that led him to me, over and over throughout my childhood.

Every day my mother, who did not complete the tenth grade, told me that I was just like my father who loved books (although we had no books in our house). She said my father wanted to go to college (but he had to go to work to support his family). He had been a high school graduate, a remarkable accomplishment for the son of depression-era immigrants who spoke very little English. More important, he had graduated from Central High School, the place where smart kids went to public school. As I write this, I am wearing the plain gold high school ring my mother kept in a drawer after it was cut off my father's swollen hand when he died. The lettering is almost all worn away, but I can still see the "30" designating his year of graduation.

My father worked for the post office (a secure civil service job that allowed you to take care of your family, I was told). But he had friends who had gone to college, including a nice Negro man named Foster Millen who worked with him. Although my mother never socialized with anyone who was not Jewish, and I never met Mr. Millen, she seemed proud every time she told us the story of Foster Millen's visit for dinner. She always used his full name and referred to him as a "nice Negro man" whenever she mentioned this story. Many years later I found a letter my father had written from England, where he had been stationed during the war. He describes a visit to the library at Cambridge with such pleasure that I do believe he did love books. A family story claims that all his books were destroyed by a fire where they had been put in storage during the war. But when we were growing up there were no books, no pictures on the walls, and no joys that I can remember inside the walls of the row house in Philadelphia.

It was outside the house that I found my pleasures, especially playing in the breezeway. It was there that it happened, one evening in the summertime. Barry, Alan, and I had been playing stickball, but the broomstick we usually used had broken, so Barry got a baseball bat that his father (who my mother called "Ray the Schlimazel") sometimes used when he and Alan's father played for the neighborhood softball team. Ray was a dark shadow of a man who never smiled and rarely spoke. When he was angry at Barry his face was very red. He had huge, thick arms and a stocky body that was very hairy. The hair was all over his arms and it stuck out in dark tufts from the openings in his shirt. As far as I know, my stepfather never spoke to Ray, never played softball, and may never have seen or played any kind of game. But Ben was a lot taller than Ray. Until that day I would have said that Ben was "bigger."

The softball bat was too heavy for the rubber ball we used, so we set it down and decided to flip baseball cards for keeps. This had all the excitement of gambling, and it took some skill. The idea was to stand back at a distance and flip cards against the wall, taking turns. After each round the person whose card was closest to the wall won the cards that were flipped. A leaner was great, but it could be knocked down with the next flip and where it ended up was what counted. Barry was usually better at flipping cards than I was, but although I did not realize it then, this day marked the beginning of a lot a changes for me.

In 1952 Robin Roberts, now in the Baseball Hall of Fame, was the hero of ten-year-old boys in Philadelphia. The baseball cards for him and Richie Ashburn, Del Ennis, and a few others from the pennant-winning 1950 Whiz Kids who had taken the Phillies to the World Series for the first time since 1915 were the most treasured. But Jim Konstanty was something special for those who knew baseball. Here was the player who was among the first great relief pitchers. In 1950 he had appeared in seventy-four games, with an ERA of 2.66 and twenty-two saves. This was a remarkable accomplishment. Nevertheless, his baseball card from the 1950 season was much harder to find than many of the others because his accomplishments had been a surprise. Barry won it from Alan, who had run around the neighborhood for a week showing it off. His father had bought it for twenty-five cents from someone who was obviously a fool, and he gave it to Alan. Eventually Barry, calling Alan a "chicken shit" if he didn't, talked him into including it in the stack of cards he flipped. Barry won it, fair and square. He showed it to his father, who took it to work for a while, showing it off to his friends until Barry convinced him to bring it home. Now it was in Barry's stack of cards, usually on top. But for the last month he would not flip it.

On this summer evening I was in a groove. I was winning more cards than I was losing, and Barry was getting upset. He decided that to change his luck he'd flip the Konstanty. And he threw a leaner, right over a close-to-the-wall flip by Alan, who could not believe it. Konstanty smiled at us as he leaned against the wall. Now it was my turn. I let Wally Jones fly and he hit Konstanty in his wire-rimmed eye-glasses. Big Jim Konstanty fell with Wally Jones on top of him. We ran to look. Mine was touching the wall, beating both the others. I scooped them all up. What happened next is a blur.

Suddenly Ray was there, red-faced, in the breezeway where I had never seen an adult before. He was demanding the card. I was holding it on top of my stack, my thumb pressed to Konstanty's face. The sun was almost gone. The air was cooler than I had thought and I shivered as Ray came closer. I don't know what I said, but I would not give up the card. Barry was yelling. Alan was gone. Ray picked up the thick wooden softball bat and hit me with it. The blow glanced off my head. At first it was dark, then I saw colors, then blood running, dripping on the grass, on my hands. I was alone and my cards were scattered on the ground. Big Jim Konstanty was gone. I left the rest of the cards forever in the breezeway and went home crying, but not from the pain in my head. I was outraged. My sense of justice had been assaulted. My dignity breached. Barry's *father* had hit me! In the breezeway! All the rules were broken. This is the only time in my life that I remember asking my stepfather to help me. I wanted his loud voice to overpower Ray, like it had done to me so many times before.

I stood in the living room of our row house. My mother was, for one of the few times I can recall, very quiet. Ben was pacing up and back saying it was "better not to make trouble." I said I wanted him to demand the card back. What I really wanted was for him to stand over Barry's father and threaten to pound him into the ground if he ever laid a hand on me again. I wanted Ben to be outraged and to take care of me. Before I could say it I knew that it would never happen. I knew that he could not do it, so I did not bother to ask. Ben would not confront Ray the Schlimazel and I was powerless to do anything about it. That night as I lay in my bed, I considered the possibility that I could take care of myself better than they did. That was the night I decided that I would try to be like my father. I would take the chance that I could be like him and not die.

For the rest of the summer I took long walks to the neighborhood library, about two miles from our house. I wanted to find out what it meant to love books enough to have so many that you would have to find a secret place to store them if you had to go away. Now I spent my afternoons there, usually alone, rather than in the breezeway. I rarely took books home, usually preferring to read them at the long wooden tables. I remember reading only *War of the Worlds, When Worlds Collide,* and books about Indiana high school basketball. I know I read a lot of others, but I only faintly recall them—something on King Arthur and, perhaps, *Ivanhoe.* I learned to love it when the librarian told people to be quiet. I would like to say that I suddenly became a member of the local literati, but that would be untrue. I would continue through high school as an adequate but undistinguished student. Yet, by the time the new school year started, I had a strong sense of my own ability to take care of myself. I knew how to find the library and I did continue to go there, always alone. It was a different kind of oasis, but it became my breezeway. I never collected baseball cards or played in the breezeway again.

I began to think about myself as my "real" father's son. I started to believe my mother when she said that I was like him, only occasionally thinking about my own mortality. Now I started to enjoy it when every new teacher would ask why my last name was different from my parents', a circumstance that was more unusual in those days, and a question that until that summer incident I used to dread every year. I began to think about what I knew about my father that could help me take care of myself.

For various reasons my mother had cut herself off from my father's family, and I only occasionally saw any of them. As an adult I have learned a few more things about my father and his family, but growing up I knew little more than I have said so far, other than one important fact. After he graduated from high school, before he married, took his civil service job, went off to the war, and died, my father worked on a merchant marine ship, shoveling coal in the boiler room and "seeing the world." Now I had another image. It was very physical. I imagined him down below, with bulging muscles, sweating, and only late at night reading books in his bed, like me. It was enough so that I could now think of him as a physical being too. I studied a picture of him, looking for myself.

As I began to grow and enjoy the pleasure, different from reading, of physical work and competitive sports I thought of him. When I played high school football my mother and stepfather never saw me. I was glad because I imagined that my father did. When I worked in a grocery store, I loved to be in the hot warehouse, lifting each case of twelve heavy glass soda bottles in sturdy wooden boxes, thinking of my father sweating as he shoveled.

For a high school English class I was expected to do a research paper, and thinking about my father gave me the courage to explore my world. I learned to use the feelings I had experienced on that cold summer evening in the breezeway to express my outrage at injustice. This was 1958, and despite the fact that Martin Luther King Jr. had already been on the cover of *Time* magazine, I recall no conversation at school or elsewhere in my neighborhood about what was happening as the civil rights movement exploded into popular consciousness, much less about black writers. For reasons I don't remember, I proposed to my English teacher a paper on "The Negro in American Literature." I do remember her telling me that it would be OK, if I could find anything, and indeed there was nothing in our school library. The neighborhood public library that had been my oasis was in this case of little help, although I did get referred to the main branch of what was in fact a quite wonderful Philadelphia Public Library. Then I had an idea that made my heart pound! What if I called the NAACP and asked for help? I found them in the phone book and someone said I could come down to their library. It was in a part of town that still remained a mystery to me. It had more than a faint aura of something dangerous. Would it be safe?

I knew that there were black neighborhoods and schools, but I had very little experience outside my own neighborhood. When we played football against one of the black teams there were always rumors about how dirty they would be, about razor blades in their wrist tape, and so on, and I had long since figured out that this was nonsense. But still, Negroes were completely outside my everyday experience, except as the domestic workers I saw taking the trolleycars, or the men dressed in suits who I sat near in the bleachers at Phillies games when Jackie Robinson and the Dodgers were in town. Now I remembered Foster Millen and thought of him with my father. Of course, the idea of being comforted by the thought of my father having dinner with a "nice Negro man" is now an embarrassing one. But for all its condescension, when I was a teenager in the 1950s it was just the kind of counsel I needed.

The small NAACP library was upstairs somewhere in a neighborhood I had never been to. I think it was only one room, but on the shelves were more books by Negro writers than I had ever heard of, let alone seen. I was surprised to find the librarian to be as familiar and helpful as the one at my branch library. I returned many times. I don't have the paper I wrote, and I don't even remember which books I read. But I do remember the smell of them, a smell that I have always liked about books found on library shelves, a smell that I imagined my father had smelled. I do not know if it is literally true, but I have often thought that I must have first read in that poorly lit library the words of Richard Wright in *Black Boy,* published in 1945, describing his own reaction to a library book: "Yes, this man was fighting, fighting with words. He was using words as a weapon, using them as one would use a club." I could club Ray, and all the indignity and injustice of the world, with words. Taking care of myself included learning to use words. I knew what it felt like to be powerless. I knew what it felt like to experience rage. Now I learned that people could write about it.

I learned to seek counsel from my father in ways that did not seem at all unnatural. I simply asked myself, "What do I think he would do?" He never got upset when I had a problem. He never panicked. He never raised his voice. He kept sending money from the VA, paying my bills and giving me time to get better at taking care of myself. He paid my college tuition. When I was told by a guidance counselor that based on my test scores I probably would not be able to get into college, much less graduate, I never believed her. I already knew that I would go to college and figure out how to do it once I got there. I knew that I had no choice; it was my destiny. It had been my father's desire for himself, and if I was going to be myself, I had to go to college. Since then I have never been able to put much faith in the ability of tests to predict the future.

He never did tell me why he died. But now I am much older than him. I would love to talk to him about the things I have learned about justice and dignity, about the power of people to care for themselves, about the beauty of the struggle against arbitrary power, and about words. I would love to know what he thinks now about all the books and movies I have seen. I want him to browse through my collection. I want him to know my wife who would be his friend, as she is mine. I want him to know my grown daughters and his great-grandchildren. But he is too young for all of this. Ever since that cold summer evening my father has been alive and young. For a long time now I have been older than my father, stronger than my mother, braver and smarter than my stepfather, and taller than myself. I can see it in the bathroom mirror.

REFERENCE

Wright, R. (1945). *Black boy: A record of childhood and youth*. New York: Harper.

Chapter 4

Remembering the Origins of a Constructivist Psychologist

James C. Mancuso

Rememberer: Critical incidents do set up the framework of salient self stories that we reauthor and reenact throughout our lives. The reauthoring and the reenacting might embellish and vary the story in potentially infinite ways, but the same basic structure is retained in each variation. I can remember this incident, and I frequently have repeated this story—like the theme in the movement of a symphony.

Dad and I were at the home of my mother's parents. I must have been about four years old, since Grandpa died when I was five. Uncle Pat took me into his barber shop, which was attached to the house, and there he carefully shaped my hair, as he had been doing since I had had my first haircut. When I returned to the kitchen of my grandparents' home, Grandpa noted that I was pouting about something. He and Dad inquired about my expression of displeasure. Using the terminology of the barbering business of the day, I ruefully reported, "Uncle Pat didn't wet my hair."

By this announcement I had intended to report that Uncle Pat had neglected to douse my hair with the wonderfully scented contents of one of the bottles of hair tonic that lined the long shelf in front of the chairs.

Grandpa expressed exaggerated sympathy with my plight. As he did so, he went to the kitchen sink, filled a glass of water, and came over to me and ceremoniously "wet my hair." I can remember myself as amused at his transmutation of the meaning of my ambiguous words, as were the others who shared the event.

Dialogue Partner: How can you put together all those details regarding something that happened to you when you were four years old? How did you know that Uncle Pat had cut your hair from the time of your first haircut? How do you know that the hair-wetting took place in the kitchen? How do you know that you were amused? How can you characterize your grandfather's tone as "exaggerated sympathy"? Furthermore, why do you remember and retell this story, and not another story?

Rememberer: Since I think your last question gets to a major point of what I am trying to say, I first will explain remembering of this story by claiming that, in one way or another, I have over and over reauthored the essential parts of this story as I have made my self-presentations.

Regarding your other questions, I believe that our understanding of the process of remembering has taken us way past the point where we can try to make the claim that any remembering is a matter of reading off some kind of internal videotape of what happened back then, so long ago. If you are trying to demand that my story should qualify as some kind of *retrieval* or some kind of *recall* of something that was imprinted into my neural system back then, then you are expecting a process that *never* happens.

When a person expects a remembering to render an "accurate" reproduction of a previous event, the suggestion is that he or she is using the "videotape" metaphor. The most convincing current psychological formulations about remembering would show more affinity for engineering or architectural metaphors: the attempt to return to an original shape, a reassembling of some kind of structural units. As we tell stories, we try to build a good story—a linguistic assemblage that gives all the structural parts that we expect in a good story. When we put together a story we want to provide a setting that locates the episode, introduces characters, etc. Then we want to have a segment that sets out a beginning, something that can be seen as the cause of the continued action. Then we want to have a goal that defines the purposes of the protagonist's action. Then we would like to have a statement of whether the protagonist reached the goal. Something should be clearly identifiable as a cause of the outcome. Then a teller of a good story winds up by setting the outcome into a broader context, perhaps including a global ending that ties the episode to other forthcoming episodes. This structure of stories can be discussed as *story grammar*—the "parts of speech" of a story and their arrangement.

Let me delay giving a response to some of your other questions. Let me remember another interaction with my dad. I could fill in the time slot in the setting part of the story by saying I was eight years old. I assume that I was reading, so I must have been at least seven years old. Dad left for the sanitarium shortly after I turned ten.

> Dad asked me, "Is there a boy named Feeney in your class?"
> I knew that this was the start of some kind of game, because he showed the same kind of smile he had shown when he and Grandpa had wet my hair.
> "Oh yes, John Feeney."
> "His dad is a foreman on the three o'clock shift at the mines. He told me that his boy is the best reader in your class."
> "He can't be. He sits in the fourth row. I sit in the first row," I countered vehemently. I was sure of myself.
> "Then either his dad must have been trying to brag, or his boy must have been telling him a big story."
> "Well, you can come to the class any time to see where he sits, and to see that I sit in the first row."

Dialogue Partner: Again, you toss in the phrase, "I was sure of myself."

How can you ascribe that feature, *certainty,* to your self at that time, when you can't even tell me precisely how old you were? If *outcome* is a part of the grammar of narrative, why didn't you tell me whether your father accepted your claim that you were a better reader than John was?

Rememberer: Good points! I thought you were going to ask me to explain why I can remember easily the evidence that I gave to prove my reading superiority. I also should point out that I can't remember John Feeney as a person, but I can remember his exact location in the next-to-last row of those screwed-down desk-chair sets in which we sat.

Let me tell one more story. It will be easier to answer your questions if we have all three of the stories to consider.

> Again, I had to be about eight years old. It was a dreamy summer evening—a Sunday. I have the impression that my father had awakened me from an afternoon nap. I was home alone with

Dad. The rest of the family was out for some function or other. I can't remember where they might have been.

Our household maintained a very productive garden, and we had all kinds of food-producing animals. Dad had me help him with the evening chores. I thoroughly enjoyed working with him, whenever I could. Again, I can readily remember the happy glow of that late afternoon.

I made this self-presentation: "Dad, I must learn to do all these things, because if something happens to you, I will need to be able to do this work."

That evening he took me along when he went to play cards with one of his buddies. During one part of the conversation, he told his buddy what I had said. I remember that as one of the most pleasing events in my life.

Dialogue Partner: Again, you assign all kinds of features to your self. How can you be so sure that you were able to construe your self in those ways at that time? That was a very long time ago, and you are giving some very specific details. And, here you told about outcome in some detail, whereas you didn't when you told the "Among the Best Readers" story.

Rememberer: Your last concern, about the specification of outcome, points up the kind of processing most of us follow when we tell stories. In many instances, a narrator will leave out one of the parts of a story he or she recounts. In many of those instances, the narrator might have filled the story part as he or she remembered the story, but does not verbalize that section. The contents of the part might be judged to be too obvious, so that verbalizing that section would be redundant. The narrator will expect the listener to fill in the slot. As we tell a story, we expect that listeners will process verbalizations as if they were "reading the narrator's mind," that is, "following his or her construction processes."

Did I, at the time of the incident, construe my self as I now construe the person I am describing—my eight-year-old self? Again, that question must be irrelevant. There is no way to check out the "reality" of that prenarrative self. We can relate to that putative event only as I or other persons would remember it. I have verbalized this story dozens of times—to my self and to other persons. More than that, I have acted out that story repeatedly during my life.

   Indeed, I think that I could characterize a good part of my life in terms of retellings of these three stories.

   First, more background: Dad came to the United States in 1922. He went to the anthracite coal mining regions of Pennsylvania. There a cousin of his introduced him to the man who would become his father-in-law—my mother's father. My mother's father hired Dad to work with him. Basically, Grandpa was an employer, because he would contract with the mine owners to excavate a seam of coal that ran off the main shaft. They were paid by the load. My father's ability to work was legendary. Everybody spoke admiringly of his capacity for work. Of course, as far as my grandparents were concerned, he was the ideal candidate for becoming the husband of their oldest child, my mother. She, likewise, was regarded as an indefatigable worker. They both understood the old Italian immigrant traditions. They both were regarded as physically attractive.

   The marriage, however, was flawed. Before the marriage, my mother had gone well down the road to becoming *americanizzata*. She knew that she was being wheedled into marrying a "greenhorn," even if she did appreciate his famed capacity for work.

   Five children came, with barely a breathing space between each of them. The fifth child, who had been born with multiple physical defects, died after eighteen months. Within two years of that child's death, my father was sent to the state-run tuberculosis sanitarium, where he died after nine months of wasting away with anthracosilicosis.

   Dialogue Partner: So, you could say that when you indicated that you were in preparation for "something happening" to your father, you were working as if you had had a premonition! No wonder that story is one that you have retold many times.

   Rememberer: Well, I wouldn't accept that kind of interpretation. Nor would I bring in something like a death wish about which I have experienced guilt—an interpretation that would make a psychoanalyst's heart thump.

   You should also know that after Dad's death, my mother arranged to have us placed in child-rearing institutions. My brother and I were placed in a farm setting, where we learned to do all the farm work in the grand Pennsylvania Dutch tradition. Many of the boys who came to The School showed signs of severe homesickness. I didn't experience anything like that. There were some beautiful farms in the area where I spent my earliest years, and we often visited one that was owned by one of my father's friends. Such visits sparked his telling stories of his rural life in southern Italy. In addition, those visits would nurture his fantasy about buying a piece of country property.

When we went into The School, I could feel that my father, by his death, had granted me the opportunity to live in his fantasy. Further, as the "Helping with the Chores" story indicates, I had already aligned farm-type work with the positive pole of my *negative-positive* construct, and I enjoyed chores such as milking cows. That is, I already had the constructs out of which to build anticipatory self-constructions that I could present to the boys and the houseparents at The School.

Dialogue Partner: No wonder you can remember that summer afternoon so readily.

Rememberer: Indeed. But let's look at the "Among the Best Readers" story. A few other details about my father: I can remember incidents in which he resorted to physical violence to my mother. In my later years, as I remembered those incidents, I could attribute his actions to provocations. She needled him incessantly. She was the sophisticate! To her and to her friends, his violence further proved that he was the "greenhorn"!

Despite my having seen my father become quite violent, my rememberings of my interactions with him are generally of a very benign quality. If I were seeking sympathy, he was much more likely to offer it. I was subject to severe headaches from an early age, and it was he who made the more serious efforts to comfort me. I can remember him standing over me, holding my head when the pain-induced nausea produced vomiting. I don't know why that practice grew up as a part of the tradition, but there was something very comforting about his doing that.

Dialogue Partner: You're getting off the track. You were talking about being able to milk the cows when you went into The School.

Rememberer: Not really. I was trying to lead into the business of my pride in being an able milker. I always took on the difficult-to-milk cows and would show off my mastery of those beasts.

And that relates to the reader story. I remembered the reader story many, many times in my life—among the best readers, among the best milkers, the best pie-maker among the other students in the baking curriculum, and on and on. The "Among the Best Readers" story was retold—reenacted—dozens and dozens of times.

Dialogue Partner: You must have been intolerable!

Rememberer: Well, in my reconstructions I didn't construe my self as *intolerable*. If I undertook something, I wanted to become very skilled at doing it. Otherwise, I wouldn't spend too much time at it. For example, our family never encouraged us to develop athletic skills, so when I did get an introduction to athletics, I participated minimally, because I was a long way from being regarded as among the best.

The interactions between my father and myself, of course, took place within a context. My Americanized mother's rudimentary constructions of class struggle provided an ever present strand of the context, as well. That strand also elaborated the meanings of the narratives that Dad and I enacted. My mother had a strong mastery orientation, so that she became a very, very skilled seamstress. Of course, it was the middle-class ladies, from the upper end of town, who would come to our house with a pattern and cloth, which my mother would sew up and fit to the client. She learned something about class distinctions!

My remembering of one of her oft-repeated phrases also repeatedly takes place: "You're not going to stay at 992 Ash Street and take shit from people for the rest of your life."

The combination of my father's gentle teasing to prod me toward being "among the best," coupled with my mother's dramatic pronouncement, provided the text for thousands of my little self-narratives.

Sometimes the efforts to work with those narratives proved calamitous.

Dialogue Partner: As I said, you must have been intolerable.

Rememberer: I know that I was perceived to be so on many occasions, but I experienced severe disappointment whenever anyone indicated that they could not endorse my presentation of self as *among the best*—particularly if they construed my efforts as justification for regarding me as *arrogant*.

Failure to gain social warrant for my self-presentations has been the source of some very strong invalidation reactions. I can go back to my grade school experiences. As noted, my mother was a 200 percent pusher. She had sent all of us to preschool, which was very unusual for an Italian immigrant family. That experience, along with the ways we were treated by our extended family, assured that we would be unusually successful in school as soon as we arrived.

You asked why I was so certain of where John Feeney sat in my classroom. That certainty, I would guess, is an example of later learning acting to fortify the remembering of an earlier event—kind of filling in the slot with constructions that were developed after the event. Doing this solidifies the structure of the story so that the story is remembered in greater detail long after the event took place.

I didn't understand the situation at the time, but looking back, I have become convinced that our school district was administered by educators who had totally succumbed to the ideologies of Teachers College, Columbia University. Each grade was segregated not only into high, medium, and low classes, but also in five rows, according to the results of a major testing program that was conducted at the end of each school year. Thus, every child in the grade who had any idea of competition knew where he or she fit on the *dumb-smart* judgment scale.

I usually sat in the fourth or fifth seat in the first row of the top class. There were three or four other children from Italian immigrant families in our class, and a sprinkling of children from the Slavic immigrant families. The remaining children in a class of about twenty-five children were from Irish and Anglo-Teutonic backgrounds. My row was filled out by children with names like Walters, Richardson, Newell, etc. Remembering my mother's colorful admonition, I knew that if I did not excel them, these were the people who would eventually "give me shit." It was a constant struggle, made more complex by the fact that the Irish-background teachers were totally befuddled by having a vowel-ending name in that first row. I can easily remember incidents in which the teacher would assign a special, honorific task to the others in the first row, acting as if I were never there, alerting me to the need to demand recognition as one who ranked "among the best."

Dialogue Partner: I keep saying, you must have been a serious pain in the butt.

Rememberer: Sure, but have a little sympathy, please. Others frequently had the privilege of offering invalidations of my self-presentations. Remember my headaches! Did I have headaches? I can see my little self jumping out of my seat, trying to race to the bathroom and vomiting in the aisle in the back of the room, then the teacher impatiently sending one of her prize pupils to call the janitor to clean up the mess.

The biggest blow came at the end of the sixth grade. They gave us special exams. They called them "Speeder's Tests." Only select kids from the entire school district—about forty of us—took the Speeder's Tests. From that group they selected about twenty who were then given a special program in which they completed seventh and eighth grade in one year. I was one of the candidates. I knew, however, that eventually I wouldn't partake in the program, because we already had been admitted to The School, and we were to leave home at the end of the academic year. When the results were in and announced in class, I was not one of the finalists. I can remember the scene the next day. My mother kept me home because I had one of my grandest headaches. One of the girls in our neighborhood came to our house after school to say, "The teacher was looking for you today. She said that they had made a mistake in not letting you know that you were selected to be a speeder."

Dialogue Partner: So you're going to blame your father for making you an arrogant little monster who suffered from headaches?

Rememberer: Come off it. That isn't the point. I am trying to show the connections between significant story-creating incidents that have a tremendous effect as we recreate our anticipatory life narratives. It has nothing to do with blame. My parents were "telling their life stories," and they passed on to me the construct system with which to create my self-narratives. How can we talk about *blameworthiness* when we are talking about a barely literate man, who left behind his family and all with which he was familiar, and then literally worked himself to death for the family to which he had committed himself?

Dialogue Partner: All right, how do you fit in that story about the wetting of your hair? How is it that you re-remember the features of that story?

Rememberer: I want you to remember that I indicated that when I remember that story, I attribute a kind of teasing amusement to Dad and to Grandpa. I also attribute the same feature to Dad in the "Among the Best Readers" story.

I can ascribe that feature to many, many interactions with my father and my uncles. They all seemed to have adopted the tactic of a kind of teasing by-play to provoke us into a reciprocal repartee. They enjoyed getting me to react in the same way.

I think that those games gave me a series of constructs to use in the self-constructions that would guide my self-presentations. First, they made it clear that if we were taking our self-constructions as realities, they were in a position to withhold validation.

In effect, "You think that your self-construction as a flower-scented little boy is a necessity. I will offer my interpretation of what you should be. *Wet* can mean what I wish it to be. Your interpretation does not necessarily end the categorization process."

Second, they made it clear that the interpretation of words depended on the context in which the words were used. The listener must have the option of constructing his or her own personal construction in the context of the conversation.

Dialogue Partner: Wow! You sure are trying to make something profound out of a little bit of word play.

Rememberer: Okay. Sure—very profound. Again, that is the point. What seems to be a very simple process of child-adult interaction can build some very complex structural elements into a child's psychological processing system.

I am sure that I can trace some of my most memorable life stories to that basic "Wet Hair" story.

When I was in ninth grade, the science teacher was giving a demonstration about vaporizing water and the energy transfer properties of heated water vapor. In the course of his remarks he said, "What you see there is not steam. Steam is invisible."

Wow, did we have fun. Up went my hand.

"If everyone calls that steam, then that's steam."

There I was—a fourteen-year-old semanticist. The teacher didn't like that one bit, and he surely let me know, particularly since he couldn't shut me up.

Then there were the beginnings of my psychology career. The social studies teacher put a multiple choice question on one of the tests:

"Learning is:"

and two of the four choices were as follows:

(1) experience, (2) a change in the nervous system.

I chose the second choice. He marked me down one.

I went to the library and dug out a piece that talked about learning and synapse changes. I talked to the health instructor.

In the next meeting of the class, I asked for the floor and protested his having marked me down. We had a real verbal brawl. It ended when he convinced me to conclude my effort: "If you don't sit down and shut up, I'll come back there and knock you into that seat."

Dialogue Partner: Did you have a headache that day?

Rememberer: I can't remember if a headache followed that interaction. During my high school, college, and graduate school years I went through a long period of very severe headaches, so it would be quite impossible to associate all of them to one or another arousal-inducing invalidation.

Many of those headaches gave me the occasion to remember the comfort of my father's hand on my forehead as I struggled with the nausea that came with my most violent headaches.

Of course, I thought of him repeatedly on many other occasions. When I moved on into adulthood, I tried to reconstruct his hopes and dreams when he left Calabria and came to Pennsylvania to start a family. As I passed the significant milestones in my life and career and when I received some kind of recognition for what I had done—when I started my first paying job as assistant pastry chef at a fine hotel, when I was selected for a special program in the U.S. Navy, finishing my doctor's degree, getting book contracts, career advancements, special awards, and so on—I would think of how he might have reacted had he been able to share those moments. I am sure that in those instances I was rescripting that summer afternoon with the animals, and Dad's recounting my declaration to his buddy.

Dialogue Partner: Indeed, but did you think of him when you annoyed people by pushing on your superiority? Did you think of him when someone let you know that he or she had judged you as arrogant?

Rememberer: Well, that takes me back to the "Wet Hair" story. I would speculate that ultimately experiences like that helped me to understand that anyone with whom I would interact would be expected to apply his or her construct system, and I could not expect that the enactments of my anticipatory self-stories would inevitably evoke the constructions I had tried to evoke. Everyone has his or her personal construct system. I could expect that I would encounter dialogue partners who would use a construction of *wet* that would be quite different from the construction I had used when I used the word *wet* as a signifier! If I had made a particular enactment, anticipating that my dialogue partners would construe me as highly competent, there would be some persons who would place me at the *arrogant* end of their *arrogant-humble* construct.

Indeed, I am willing to claim that experiences such as that in the "Wet Hair" story shaped my professional commitments. I think that those experiences attracted me to trying to understand the processes by which persons place alternative constructions on what would be regarded as "the same" inputs.

Dialogue Partner: Now that's really stretching it! You aren't going to tell me that there was a connection between the "Wet Hair" story and your advocacy of a contextualist/constructivist perspective on personality theory?

Rememberer: Well, you judge that for yourself. Here's another story.

> When I started graduate school, my classmates were clearly some of the most well-prepared psychology majors in the United States. My first semester there was really rough. I had a rather easy time of it in undergraduate studies, and I needed to reorient my entire approach to study.
>
> One of my most important professors was a young man who was making his name as a researcher into "perception and personality." Silly stuff, coming from a kind of mashed psychoanalytic theory. Would a person with "repressed sexual impulses" show a long reaction time—take a long time to perceive—a word like *clitoris* when flashed on a screen for very short durations? During his section of our introductory seminar, this professor presented scores of studies completed by himself and other investigators. It wasn't my favorite section of the seminar.
>
> A different professor guided the section on perception. He emphasized the "transactionalist" approach to perception, the precursor to modern studies of cognitive processes. This material produced vibrations that harmonized with my existing construct system. Here was a set of studies that demonstrated that "illusions" were a matter of attempting to apply to an ambiguous stimulus pattern that which the viewer already knew. Today, I would say that the person viewed the situation and construed it in terms of his or her already existing personal construct system.

That section of the first-year seminar was the highlight of the year—in terms of spurring my involvement and in terms of my achievement.

During the second year of graduate study I took an advanced seminar in personality study with the "perception and personality" professor. Each of us was to present a paper on a topic from the professor's list. I chose to present a paper on what was then called *person perception*.

I was able to gather the material to make the case, in the language of that day, that one could describe personality in terms of perceptions of self and others in social situations. This approach, of course, minimized the idea of "hidden forces" as distorting influences on the ways in which persons construed inputs. In my reading I came across a statement that provided a unifying thread for my paper. I am sure that I was reenacting the "Among the Best Readers" story when I triumphantly concluded the oral presentation of my paper by quoting one of the then-esteemed authorities (call him Blakesly) on the subject, to this effect:

"In conclusion, I would agree with Blakesly who proposes that we are on the wrong track when we attempt to discuss perception *and* personality. We now can move toward affirming the position that the way in which we perceive persons *is* personality."

The professor did not threaten to knock me back into my seat, but his mocking reaction did remind me of my ninth grade social studies teacher!

About one and a half years later, that professor supplied the personality study question for the examinations given preliminary to our presentation of a dissertation proposal. His question was something like the following:

"Justify or refute Blaksely's claim that perception is personality."

It happened that the evening before I had taken the exam I had read an article about personality as an expression of a person's perceptions of self and others.

To top things off, an incident during the examination period again evoked my "Among the Best Readers" story. One of the students, whom I perceived as having gained special attention from some of the professors, revealed that he had little idea about how to frame the response to the questions. During the examination he said aloud something like, "Who the hell is Blakesly?"

I am sure that my reaction, at that point, was something like that which I had when I had asserted to my father: "He can't be a better reader than me. I'm sitting in the first row!"

Chapter 5

Teaching by Doing

Donald P. Spence

It was the day after Thanksgiving and we were snowed in. We had come up to our summer house in Connecticut on Thanksgiving eve and watched the snow gradually build up during the night as we unpacked the car and made our beds. By the next morning the snow had stopped and the house was freezing. We started a fire in the fireplace and took turns walking our things up the hill to where our friends the Smiths lived—they had heat and hot water. By the middle of the afternoon we were all assembled and finished off the dinner in a burst of "We're Gathered Together" around the piano. I think we slept at the Smiths' that night—crowded but comfortable.

The next day the snow had stopped but the roads were still unplowed and no one was moving—except my father. He surprised us first by turning up at breakfast fully dressed, coat and tie, and surprised us again by telling us that he was expected at a planning meeting with some of the other faculty from Teachers College. The meeting was somewhere in Pennsylvania. This came as a complete surprise to us and we waited patiently for the end of the joke—he had been born on April Fool's Day and springing practical jokes was one of his frequent activities. But as time wore on, it seemed clear it was no joke but, on the contrary, serious business, an adventure I couldn't quite believe in but which seemed to be happening.

After a quick breakfast, he set forth, planning to walk down to the paved road (about half a mile) and then thumb his way to the Westport station (about ten miles). From there he would catch a train to New York and then make connections for Pennsylvania. When we next saw him, he told us he had been a little late but nothing serious.

All this happened just when I was starting high school in the late 1930s. Many years later, I learned more about the meeting and discovered that, while important, it was far from essential; a group of faculty was meeting in order to plan its lectures for the remainder of the term. Another meeting could easily have been arranged. In fact, by the time I heard the full story, I was also teaching and planning similar meetings, and I had began to realize quite well just how movable such meetings could be and how, if need be, the course would survive even in their absence. The older I got, the more unbelievable the Connecticut episode appeared to be, and I began to wonder whether there was another reason for hitchhiking off in the snow. Surely something more urgent than an ordinary planning meeting.

But I think that *was* the whole story. And my suspicion (and perhaps yours) that there must have been more to it tells us something important about the difference between the 2000s and the 1930s. Today is a much more cynical time and we have trouble believing that any faculty member—junior or senior—would set forth on a snowy morning, without a car, to fight his or her way to the station (not knowing when the trains were running) in order to make a meeting that could easily have been canceled (and might have been by the time he arrived). But this is the present speaking. Back then, during the depression, people such as my father saw nothing unreasonable in making this kind of effort; any number of his friends would have done the same thing. This kind of selflessness was entirely in character; it was to have an enormous impression on me and led directly and indirectly to any number of things I have done since without ever wondering quite why.

Setting off on this kind of adventure that snowy morning in Connecticut was entirely in keeping with Ralph's sense of obligation and moral responsibility. (We never called him Father because we had been brought up in a progressive school environment where everyone was equal). He believed that a job was a job and you never asked, At what cost? or For whom? or What is it worth to you? I am sure now that it was Ralph's example that led to my preoccupation with saving lives (in both literal and figurative senses; I'll say more about this in a minute). The word *example* is important here because he never preached his beliefs. Had he done so, I think the effect would have been much less telling; having this kind of example in front of me was a lesson many times more powerful than any number of lectures.

Another memory: I was sick in bed, my mother was in the hospital, and Ralph was planning to go out for the evening and play bridge with some friends. I pleaded with him not to leave and, with almost no hesitation, he offered to invite the bridge group to our house. He didn't surround the offer with "maybes" or other conditionals; he simply said, "I'll invite them here" and that was that. I was overjoyed; not only would he not leave me, but I could go to sleep to the sound of laughter and merriment. Looking back on this moment, I can see the same kind of selflessness at work: you do it but you don't talk about it. Not only did he leave out the "maybes"; he also made no attempt to bargain with me or make a moral point. By doing and not saying, he showed me that actions can often speak much louder than words.

My father was a lifelong student of John Dewey and believed very much in the progressive school movement and the wisdom of learning by doing. The joke at the time (and he told it on himself many times) was that those who can, do; those who can't, teach (he was a professor at Teachers College for almost all of his working life). But much as he appreciated learning by doing (one of Dewey's main principles), he also believed in what might be called teaching by doing (as in my two examples). And perhaps because he believed strongly in the power of action over language, he never found a way to write about his beliefs. The irony is obvious: if you believe that language somehow diminishes what you think, your only means of influencing others is by example. I think it may have been for this reason that he published almost nothing during his forty-year career as a college professor. But because he was a man of few words, his influence on me was, I think, all the stronger.

His interest in Dewey led to one of our few disagreements. During the last months of World War II, my outfit in the mechanized cavalry had been doing its best to keep warm in French barns and farmhouses during one of the worst winters in Europe since the turn of the century. Our unit had just been pulled back from the front (we had been rushed in to reinforce the southern edge of the Battle of the Bulge). We were catching up on our sleep and eagerly going through our mail. A wonderfully heavy package had just arrived from home—cheese, I thought, or even better, chocolate—but my hopes were dashed to find only a book. And not just any book, but Dewey's *Human Nature and Conduct!* Food for thought, maybe, but not exactly edible or nourishing. I immediately fired back a V-mail note to my father and asked him what he thought he was doing. Here we were in the middle of mortal combat, suffering from trench foot, sniper fire, and worse. The last thing we needed was a book on philosophy. I forget what his answer was; perhaps he thought it would take my mind off the fighting. (It is also true that as time passed, I learned to rank Dewey among my favorite authors, but largely because of *Art As Experience;* I never went back to *Human Nature and Conduct*).

The memory of him setting off that snowy morning in Connecticut has come back to me many times, in part because it stands for many similar examples of action without words. When I was around three or four, we were swimming off a raft and I accidentally knocked a towel into the water. It immediately began to sink and seconds later, I was surprised to see my father diving after it. There were times, I learned, when talk only gets in the way and makes the right move even more difficult, if not impossible. Emergency squad medics know this lesson well: Talk is for later—or for the classroom.

One of the many meanings of watching Ralph set off to hitch a ride is this: Don't be discouraged by the way things look; you can do almost anything if you want it badly enough. Sheer effort and persistence can accomplish miracles. One corollary was this: If you don't know something, teach yourself. During my internship in clinical psychology, I designed and built my own tachistoscope from pieces of an orange crate and a spare shutter. Many years later, when I started doing psychotherapy research on the computer, I taught myself the programming language C when I found existing programs did not do the job. Ralph's example had something to do with each of these initiatives.

But perhaps the most direct outcomes of the Connecticut memory were two life-saving adventures. The first took place not long after I was discharged from the Army when I was working at a summer camp. It was our day off and two of us had gone to meet some other counselors at the edge of a rocky stream (called, fittingly enough, Ralph's Chasm). They were putting out their campfire when we found them and then we all hiked back along the canyon's edge to the car. The leader had the one flashlight. Suddenly we heard a shout and discovered that he had stepped over the edge and had slipped some distance down to the stream below. Without thinking twice, I headed down in the direction of his voice, moving by feel, grabbing whatever I could in the way of roots and branches to slow my fall and guide me to the bottom. I heard him call every so often, and I could hear the stream noise getting louder. With great luck, I found him in the dark, essentially unhurt, and together we scrambled up the bank and re-joined the others. He had fallen face first in a large pool of water. Although he had broken no bones, he came out of it with two enormous black eyes that made him look something like a bewildered raccoon. It was only many years after this happened that I began to connect this adventure with Ralph's sudden departure on that Friday morning.

The second piece of lifesaving took place one summer day on the Hudson river. We had just moored our sailboat when my friend Howard came by in a power launch and offered to take us upriver for a swim. We anchored several miles north of Nyack and some of his passengers set out on rubber rafts. They hadn't bargained on the tide, which was running strongly upriver; very soon they had floated a fair distance from the boat and Howard jumped in to bring them back. He found them easily enough but in trying to tow them back, swimming against the tide, he started to tire quickly. He began to holler and thrash around. I had no idea how to start his boat but instead, I found a long piece of rope which I tied to the railing, dove overboard carrying the other end, and swam easily and quickly (with the tide) to meet Howard and bring him back to the boat. He could then motor up and pick up the others. By the time I reached Howard I had run out of rope, but he was only a few yards beyond the end. I grabbed him in the cross-chest carry I had learned during one of the summers I had worked at the camp and was just able to tow him far enough to reach the floating rope end. We both grabbed the rope and those on board pulled us back to the boat. Soon after, we hoisted the anchor and picked up the rafts. Everybody was safe.

These are the literal examples. But I have also spent a lifetime treating patients in psychotherapy and psychoanalysis and that may count as another kind of lifesaving. One of the reasons I may have been attracted to psychoanalysis is that it believes in using words sparingly and teaches that the less you talk, the more impact you have when you finally do. This would have appealed to Ralph. But I think he would have preferred something even less verbal.

It is probably clear by now that Ralph, despite his occupation as a professor, was also a man of few words (as was his father, who was, if anything, even more silent). Not only did he publish very little, around the house you almost never heard him speak. Sometimes, after a family disagreement, he might bring the problem up again in a letter, but he would never refer to the letter when we next saw him. It was as if written and spoken language existed in two separate domains with written being a little more reliable (and perhaps safer as a result). But words of any kind always came second to actions; not only did these speak louder but they contained more of a moral presence. Language was cheap and often untrustworthy. I once invited a college friend to stay over for the night and, largely out of nervousness, he spoke almost nonstop all through dinner. I could see my father becoming more and more unhappy in the face of this flow of words and after he left, Ralph never mentioned him again; loquaciousness of that kind simply couldn't be trusted.

Actions not only spoke louder than words but they seemed stronger if they weren't talked about. Language, in some way I only vaguely understood, could diminish what it described and this rule was especially clear in the case of excuses. It is easy to imagine the doubt that welled up in my father after hearing any after-the-fact explanation, no matter how sincere, and I have come away with a similar impatience. Early on I learned that mistakes were best followed by silence and I remember very few times when I was called to account, the reason being that Ralph simply didn't believe in explanations, probably because they were too easy to fabricate.

The same suspicion of symbol systems such as language also carried over into money. I have a sense that barter—the exchange of goods—was often preferred during the 1930s to buying and selling and I clearly remember one winter vacation when we exchanged our apartment in New York for a house in Vermont. Both families had a good time. Another exchange, several years later, worked out badly. I had arranged to trade piano lessons for tutoring on the Army intelligence test because my piano teacher was afraid of being drafted and wanted to get as high a score as possible when the time came to take the screening examination. As it turned out, we were each too kind to the other and not much learning took place.

Were there any drawbacks to this kind of upbringing? Three stand out. Growing up with the sense that action makes the difference, I never learned the importance of careful planning and how it could often save time down the road. And I never learned when to defer to experts or when to delegate a tough problem to someone who had more experience or better training. Part of my heritage, due partly to Ralph and reinforced by my progressive school education, was that any problem could be solved, sooner or later, and experts were often not worth the time or money (or the patience needed to frame a complete account of the problem). As a result, I ended up wasting a good deal of time learning new skills that I used only once. I began to admire those who could delegate well and who were able to use language to enlist and inspire others.

The third drawback concerns language itself. It took me many years to begin to trust it fully and to realize that action, no matter how immediate, was severely limited in its ability to convey multiple meanings. I began to admire those who used words well and who could use language to make an experiment (or a patient) come alive and exist again in the mind of the reader. But I also kept hold of a sense of the fraudulent and a keen awareness of when words got in the way and how easily nonsense could take over. It's probably no accident that my last book is titled *The Rhetorical Voice of Psychoanalysis*.

Chapter 6

Every Kid Deserves a Chance

George S. Howard

I grew up in a role-reversed family. My mother was an analytic, achievement-oriented, hardworking Yankee disciplinarian. My father was a laid-back, easygoing Southerner whose great loves in life were fishing, hunting, and baseball. I'm now a psychologist who has spent the lion's share of his personal and professional lives trying to figure out how to maintain some measure of peaceful coexistence among many of the seemingly incompatible traits that I apparently inherited from my two very different parents.

My dad grew up in rural Virginia in the 1920s and 1930s. I grew up in urban New Jersey in the 1950s and 1960s. In 1960 my father was the greatest hunter and fisherman who ever lived—I was well on my way to becoming the greatest basketball player who ever lived. Okay, so maybe I was a bit susceptible to overstatement and hyperbole as a twelve-year-old. But when I was a child, my dad could do no wrong in my eyes. Anyway, my great love was basketball—and my father went to just about every game I ever played. While he was always behind me 100 percent, he really didn't know squat about the game. Thus, I had to rely upon my coaches to master the finer points of hoops. But my dad was always ready to offer his honest, supportive analysis: "Good game, boy," or "Your man kinda ate you alive tonight, boy." My dad and I did okay in basketball, but there was no real connection there.

My father could have molded me into the second coming of Isaak Walton, had I any talent or interest in fishing. But Bayonne boys bleed basketball—not bait, bobbers, and bluegills. My dad and I remained star-crossed fishers. No problem, really, as my dad simply adopted my cousin Richie as rightful heir to his fishing fortune. Richie now *is* the world's greatest fisherman—and he and my father still tell one another the lies that prove it.

My dad was smart enough to realize that the place where we were most likely to make a father-son connection was on the baseball diamond. In my first year in the Bayonne Little League (Charley Hattenberg Minor League), my father volunteered to be the first base coach. With that period for germination behind us, by the summer of 1960 we were ready to bloom. My dad was the team's manager, and I was the first baseman on a talented Ace Auto Service squad. One of the reasons that Ace Auto was so good was because our manager picked up a slew of good black kids whom the other managers seemed to be avoiding in the league draft. While blacks represented less than 10 percent of the players in our league, Ace Auto was about 30 percent black. They were nice kids and good ballplayers, so our team was thrilled to have them.

The parents of the kids on our team really, really loved my dad. He was the kindest, most patient, most generous manager that you could imagine. He never put any pressure on any player, but we were talented enough to win almost all of our games even without being pressured to do so. My father always had a terrible time remembering names, so he called every kid on the team "son." Except for me—I had always been called "boy." It was a family thing. My dad had always called his younger brother Orman "boy" also. I remember meeting Orman for the first time. My dad hugged him and said, "Howdy boy! Sure is good to see ya." Uncle Orman bent down to greet me and all I could ask was, "You 'boy' too?"

Anyway, my father left home for baseball games about two hours early. He ran all over town picking up parents and kids who didn't have cars, kids whose parents weren't able to take them to ball games, and a gaggle of "neighborhood kids" who just wanted to watch their friends' baseball games. My dad drove a huge, twelve-year-old 1948 Kaiser. We sometimes put seven or eight kids in the backseat alone. You see, this was before the invention of the seatbelt, so no one even imagined that backseats had a maximum safe occupancy. My dad would even take parents and kids home after games—unless, of course, he was umpiring the next Little League game.

So there we were—this one, big, happy Ace Auto family. We were winning, having fun, learning good sportsmanship, and experiencing a sense of community. Everybody was happy. Well, not quite everybody—my mom was steaming mad at my dad, and she was getting ready to unload on him big time.

The next part of this story is difficult to write, because my mom can come off looking like a real witch, unless I explain our family's situation very carefully. My father dropped out of school in Virginia during the third grade. He worked at any job that he could get to help his family make it through the Great Depression. My mother graduated from high school in New Jersey and then completed the course of study at Catherine Gibbs Secretarial School. Both my parents continuously held full-time jobs until their retirements, with the exception of the three or four times that my father was laid off from his jobs as a laborer. My mother always held more skilled jobs than my father, and she also earned higher wages than he. While my dad helped a little with spelling and geography in our early grammar school years, I'd say that 95 percent of the help we received with schoolwork came from my mom and her relatives. Approximately 80 percent of the shopping, cooking, and housecleaning tasks fell to my mother. Finally, about 95 percent of the parenting and disciplinary work was also performed by my mother. While my mom was naturally more energetic and ambitious than my dad, she chafed under the great disparity between what each of them "did for the family." Had I two parents like my mother, I might have become a neurotic, overachieving workaholic. With two parents like my father, I could have become the world's most laid-back, easygoing bum. But let me get back to our story.

One Saturday afternoon, three hours after another great victory for Ace Auto, my dad and I happily waltzed in the back door to be greeted by a withering attack from my mother. Since my father was the target of her rage, I slipped into a bedroom and listened to my mom's avalanche of assaults. Sure, he had a forty-hour-per-week job—but so did she. Who did all the cleaning? Who did most of the cooking? Who gave all the help with homework? Who did all the planning, organizing, bill paying, and any other family task that happened to come along? Shouldn't she be entitled to an hour or two "off duty" each week? Why did she have to do everything for this family while he went on fishing trips, hunting trips, and was everyone's favorite Little League manager? If it weren't for her work, their three children would be poor, undisciplined, and uneducated. Didn't those other kids on the team have fathers who could manage Ace Auto? Why did he have to be every kid's favorite surrogate father, while she staggered under the burden of too many jobs? My father only said one sentence in reply: "Every kid deserves a chance to play baseball!" He then walked out of the house.

My parents fought with each other every six or eight months. This particular confrontation was a little shorter and a little more one-sided than most. However, they all ended in the exact same way. My father simply walked out of the house. After a ten to twenty-four hour cooldown period, he was back. I never knew where he went or whether he and my mom sorted things out upon his return, or whether these blow-ups ever produced any changes in their day-to-day relationship. When he came back, I was more than happy to repress the fact that he'd ever been gone.

While I always loved my dad, as an adolescent I didn't always respect him. My teenage years were a time when I worked as hard as humanly possible to get an education—to prove to myself and the world that I was anything but a bum. During this time I felt inferior intellectually to my classmates, and my father's lack of education hung like an albatross around my neck. I often was mortified by the lack of sophistication in much of what he said. But my friends just loved him. He could tell absolutely amazing stories—about fishing for 'gaters down in Dismal Swamp, about outrunning revenuers while trying to deliver a load of hooch in North Carolina, about cracking GIs' skulls in bar fights when he was an MP in Newfoundland, and the like. All my New Jersey friends thought he was "a trip." I thought he sounded like something out of the *Li'l Abner* comics. I tried to minimize contact between my father and my friends—but that was a losing battle because of the appeal of my dad's tall tales and his natural love for all kids.

I guess you could say that I bought my mother's construal of the world—hook, line, and sinker. It wasn't as if my father opposed my academic ambitions. Rather he was completely clueless about them. For example, after my high school graduation ceremony he came over, put his arm around my shoulder, and whispered, "I'm right proud of you, boy. I never thought you'd make it!" Make it? High school!? For an instant I wondered if he was hassling me. Then I realized that he was being completely sincere. If you're still in the third grade, everything in high school must sound like Greek—and Latin, and trigonometry, and physics, and calculus—to you.

Not only had my mother completely transferred her thirst for academic achievement into me, she also convinced me that I wanted to be *at least* one-half of an equal marriage partnership someday. She did not raise me to be a slackard—neither intellectually, nor as part of a relationship. For about three decades (roughly between my sixteenth and forty-sixth birthdays) I developed into the kind of man/husband/father that my mother had in mind. My father isn't at all displeased with the kind of person I've become—a bit amazed perhaps, but not at all displeased. In fact, I think I've grown into the kind of man I'd hoped to become.

However, over the last three years, I've noticed that I've become so much more like my dad that it's almost scary. First, I've come to look a lot more like him. Sometimes, when I catch a glimpse of myself in a mirror, the image looks more like my father than it does me. Second, I've just had hip replacement surgery. The experience reminded me so much of the hip replacement operation my father had twenty years ago. (He waited ten years too long before he got his operation.) I looked so much like my dad had, as I limped along before my operation. After surgery, as I moaned in pain whenever I changed positions, it startled me how much I sounded just like my dad. But there was one way in which my dad's hip replacement experience was different from mine. He was a pioneer—I simply followed in his footsteps. As soon as my orthopedic surgeon said that my X ray showed substantial deterioration in my hip cartilage due to arthritis, I called my father.

"Dad, tell me the truth. Has your artificial hip given you much trouble over the years?"

"Boy, sometimes it's the only part of me that don't hurt."

I was still frightened by the operation, but one day later I was scheduled for surgery. If you can't believe your own dad . . .

However, the most dramatic way in which I've become more like my father is in the way I use my leisure time. I am no longer a seventy-to-eighty-hours-a-week-hell-bent-on-success-psychologist. My son John (thirteen) would love it if I'd coach his soccer team, but I've never played the game and I have no feel for it. Similarly, my son Greg (eleven) would love it if I would take him fishing. But for me, fishing is like watching grass grow or paint dry—minutes seem like days. However, I've coached Greg's fourth, fifth, and sixth grade basketball team the last three years. It is now, by far, the most enjoyable activity in my life.

First I take ten enthusiastic little boys and get them flying up and down the court. Then, little by little, I mold them into a cohesive, well-oiled machine. Well, at least I try to get them all running in the same direction. Everybody plays the same amount—and everybody has lots of fun. Because their parents and friends are in the stands, my poor little whippets are already under more than enough pressure. Thus, I'm a cheerleader, a teacher, a clown, a storyteller, a tease, and a patient listener. I think of all of the players as my sons, and it is amazingly easy to treat each one of them as if he was my own.

We win more games than we lose. We have not yet won a championship, but nobody seems to care. While I may not be the best basketball coach in the league, I know that I am the best psychologist among the league's coaches. Somehow, seeing my "sons" become happier, healthier, more competent, and more self-confident as each season progresses seems more rewarding than winning championships. Like I said, I'm more of a psychologist than I am a coach.

As you can imagine, the parents of my players talk with me quite often during the course of the basketball season. They are sometimes lavish in their praise of the experiences that their sons are having on our basketball team. I love hearing their comments, but I always get very embarrassed and tongue-tied. My "sons'" parents seem confused as I can only stammer in reply, "Every kid deserves a chance to play basketball."

BEING THERE

My dad didn't die on June 12, 1997, but he might have. After all, most men don't live past their eighty-third birthday. I guess he and I are lucky that he's still with us. With a little less luck, I would now be devastated because there are still some important things I've not yet told him. What kind of things? I don't know! I feel I should say lots of things to him. I just can't seem to put them into words.

I flirted with becoming a monk many, many years ago—from 1966 through 1971. As part of training, the Marist Brothers tried to take their novice brothers away from "the world" and an important part of the world was their family. I was eighteen, and I was allowed to see or talk with my family only once a month. Those few hours with five to fifteen people were formal, frenzied, and frustrating—nothing of importance could be said. I really was being removed from my family, as no communication means no connection.

There were two classes of membership within the Marist Brothers, the working brothers and the teaching brothers. Working brothers tended to be poorly educated and performed the enormous amounts of manual labor needed to support the order's primary function of teaching. The teaching brothers ran the order.

On one family visitation day, my dad got talking to some of the working brothers. The next thing I knew he had agreed to contribute one of his two weeks of vacation that year to perform manual labor with the worker brothers at Camp Marist in Vermont. All seventy monks-in-training and all the worker brothers spent the first week after final exams at Camp Marist. There were thousands of jobs to be done to get the camp ready for the summer. What luck! My father's vacation fell on the one week that year that I would be at Camp Marist. What are the odds? This was in mid-May, prime trout fishing season, and my dad *chose* to donate that week?

Our Master of Novices was possibly the most sour, joyless, human being to ever tread God's green earth. Talk about being typecast! Well, Brother Master found it curious that my dad couldn't find any chores around his own home, and felt compelled to donate a week of service to a religion of which he wasn't even a member.

We all worked hard each morning and relaxed each afternoon. The Master assigned me to clear underbrush on our third morning of work. Fifteen minutes into the job, Brother John (a working brother) desperately needed help with a plumbing job he was doing with my dad. Would I please come and help? The next day, I was assigned to scrub the dining room floor with three of my buddies. We were all pleasantly surprised when Brother Sylvan (another working brother) announced that there was a delicate tree-cutting project that demanded my father's and my expertise (mostly we carried logs back to the dump truck as Brother John cut up the fallen tree). There were gales of laughter and volleys of good-natured abuse from my peers when Brother Sergius announced the next morning that I had to stop painting canoes, as my unique carpentry skills were needed for a particularly tricky project. I held boards as my father sawed them. And since neither of us lost a finger that morning, perhaps I was more skilled at carpentry than the other novices had playfully alleged.

If your title was "The Master," you would need godlike wisdom to appreciate a higher plan at work, when that plan came disguised as underlings changing your work assignments. Sadly, no one ever accused Brother Master of being overly wise. So it wasn't a complete surprise when the Master announced that hell would freeze over before another of Brother George's work assignments was changed to allow him to spend more time with his dad.

Perhaps an association was triggered by the thought of hell freezing over, but at 8 a.m. the next morning I found myself up to my neck in freezing spring lake water. We were fastening together countless sections of a quarter-mile-long floating raft, bolt by bolt, nut by nut. Presumably the other nine freezing novices were just the victims of bad luck in their work assignment—I felt I was being punished. "For what?" I raged. Long after all my reasonable peers climbed on the raft to fight off the numbing cold, they implored, "Come on, George, get out. Don't be a jerk." With impeccable nineteen-year-old logic I thought, "It's the Master who'll look like a jerk if I lose a few toes to frostbite."

Then I experienced the one and only quasi-religious vision of my life. I turned my eyes toward heaven in prayer, and the vision appeared. I saw my father framed against the clouds. I was startled initially, but soon realized that this was no vision. My dad was standing on the roof of a cabin that had been hit by a tree the previous winter. He and four working brothers were joking around as they hauled their tools up to fix the roof. My dad wasn't gonna let some jackass Master ruin his vacation—or keep him from getting an important job accomplished. That's the trait that the working brothers had immediately recognized in my dad. Seeing him as a kindred spirit, they had adopted him.

"Hey guys. Give me a hand. I'm freezing. Get me outta here. Come on. Pull me out."

I lay on the partially assembled dock for a long time. How curious that a nineteen-year-old boy would be surprised to realize that his dad had always been there for him.

How curious that a forty-nine-year-old man would be surprised to realize that his dad wouldn't always be there.

Chapter 7

Responsibilities

Alan C. Elms

The year is 1938; the season is fall; and the place is De Leon, Texas. De Leon is a town of a thousand people, with two blocks of stores and a movie theater on Lower Main Street. Out near the edge of town, on Sipe Springs Road, are Holdridge's Market and the Elms Garage. An old open-doored delivery van is just now backing away from Holdridge's, the best place for barbecue in De Leon. In the front of the van are a young man named Vernon and his even younger wife, Letona. They have been married for nearly a year. They don't use the van for any sort of business; it was cheap, and it moves. Letona is, as folks say around here, in the family way. In a few more weeks she'll give birth to their first child. Vernon glances at her anxiously as he straightens out the van and heads down Sipe Springs Road.

From the corner of his eye, Vernon sees a car turn onto the road from a side street. Vernon knows the road well; it leads due west to the farm he was born and raised on, a few miles from De Leon. But the other driver seems uncertain which way to go, or even which side of the road to drive on. The car is coming directly at the van, so Vernon veers right to get out of the way. But the other driver turns in the same direction; they are still on a collision course. Vernon turns toward the left and the other driver turns that way too, in mirror image. By now they are too close to avoid colliding. Vernon stomps on the brake, but he knows he won't stop in time. He lets go of the steering wheel and turns to put his arms around Letona, shielding her body and the baby from the crash.

Car and van bang together. Both motors stall. Dust swirls as people run toward the accident from market and garage. Vernon feels a little sheepish as he pokes his head out to check the damage. The vehicles have met head on, bumper to bumper, at a braking speed of five or ten miles per hour. The other driver, who looks to be about fifteen, gets out of his car and shrugs. At worst they have two banged-up bumpers. Vernon glances back at Letona before he gets out. She is wide-eyed, but she and the baby are safe.

Less than a year later, on a warm summer evening in northeastern Arkansas, Vernon and Letona sit in the kitchen of their log cabin. It's also the dining room and the guest room; the other half of the cabin is their bedroom. The baby crawls around the plank floor. Occasionally he glances up at the visitors, who are seated at the kitchen table facing Vernon and Letona. Outside, the woods are alive with a creaking chorus of dry flies and the bass calls of distant bullfrogs. The visitors have been making music with Vernon, blending their guitars and harmonicas with his mandolin. Now they've leaned the guitars against the wall while they talk eagerly to Vernon. He listens, occasionally putting a question to them. Letona has already cleaned up the supper dishes. She is not a musician, but she has enjoyed the men's playing. She sits quietly, keeping an eye on the baby, while the men talk.

The more talkative of the two visitors is a man named Wayne. Wayne's hometown is Drasco, way up in the mountains. Vernon's Uncle Henry and Uncle Charlie live around Locust Grove, the next town along the road, so Vernon knows some of Wayne's folks in Drasco. A year ago, when Vernon and his cousin Lester auditioned at KARK in Little Rock, they ran across Wayne at the station. He was hardly more than sixteen at the time, but he already had a regular program there. Though Vernon and Lester had been performing for several months on a little station in Texas, KARK would be a real step up for them. They got a tryout for a week, on a 5 a.m. farm show, and people seemed to like them. Wayne was particularly impressed with Vernon's mandolin playing. But the show's sponsor didn't care to pay them real wages, and they were losing money on their hotel bill, so they quit.

From Little Rock Vernon went back to Letona's home territory in the Ozark foothills. He cleared the land and cut the logs to build this cabin. The cabin is in the middle of a second-growth pine forest at the edge of Pierce Mitchell's farm. Mr. Mitchell is Letona's father, and he has given three acres to her and Vernon as a wedding gift. Wayne has never visited the area before, so it has taken him all afternoon and into the dark of the evening to travel the twenty miles from Drasco. Wayne and his friend have had to come over Dean Mountain on foot, cross the White River without benefit of a bridge, and ask people up and down Mitchell Holler where Vernon's new cabin might be found. Wayne is one fine harmonica player, and his friend picks a halfway decent guitar, so Vernon has enjoyed their visit. Now Wayne is leading up to a proposition.

Wayne has had enough of Little Rock, he says. It's small potatoes and he's ready for the big time. Memphis, or the Grand Ole Opry in Nashville, or heck, maybe even Hollywood—some folks say that would've been Jimmie Rodgers' next stop after New York if he hadn't died first. Country music is starting to get big, Wayne says, and it's going to get a lot bigger. With his harmonica and Vernon's mandolin, plus his friend's guitar and maybe a fiddle or a banjo, they'll have a unique sound. Wayne is writing lots of songs, and even just the three of them could get a recording contract as a vocal and instrumental trio—look what the Carter Family has done. They can hitchhike to California together in no time flat and cash in quick. Then Vernon can come back to Arkansas in style to pick up the wife and baby. So what about it, Vernon?

Vernon doesn't need a lot of time to think about it. Two or three years ago, he'd have jumped at the chance. He's already put enough of his lifetime into chopping cotton and threshing pecans. And he's already tried several ways to make his music pay off. In addition to the radio appearances, he's played for barn dances, taverns, even a patent medicine show for a while—mandolin, guitar, fiddle, accordion, jew's harp, banjo, you name it. But now he's a family man with responsibilities. He isn't sure he can survive as a farmer, and he's not sure he wants to farm for the rest of his life even if he could. But there are other ways to earn a living wage and stay settled at the same time. Going on the road, leaving a young wife behind with a new baby, is no serious way to be a man. Wayne is still hardly more than a gawky kid. Let him have his fun and see where it gets him. The music business is tempting, and Vernon may still be able to pursue it part-time over in Batesville or back in De Leon. But Nashville! Hollywood! Thanks for thinking of me, Wayne, but no thanks. Much obliged, and y'all come back.

Wayne and his friend sleep on pallets on the kitchen floor that night. They leave after biscuits and gravy the next morning, headed toward Hollywood.

Who were these people, and why am I writing about them? Vernon and Letona are my parents. The baby in the womb in that delivery van, the baby crawling on the cabin floor, was me. Wayne's last name was Raney, and his friend's name was Louie Clark. I don't know much more about Louie than that, but he never gets any speaking lines in the story anyway. I first heard that story when I was ten years old, the year Wayne Raney recorded his only number one hit. Wayne had indeed gone off to Hollywood after his night at our cabin, but Hollywood didn't work out. He persisted as a musician and song-writer in various locations, recording a number of songs that enjoyed modest success at best. In 1949 the country music stations we lis-tened to began playing a song of his, "Why Don't You Haul Off and Love Me (One More Time)." As the song grew more and more popu-lar, my parents recounted the story of how Wayne had tried to talk my father into going on the road with him.

They told the story with a kind of amused pleasure, in my mem-ory—pleasure that they knew this fellow on the radio, pleasure that he'd finally achieved a degree of success in the music business, plea-sure that he'd written such a listenable song. I never heard the story as expressing any sense of regret on the part of either of my parents. There may have been some such feelings below the surface—a feel-ing on my father's part that if he'd gone with Wayne, he could have been a contender, feelings in both parents that if Vernon had stayed with his music on a professional basis, we'd all have led more inter-esting and perhaps more comfortable lives. But the unspoken mes-sage I got as a child was mostly that the story showed my father's sense of responsibility to family.

That message was strengthened by what we gradually learned of Wayne Raney's later career. He never suffered the sort of tragic fall or abrupt end that country musicians have often confronted. On the other hand, he never reached the heights that he'd hoped for. He did have a few other minor hits after "Why Don't You Haul Off and Love Me," and played with the Delmore Brothers on their most popular records. He continued to get radio jobs as a singer and a disc jockey, including many years on Cincinnati's WCKY, whose powerful trans-mitter reached a large part of the South and Midwest. His bluesy har-monica playing enabled him to sell several million harmonicas through radio commercials and print advertisements. When I first visited the Country Music Hall of Fame in Nashville in the early 1980s, there was no exhibit for Wayne Raney, but the museum gift shop was still selling harmonicas embossed with his signature. His later writing and recording career focused mainly on gospel music. In that field his only real hit was a song that he wrote and performed seriously, but that was later recorded tongue-in-cheek by such artists as the Greenbriar Boys and Linda Ronstadt: "We Need a Whole Lot More of Jesus (and a Lot Less Rock and Roll)."

As a teenager, I came to want a lot more rock and roll, and a lot less Jesus, than either Wayne Raney or my father. The sort of country music my father had played professionally as a young man, the music on which I had grown up, was now painful to my ears. For several years I had a hard time appreciating my father's viewpoint on just about anything—music, religion, politics, family relationships. It was clear to me that he didn't much appreciate my viewpoints, either. We had grown up in different times, we held different values, and out of those differences grew a major and mutual lack of understanding. But whenever I heard the story again about Wayne Raney's visit to our log cabin, or told it to someone else, or just thought about it for some reason, it reminded me of one important aspect of my father's character that I could still value: his sense of responsibility. At a time when I needed to find something to value in him, that story spoke clearly of his willingness to sacrifice a major part of his own ambitions for the sake of me and my mother.

In Henry A. Murray's polemics about what personality psychologists ought to study, he advocated among other things more attention to what he called "serials." We shouldn't study just separate bits of behavior if we want to understand a personality, Murray said. We shouldn't stop even at the next level up, the psychologically meaningful incident, which Murray called a proceeding. Rather, we should examine whole sets of related proceedings in an individual's life— meaningful incidents that are related to one another, that reveal the development and persistence of certain personality patterns over time. Throughout his life my father has displayed in many ways a persistent sense of responsibility to his wife, to his children, to his extended family, to his friends, often even to total strangers. All those ways of behaving responsibly can be seen as a long-running serial, in Murray's sense of the word. I could cite many episodes in that serial, mainly ones I've seen firsthand. But besides the Wayne Raney visit, the episode most personally salient to me is one I couldn't have observed di-

rectly: the story I started out with here, the collision on a road in De
Leon.

In contrast to the Raney visit, which became a frequently told family legend, this story was spontaneously told to me only once. I heard
it during my late teens or early twenties, and now I'm not even sure
which parent told it to me. When I told the story back to them recently, to check the details, my mother said it must have been my father who told me, and my father quickly changed the subject. The
story does involve a topic my parents didn't usually discuss with us
children: pregnancy. It was perhaps an even more awkward topic to
discuss with me, since I'd been the fetus in question. It may have been
an especially sensitive matter for my father, because it involved his
taking his hands off the steering wheel at a crucial moment—a behavior that some people might interpret as showing that he'd been momentarily confused or hadn't yet fully understood, in 1938, how cars
worked. But to me, hearing the story for the first and only time from
one parent or the other, it reinforced my feeling (at a point when I
needed the reinforcement) that my father had felt his responsibilities
toward my mother and me from the very beginning of my existence,
and had unhesitatingly carried out those responsibilities in spite of
potential danger to himself. So here I had two distinctive incidents
with a common theme, displaying a recurrent pattern in my father's
life. It's a pattern I've tried to emulate in my life, not only in my own
parenting but in a broad variety of relationships with other people. It's
a pattern that has been important for me to feel I share with my father—important because of what it shows me about him, and because
of what it shows me about me.

Sometimes, though, I've felt my father was *too* responsible, or expected me to be more responsible than I wanted to be. For over a decade after we lived in that cabin in rural Arkansas, he worked at one
kind of job or another without ever settling into something he really
liked. He needed to earn enough money to support a growing family—eventually there were seven of us kids—but he couldn't do it by
small-scale farming. At the same time, he never quite got his farm-
boy background out of his system. He'd soon tire of city life whenever he got a skilled job there, and then we'd move back to the country for a while. Eventually he worked out an arrangement that made
him happy. He got a day job at a western Kentucky uranium process-

ing plant, maintaining the electrical system. (Talk about being responsible!) After hours and on weekends, he farmed a couple of acres to provide fresh vegetables and fruit for the family, as well as to give himself the satisfaction of growing things and working in the fresh air. He expected us older kids to help with the farming—planting and watering and weeding and whatever else needed our attention. At the same time, he expected me as the oldest child to go looking for spare-time jobs, such as weed whacking or topping tobacco plants or grocery store clerking. I much preferred to spend my nonschool time reading and writing, and I felt much put upon by his expectations that I do "real" labor for at least several hours a week. I also felt that he looked down on me for my irresponsibility, as much as I looked down on him for his unnecessary sternness. Those feelings added to the friction between us during my adolescence.

Then one of my father's older brothers told me a story about him. In his early teens on the family's Texas farm, this brother recalled, Vernon was sometimes nowhere to be seen while the rest of the family was working hard. He didn't come to the fields when he was supposed to, and he didn't respond to calls. Finally he'd be found on the roof of the farmhouse or the barn, or somewhere else out of sight, reading a book. Vernon just loved to read, the older brother said; he'd read anything he could get his hands on. Later in his teens, of course, after his mother died and the survival of the rest of the family became a more difficult proposition, Vernon didn't have time for such frivolities. He pitched in without objection, doing his share of farm labor and more. He was a responsible member of the family.

When I first heard that story, it just seemed funny to me. I took a secret adolescent pleasure in discovering that my father hadn't always been as perfectly responsible as he now appeared. But when I told the story to one of my high school teachers, whom I regarded as a wise mentor, he suggested an interpretation that struck me as quite insightful. The story showed, my mentor said, that my father was much the same as I, or that I was much the same as he: in the right place at the right time, we'd both rather read books of almost any kind than chop weeds. Maybe Vernon didn't regret letting Wayne go off to Hollywood without him and his mandolin. But he probably did regret (and even resented, at some level) not having had more time to climb up on the roof in the hot sun and read to his heart's content.

In his long retirement from the job of maintenance electrician, my father has continued to farm with pleasure. At age eighty-six, he still cultivates a very large garden, regularly planting new varieties of fruit and nut trees as well as the latest hybrids of tomatoes and sweet corn. Because of arthritis and partial deafness, he rarely plays his mandolin or any of the other instruments he keeps around the house. But he does a lot of reading now, and some writing as well. In studying personality, Henry Murray searched not only for repeated instances of one broad pattern, but also for the diverse behaviors that display a person's individuality, a given character's true complexity. My father is a very responsible man, and he is much more besides. And so, as my father's son, am I.

Chapter 8

On Coming to Understand My Father: A Personal and Professional Journey

William McKinley Runyan

What is an appropriate way to write about a close personal relationship with a much loved father? How much to be personally expressive, to be analytical, or to be evaluative? I want to be "objective" in the sense of not telling untruths, of not distorting the facts, yet at the same time, I do not want to feign a cool neutrality that doesn't exist. I begin with the emotional-expressive side, which preceded all the others, and is still probably the most relevant. This is followed by a brief intellectual analysis of aspects of his life that might not have been pursued without the invitation to contribute to this book. Finally, I will begin exploring how my experiences with him are related, if at all, to the kinds of work I have done and would like to do.

In proceeding, I do not want to claim any full or final understanding of my father or our relationship. There are many issues touched here just on the surface, with ideas leading to other thoughts and feelings swimming to the surface behind them, in a seemingly unending procession. In laboring over this chapter for a number of months, I have been struck by how much these thoughts and feelings about my father are a contingent historical process. While there seems a relatively stable core of positive emotions and feelings toward him, my thoughts and interpretations are shaped by a surprising array of observations, experiences, comparisons, theories, and conversations. I see a mother from India walking down the street in Berkeley carrying an infant over her shoulder, and see the placid face of the child bobbing along, and am reminded of having such a feeling of being safe, secure, in relation to my father. Or Frank Sinatra dies, and I am struck at the dramatic contrast of his tough guy bravado with the style of my father. Or I hear a talk on intellectual historian Isaiah Berlin raising questions about the origins of his unusually sweet temperament, and about his avoidance of conflict, and am struck by how both of these features ring true in trying to understand my father. As part of this contingent process, I would like to thank those who shared in thinking and talking about my father in recent months, and who raised valuable questions and insights, including my mother, my brother John, Aunt Martha Conrad, Patricia Byrne, Stanley Renshon, Karl Engelhardt, Mary Coombs, and Nancy Unger, as well as helpful discussions with Ted Sarbin about other chapters of this volume.

THE EMOTIONAL RELATIONSHIP WITH MY FATHER

How did I feel about my father? As a child, I don't remember talking much about my parents to classmates in grade school, although I was pleased to have friends come over to my house to play or for a birthday. By high school and college, as adolescents talked more about parents and how difficult they could be (as well as vice versa), I would simply say I had a good father, a kind father; it was distressing to hear of the terrible things that some kids experienced with their parents. Here, however, I'd like to convey two later expressions of my feelings about my father, one from a letter written to him in 1987, and the other, excerpts from a statement prepared for his memorial service in 1995. The context of the letter was that after visiting home in Hudson, Ohio, for Christmas, I had gone to a professional meeting in Chicago, where my parents had met each other as students at the University of Chicago in the fall of 1938.

May 3, 1987

Dear Dad,

After I left home this Christmas vacation and went to the American Historical Association meeting in Chicago, I was hit with a flood of thoughts and feelings which started while I was walking around the big Marshall Fields store on Michigan Ave.

The essence of it was that I was flooded with the feeling that you've been a wonderful father. . . . I feel like a gift has been given to me, which it is now my opportunity to pass on to others. Sometimes when I do something kind for someone else, I think this is how my father would have done it, or I learned how to do this from him.

I hadn't appreciated so forcefully what you meant to me as a father, and got choked up thinking about it. (I was touched that before I'd left, besides gifts for Christmas, you'd even shined my shoes. My feeling is that I ought to be shining your shoes.)

From big things of care, considerateness, unpretentious love and kindness, financial support, respect and good humor down to the smallest things of even shining my shoes before I left, I wanted to let you know that this occasionally does get through my thick head, and I appreciate it.

Your loving son,

Mac

I wrote a longer letter to both of my parents in 1994 expressing in more detail a number of things I remembered and appreciated about our family upbringing, but I don't have space to go into that here. By the early 1990s, my father, who had been extraordinarily healthy until then, and remained active playing tennis, platform tennis, and taking long walks with my mother, had started to suffer from Parkinson's disease, which affected his ability to get around, and eventually his memory and cognitive abilities as well. In December 1993, they moved out of the house in Hudson, Ohio, which they'd built in 1961, and moved to a retirement community, Kendal, in Oberlin, Ohio. My father died from a stroke on September 24, 1995. His memorial service on September 26, 1995, at Kendal, gave me a chance to try to convey a brief account of his life and what he meant to me, parts of which are adapted below.

A Few Moments in His Life

My father was born in 1916 and grew up in South Haven, Michigan. He graduated from high school in 1933, where he was valedictorian and president of his class. He was an excellent athlete, being quarterback of the football team and star of the basketball and track teams. He was voted Most Athletic, Smartest, and Best All Around. The caption next to his yearbook photograph is "We know him well— no need of praise." (Not bad for a high school yearbook.)

He played football at the University of Chicago when they played major college football, having a career-ending knee injury returning a kickoff against Ohio State, and also playing against ex-President Gerald Ford when he played at the University of Michigan. After graduating from the University of Chicago in 1937, where he was president of Alpha Delta Phi fraternity, he received his law degree there in 1939. He volunteered for the Navy in World War II, and served as an officer for four and a half years in both the Atlantic and Pacific theaters, and survived having his ship torpedoed and sunk early in the war. In 1943, he married my mother, Elizabeth Runyan, who had met him on a double date while she was a freshman at the University of Chicago. They had two children; I was born in 1947, and my brother John in 1949. After working briefly in the New York area, he began a thirty-five-year career as an attorney with Goodyear Aerospace and then Goodyear in Akron, Ohio, from which he retired in 1985. Some of my personal impressions of him, written out late the night before the memorial service, are as follows.

Some Personal Impressions

What kind of person was he? I feel like one of the most fortunate people in the world to have had him as a father. He had a truly extraordinary degree of goodness, honesty, and kindness, even innocence in a way, and an extraordinary lack of egotism, vanity, or selfishness.

As a psychologist and professor at the University of California at Berkeley, I'm supposed to see things as complex and multilayered, but I seem to have such uncomplicated feelings toward my father: pure affection, pure respect, and pure appreciation. I don't seem to find any dark hidden layer of anger or resentment toward him, and I believe that is because of who he was.

The book *Golf in the Kingdom,* by Michael Murphy, says that sports is a way that men can express their love for each other. And that is the way that it worked in our family. At the beginning, I remember him playing catch with me with a football and baseball on the sidewalk in front of our house, moving back one square at a time until able to do so at ever greater distances. After that there were endless hours of playing, coaching, attending our games, and discussing each play and player. I felt support and encouragement, yet no pressure to perform, not even being aware until much later of what an athlete he had been in his own right.

Memorial services often have laudatory comments about the deceased, but it has long seemed to me that it would be good to express these feelings directly to the person, which I've tried to do in recent years to both of my parents. I feel I received an enormous amount of love from my father, that I appreciated it and expressed that to him as best I could, and that he received my love and respect. In some ways, the circle was completed. Sometimes, I think such goodness can spread in waves through the people it touches.

In conclusion, by the time my father moved to Kendal, he had somewhat declined physically and cognitively. However, he accepted the impositions of old age with grace and dignity. My mother, who was central to his life, did a heroic job in caring for him in recent years. No matter how impaired he became, his kind and gentle temperament remained. . . . He taught us, or he taught me at least, something about how to live, and how one might die. Reflecting on him raised questions in me about what is most important in life, because his life demonstrated so much that seems of value to me.

I love him, and will miss him.

A Few Aspects of His Life Related to My Own Development

In an effort to be more objective and analytical about my father's life, a great many topics could be useful to explore, such as his childhood and psychological development, education, athletics, law school, years in the Navy in World War II, marriage and parenting, his career as a lawyer, leisure interests, and his participation with my mother in the Christian Science Church. Given the constraints on space, I will comment briefly on his involvement with athletics, marriage and family culture, adult interests and priorities, and finally, on my own inclinations to idealize him.

Athletics

By the time he was in high school, organized athletics seem an important part of my father's life, as he was a star of his school's football, basketball, and track teams. My grandmother kept a detailed scrapbook of his accomplishments and newspaper clippings, which I didn't see as an adult until after his death. Davis Baer, coach of football and other teams, seemed a significant person for him. I learned recently from my aunt that my father had some inclination to become a coach but (perhaps with some family pressure) pursued a career in law.

At the University of Chicago, he overlapped with some of the history of college football, as the former coach was the legendary Amos Alonzo Stagg, and a teammate was Jay Berwanger, first winner of the Heisman Trophy as best college football player in 1935. At Dad's invitation, Berwanger came and spoke to the football banquet of his former high school team in South Haven, Michigan. In later years, my father even took notes at the father-son athletic dinners at Western Reserve Academy. My sophomore year, he wrote down what soccer coach Tien Wei Yang had to say about every member of the team, including myself, which was recorded as "Runyan—slow as molasses, quick reactions, small boy, tremendous heart, Cranbrook best." Cranbrook was one of our opponents, so presumably that was my best game. To me, and probably to a father, "tremendous heart" sounds good, although "slow as molasses" sounds ominous for a soccer player. I got bigger, although not much faster, and became captain of the soccer team my senior year, and cocaptain of the freshman soccer team at Wesleyan and varsity soccer at Oberlin. Thanks to my father, I was able to take advantage of relatively modest athletic talents, and enjoyed playing soccer, basketball, and tennis on high school teams, which was a central part of life at that time, and later enjoyed playing basketball and running for another thirty years.

For my father, important human virtues were expressed through athletics, such as concentration, teamwork, treating teammates and opponents with respect, regardless of level of ability, striving to do one's best, and learning to live with the outcome, whether winning or losing.

Marriage and Family Culture

He was married to my mother, Elizabeth, for fifty-two years from 1943 until his death in 1995. My sense is that they had a solid marriage, with many shared interests, values, and activities, although perhaps without the lengthy talks about one's emotions more common in later generations. While my brother and I were completing high school, she went back to school, receiving a PhD in English from

Kent State, and teaching at Kent State and Akron University in subsequent years. They had different temperaments, with he being more calm, secure, retiring, and optimistic, while she was more intellectual, cultured, anxious, critical, and socially outgoing. (If there was one Great Depression, which she had experienced, couldn't there be another one, at any time?) I can imagine them standing in a meadow in Switzerland, where they loved to travel, looking up at the sky after a rainstorm, my mother saying, "Looks like it's about to rain again," with my father observing, "I think it's starting to clear up." Their personality differences seemed complementary in many ways, although must also have grated at times. Their marriage seemed unusually secure, as the possibility of their divorcing never occurred to me growing up, and according to my mother recently, was not something they had ever considered.

One value they shared was expressed in a family culture of frugality, of being as economical as possible in order to save money for more important things like education or travel. In taking a walk through Marshall Fields in Chicago, there was no chance I was going to actually buy anything. If necessary to stop to eat at a fast-food restaurant, the strong expectation would be to get the basic plain hamburger, not the cheeseburger, not the double burger, not a bacon cheeseburger, but the simple hamburger. Only a barbarian, only an economically irresponsible spendthrift would insist on the more expensive cheeseburger—someone like my younger brother, John. In spite of this early profligacy, he managed to turn out all right. He excelled in high school in academics, athletics, and student government, went on to Harvard, and then to a career as a management and learning consultant. He is married and has two children and was president of the Leadership Institute of Seattle, and cofounder of the Leadership Group, a consulting firm in Seattle. My parents were, I would like to add, unusually generous in supporting us through our education and afterward; this was possible, perhaps in part, through this culture of frugality.

His Adult Interests and Priorities

As I work so much in the study of life histories and psychological biography (Runyan, 1982, 1988, 1997), I wonder how to compare my father with the people I spend time reading and thinking about, often those who affected cultural or intellectual history, or shaped social and political events. He seems to me at the opposite end of some continuum with "tormented genius" at one end and him at the other. He was bright but did not seem tormented, and not driven to change the world or overthrow the culture, and not needing to impress or win attention from others. My sense is that he was not driven by occupational ambitions, that working forty hours a week was enough, and that he was happiest to come home to be with his family, to play sports with us, to work in the garden growing tomatoes, corn, lettuce, or zucchini, to carefully manage family finances, to go on family camping trips, or later, trips to Europe, while reading about and planning them in advance.

My father rarely talked about his feelings or emotions toward me, but expressed them in almost everything he did, from his pleasure at meeting me at the airport, to sadness at seeing me go, to watching an endless number of our athletic events, to talking over dinner, to putting his hands on my shoulders while I was watching TV, to cleaning my shoes, to sitting and talking outside in the evenings at Kendal. I had the feeling of being loved by a father who was devoted to my well-being. As a child, I don't remember him saying, "I can't. I'm too busy." In a talk at Kendal one evening trying to sort out some family matter, he said, "We really understand each other." I hope if he has a chance to read this, it wouldn't change his mind.

In summary, his priorities seemed not to be on career aspirations, nor on cultural creation or social change, but rather on family life and performing some of the basic roles at home, work, or leisure with unusual kindness, honesty, and human decency, in a way that touched many around him. I think of the movie *It's a Wonderful Life,* with Jimmy Stewart as George Bailey, who at Christmas, considering suicide, encounters an angel who helps him see how much better off his family and community are for his being in the world. We happened to see this on TV around Christmas 1992 in Hudson. He was clearly moved by it and commented, in a relatively rare cultural judgment, that Jimmy Stewart was a wonderful man. I'm not sure how much he was responding to Stewart as a person (who in real life was unusually likeable with a self-deprecatory sense of humor) or his role in this film, but I think of similarities between my father and the good-hearted, moral, sometimes innocent characters that Stewart played in films such as *It's a Wonderful Life* (1946) or *Mr. Smith Goes to Washington*

(1939), which provide as close a model for the dynamics of my father's life as I've seen.

My Inclination to Idealize Him

Given my strongly positive emotions toward my father, I expect I may also tend to idealize him. I still see him as a wonderfully kind, loving, nurturant father, yet I am trying to integrate these positive feelings with a better understanding of who he was and how he fit into the wider world.

In saying he was a wonderful father, this is not to claim that he was everything, or taught us all we needed to learn. He was obviously intelligent, but clearly not an intellectual, a cultural critic, an explorer of intrapsychic depths, nor a social-political activist (although he did participate in community chest activities and came to oppose the Vietnam War). One thing that may have constrained him was an anxiety or worry about interpersonal conflict. He sometimes seemed to feel that he was responsible for causing it, or for resolving it, even when this wasn't the case. I don't know how this developed, but guess it might be related to adapting to conflicts in his parents' marriage as a child. Independent of this, he also had an unusually peaceful and good-natured temperament. If the rest of us would start squawking or pecking at each other, he would remain relatively unruffled, and get us to calm down. Although not a major figure in the social-political world, nor on the cultural-intellectual stage, as a loving father and kind human being to those around him, he was hard to beat.

WHAT RELATIONS TO MY WORK?

Given my professional interest in the relations of personal life histories to the kinds of work people do, I would like to begin exploring what relations, if any, my relationship with my father may have with the work I have done and would like to do.

The ways in which personal temperament and experience are related to theoretical orientations in psychology has been a richly explored subject (see Atwood and Stolorow, 1993; Elms, 1994; Fancher, 1996). As I understand it, life historical experience is an omnipresent context for the development of psychological theorizing and re-

search. Personal experiences need not determine psychological interests and careers in any simple invariant way, yet, in interaction with
scientific-intellectual processes, social-political contexts, and historical contingencies, they are often meaningfully related to the course
of psychological theorizing, research, and practice.

A carpenter's work is not uniquely determined by the materials on
hand, as wood, nails, and screws may be used to build a table, cabinet,
or chair. Similarly, theoretical and research work in psychology is not
uniquely determined by personal experience, yet personal experience
is one of the resources that can be drawn on in a multitude of different
ways.

What about the case at hand? What connections, if any, are there
between my relationship with my father, and the kinds of intellectual
work I do? My father felt like a safe and supportive base, from which
a great variety of things might be done, depending on my personal interests or inclinations. Let me mention three possible connections.

First, with the assistance of my parents, it was possible to go to a
liberal arts college, spending my freshman year at Wesleyan in Connecticut, and then transferring to Oberlin from 1966 to 1969 because
it had a sociology department, but more importantly, because it was
coed. At Oberlin, I was strongly influenced by sociologist J. Milton
Yinger, (who later became president of the American Sociological
Association in 1977), and whose book *Toward a Field Theory of Behavior* (1965) provided a conceptually sophisticated integration of
social, cultural, and psychological levels of analysis, with a little biology applied to topics in the social sciences, accompanied by opti-
mism about the uses of social science for social reform. In ways that
look to me unrelated (although who knows), Milt Yinger was a friend
of my father in high school in South Haven, Michigan, and they had
kept in touch for years afterward, leading to our families occasionally
having picnics together in Ohio.

Second, ever since college, I have generally been more attracted to
subjective, experiential, and holistic traditions in psychology, such as
humanistic psychology, the psychodynamic tradition, culture and
personality, and particularly, the study of lives (Runyan, 1982, 1988,
1997, 1998). Does this preference have any relation to my relationship with my father? Probably not in any direct one-to-one causal
chain in which people with particular childhood experiences will
necessarily have particular theoretical orientations. However, my re-

lationship with him may be one element along with my temperament, kinds of intelligences, cultural exposures, professional relationships, social-political contexts and values, and historical contexts that have led to and sustained these preferences for approximately three decades. While receiving a PhD in Clinical Psychology and Public Practice at Harvard in 1975, I was attracted to the romantic and experiential interests of Henry A. Murray, and admired and idealized him in some ways, although developed greater critical distance over the years (Robinson, 1992; Runyan, 1994). The kind of warm and nurturant relationship I experienced with my father may have made it easier or safer to explore personal and developmental experiences than might otherwise have been the case. This alone does not determine anything, but is one element that could be assembled into a preference for experience-oriented psychologies, and thus may have affected my interactions with experiential versus natural science psychologists over the years.

A third and final example to be discussed here is my exposure to the history of the science world in recent years. As a visiting scholar at Harvard from 1995 to 1997, I learned a good deal about social-political critiques of science, the sociology of scientific knowledge, postmodern and Foucauldian critiques of science, and cultural, linguistic, and material constraints on the history of science. However, biographical and psychological approaches to the history of science were dismissed by some as little more than return to a discredited "Great Man Theory of History." Something in me rebels against this view, which seems severely one-sided. Yes, social, economic, political, linguistic, cultural, and material conditions can all shape the course of science, but so too do the personal, experiential, and cognitive processes of individuals, groups, and populations.

My father died in September 1995, and I sense there was some aspect of my relationship with him that made me react against what seemed like purely "critical" positions, whether of neo-Marxist or progressive critiques of science, or Foucauldian historicizing and constructivist critiques, which, in Foucault's words, could be seen as tools used in dismantling the system. Rather than dismantling the cultural or social system as a general program, it seems to me important to differentiate between structures that are humanly helpful versus those that are destructive or oppressive. A general deconstructive program doesn't appeal to me, I suspect, for intellectual-analytical reasons, as it seems insufficiently differentiated, and I suspect also for personal-experiential reasons, including my relationship with my father, which gave the experience that some structures can be helpful, supportive, and beneficent.

CONCLUSION

In summary, I've tried to convey something of the emotional-expressive side of my relationship with my father, to more objectively analyze several aspects of his life, and finally, to begin thinking about what relationships, if any, there may be between my relationship with him and the kinds of work I do.

The problem presented for me by this chapter was how to construct a conceptual space in which to attend to and to honor the experience of being with my father, and also to value the intellectual-analytical world on its own terms (with social-political concerns also important, though given less attention here), and to at least begin exploring the question of how they may or may not be related in my own life. In doing so, it seemed important to reach the view that each can be valuable even when largely unrelated to the other. This idea seems obvious in retrospect, but was difficult to reach. Even if a relationship with one's father has no particular "scientific" value, it can have great value in its own terms. Even if personal experience and science are not related in some cases, I simultaneously hold the view that personal-psychological-experiential factors, along with social and cultural contexts, often have far more relevance for social scientific theory or research than commonly recognized.

On the side of my father and our relationship, let me end with a dream from August 25, 1997, nearly two years after his death. I was descending some steps with a landing, as in front of my house or going down to a beach, and was surprised to see my father walking up. I said, "I didn't expect to see you here." He was pleased to see me. I was delighted to see him. He, in turn, was happy that I was glad to see him. We hugged, and the dream ends.

On the side of psychology, the point I'd like to make is that psychological theory and research can be shaped by cultural contexts, by social-political contexts, *and* by personal-experiential factors, with all of these coevolving in a complex and fascinating variety of ways.

REFERENCES

Atwood, G. and Stolorow, R. (1993). *Faces in a cloud: Intersubjectivity in personality theory,* Revised edition. Northvale, NJ: Aronson.

Elms, A. C. (1994). *Uncovering lives: The uneasy alliance of biography and psychology.* New York: Oxford.

Fancher, R. E. (1996). *Pioneers of psychology,* Third edition. New York: Norton.

Murphy, M. (1972). *Golf in the kingdom.* New York: Dell.

Robinson, F. (1992). *Love's story told: A life of Henry A. Murray.* Cambridge, MA: Harvard University Press.

Runyan, W. M. (1982). *Life histories and psychobiography: Explorations in theory and method.* New York: Oxford University Press.

Runyan, W. M. (Ed.) (1988). *Psychology and historical interpretation,* New York: Oxford University Press.

Runyan, W. M. (1994). Coming to terms with the life, loves, and work of Henry A. Murray (Review of *Love's story told: A life of Henry A. Murray*), *Contemporary Psychology, 39*(10), 701-704.

Runyan, W. M. (1997). Studying lives: Psychobiography and the conceptual structure of personality psychology. In R. Hogan, J. Johnson, and S. Briggs (Eds.), *Handbook of personality psychology* (pp. 41-69). San Diego, CA: Academic Press.

Runyan, W. M. (1998). The changing meanings of holism: From humanist synthesis to Nazi ideology. (Review of *Reenchanted science: Holism in German culture from Wilhelm II to Hitler*), *Contemporary Psychology, 43*(8), 389-392.

Yinger, J. M. (1965). *Toward a field theory of behavior.* New York: McGraw Hill.

SECTION II:
STORIES OF EMOTIONAL LIFE

Chapter 9

The One That Got Away—Or Did It?

Mark B. Tappan
Richard E. Tappan

For our contribution to this collection of critical incident narratives in the lives of fathers and sons, we have chosen to collaborate in describing and reflecting on an incident that occurred in our lives some thirty-five years ago—an incident that has assumed a central place in our respective (and collective) life stories. We have chosen this approach because we think it will not only lead to an interesting story (or stories), but will also allow us to consider the different understandings that sons and fathers construct of the same critical event.

The format for our presentation is as follows: Mark (the son) will tell his version of the story first, followed by Richard (the father). In writing these accounts we deliberately chose not to discuss or share our versions with each other until they were finished, to preserve the unique character of our respective memories of this event. After completing our own accounts we exchanged them, and then we took the opportunity to talk together about our thoughts and feelings upon reading each other's account. We present selected excerpts from that dialogue in the third section of this essay.

MARK'S STORY

I was about six, and my dad and I were attending a weekend retreat for the Indian Guides. We lived in Boulder, Colorado, and the retreat was held at the YMCA camp in Estes Park in the Rocky Mountains. It was late spring or early summer.

I don't remember driving to Estes Park, getting settled in the cabin, or anything about the other activities in which we were involved. My

93

memory begins as we were fishing on the shores of a small pond on the camp property.

I loved to go fishing. I first learned to fish with my Grandpa Teal (my mother's father) during a summer visit to Indiana. He loved to fish, too, and we fished together in the ponds and creeks around the small town of Arcadia, where he lived. My dad and I had also done some fishing around home the past summer and fall, but this was probably the first time I had been fishing that spring, and I was very excited about it.

We were fishing for rainbow trout. We were using worms or salmon eggs, and because the pond had been stocked it wasn't too hard to get bites. Suddenly I had one! I set the hook and began to reel in the fish. I was very excited, and my dad was by my side, encouraging me.

I proudly pulled the fish out of the water. But as my dad was trying to get the hook out of its mouth the fish got loose and fell, flopping, onto the bank. In a flash my dad reached for the fish and tried to get a hold of it again, but it flopped quickly into the shallow water. Without a pause my dad jumped into the water to catch it—clothes, shoes, and all!—but the fish was quicker, and it was gone.

I was stunned. I was a little sad about losing the fish, but mostly I couldn't believe that my dad had just jumped into the water to try to catch that fish! My dad looked quite funny, flailing around in the water, and I know he felt bad about losing my fish. I don't remember being embarrassed; I just remember being amazed at what my dad had done, that he would do something like that for me—jumping into the water, getting his clothes wet, showing no concern for himself, only for me.

I have only very vague memories of the rest of that day. I remember cleaning a fish or two in the bathroom sink of the cabin in which we were staying (which also struck my six-year-old sensibility as quite odd and a bit funny), so we must have had some other luck that day. I don't remember anything about dinner, or what we did after dinner, or how we slept that night.

In fact, the whole incident might have faded quickly from my memory had it not been for what happened the next day. It was Sunday, and there was an informal worship service as part of the weekend campout/retreat. My dad, as a minister in one of the churches in town, had agreed to lead the service. When it came time for him to offer his brief sermon, I was shocked, again, when he started to talk about the events of the previous day, particularly his attempt to catch the lost fish. I don't really remember what he said, but I do remember that he talked about our experience together, and by talking about it publicly, and by using it as an example in his sermon, he somehow reified and reinforced the power of that experience for me, strengthening, even more, the bond between us.

I don't remember anything else about that weekend. Of course we packed up and made arrangements to head home. Maybe we even got a little more fishing in! When we arrived home I'm sure we told Mom and my sister, Nancy, about the events of the weekend, including the story of the lost fish. But I don't think my dad and I talked much more about that event that day or in the days that followed.

Nevertheless, this story has become part of the mythology of our family. It must have been told and retold enough times over the years that it became unforgettable, although I don't recall that it was ever discussed in great detail. For some reason, though, it became important enough for both my dad and me that we kept it alive, referring from time to time to "that time at Estes Park when the fish got away" in a way that we both knew what we were talking about. There was at least one birthday letter from my dad (when I turned twenty-one) that mentioned the incident explicitly as one of his memories of me as his "little boy." And I know that in recent years I have mentioned the story at least once or twice in birthday or Father's Day greetings to him.

So what does this story mean? Why is it so important to our ongoing and evolving relationship as father and son? While we had always done lots of things together, there was something about his unselfish, unselfconscious, loving attempt to recapture that fish that really struck me. For me, at age six, it was perhaps the fist time I really understood that my father loved me, that he was there for me, and that he would do anything for me. As a child it made me feel very secure and safe in his love, and that security and safety has persisted over the years. As I grew older I came to understand the story in more complex and sophisticated ways, I suppose, as a reflection of the kind of love and commitment that being a father entails. But, even so, the fundamental sense of love and connection that I felt in the moment has remained most salient, and when I think of the story, even now, it reminds me, most of all, of what it was like to be six and to love my daddy.

RICHARD'S STORY

It was a small incident but long to be remembered. In late May of 1963, Mark and I with the other fathers and sons of our Boulder, Colorado, YMCA Indian Guides tribe participated in the tribe's spring outing at the YMCA campgrounds near Estes Park. It was the concluding event of our first year in Indian Guides. Mark was six. We had attended our Indian Guides' meetings almost every other week since October. The campgrounds were picture perfect, situated in the foothills of the Rockies near Rocky Mountain National Park. Longs Peak was not far away. Spring was in the mountain air.

Probably it was in the free time in the afternoon of the day of our arrival that we went fishing in the stocked pond on the grounds. Mark could bait his hook and knew how to cast out and reel in his line. He enjoyed the adventure. His grandfather may have taught him most of what he knew. However, a few times I had taken him and his sister, Nancy, to fish in the gravel pit outside Boulder. We had packed his fishing gear for this camping trip in anticipation of experiencing this back-to-nature sport together, as father and son.

We were not alone. Other fathers and sons from their tribes were also around the pond. Many other fathers were also helping their sons rather than fishing themselves. Some put the worm on the hook for their sons, and some let them experience the slimy creature alone. Into the water the lines went. The bobbing of the floats was watched carefully. Fathers coached their sons on when to pull in and how to throw out their lines. There were congratulations and celebrations when a small fish was landed. Mark's float bobbed some and went under occasionally. Yet he had to wait for some time before he hooked a fish.

Finally, the moment of triumph came. His float went under for a moment, and Mark yanked on his pole. He felt the tug on the line and knew he had a fish. He needed no coaching. He reeled in his line like a pro. He was excited. I was elated. Mark had a fish. He had succeeded. He held up his pole triumphantly. I grasped the fish in my hand. But as I was about to hand the fish to him or take the hook out of the mouth of the fish or who knows the purpose of that long ago fateful gesture, the fish slipped from my hands, flopped once on the shore, and flipped back into the water.

Mark was dumbfounded. I was beside myself. No time to think. Adrenaline took over, and I waded knee deep into the pond, chasing that hapless fish. And, miracle of miracles, I caught the fish in my bare hands. I waded out, fish tightly clasped in my cupped hands, and handed it to Mark. There was applause from the crowd on the shore. I was embarrassed for having lost the prize, for having failed my son in this supreme test.

But Mark has not remembered this mishap as a failure. Instead, this small adventure has become a long-remembered and oft repeated tale in our family lore. What happened to the fish, how much of the story was told later in the day, how much the story was embellished when we returned home, all of these details are lost in time. In his maturity Mark has helped to keep the memory alive in the number of Father's Day cards he has sent to me featuring fish or profiles of father and son by a fishing hole or similar scenes, always accompanied by a note expressing his love and gratitude. He usually includes something about that long-ago event beside the fishing pond and how much he has prized the memory. Because it seemed to be such a singular event in Mark's life, my embarrassment long ago turned to joy. I relish the story and am forever grateful that I managed to grab that little fish that may have been too stunned to swim away.

If this incident is seen in the context of the contemporary events in the life of our family at that time, this is more than a tale of a father and a son and a fishing pond. This is an account of a father anxious for the welfare of his son, anxious that his son have a successful adventure. A tale of a father concerned about national and international events that seemed to predict a very precarious future for the world of his son, a father who wanted to protect his son from all of the future uncertainties of life. And a tale of a son who was depending on his father to do just that. This is a story of a father who felt he had let his son down in a moment of need, and from what has since been said, a story of a son who remembers the incident with pride.

Some background: In May of 1963, I was about to leave my position of ten years as American Baptist campus minister at the University of Colorado. Within a month I was to become my church's national supervisor of its ministries on college campuses in eleven western states. I would be away from home about half of the time. During the previous ten years I had often wished that I had had more time to spend with my family. Weekend responsibilities, evening meetings, and travel assignments kept me away from home for short and longer periods. My salary was also modest. So my wife, Margaret, and I agreed that this new position, which could be seen as a promotion, would provide more quality time with the family when I was home. Also, there would be a modest increase in income to meet our growing family's needs. The new position would require an eventual move to California, but that could be postponed for a year.

By 1963 students on university campuses were becoming more assertive about opposing racial segregation. There were sit-ins at lunch counters in the South demanding that long-standing traditions be changed. Martin Luther King and the Southern Leadership Conference were becoming better known. There were calls for ministers to join in freedom rides to challenge segregation in public transportation in the South. I watched and worried, and at times felt pangs of guilt that I did not become more involved in the witness against segregation in the South. I knew that some on my supervisory board would not approve of my being absent from my local duties to join a freedom ride. I also felt that my family could not afford for me to take such an expensive and possibly dangerous trip. I worried that as a father and husband I should not be away from home more and make Margaret and the kids anxious about my safety.

And then there was the increasing tension in the cold war. The Soviet Union was challenging the West. In late October of the previous year this nation had come face to face with the prospect of war with the Soviet Union as the Kennedy administration challenged their shipment of military equipment to Cuba. Our household in Boulder joined millions of others in laying in extra stores of food and emergency supplies expecting that there might be nuclear war. Our supplies were stored in the furnace room in the basement. There was constant worry among the citizenry that this impending crisis could wipe out all of civilization. Margaret and I were at a loss as to what to do, how to be good parents in the face of such an impending holocaust. We acted like everyone else, praying, laying in supplies, and worrying that the world might come to an end.

So the story of the fish that did not get away, rescued by a father for his son, is perhaps a parable of what I and fathers all over the world would like to be able to do for their sons. In this instance there was an enormous amount of guilt and anxiety on the part of this father, wishing that he could control the world and the evil therein and protect his son and family from that which seemed to be awaiting them in the future. Instead, he did manage to save face for a moment and make his son proud as he waded in and grabbed that fish that was slow on the getaway.

A CONVERSATION BETWEEN FATHER AND SON

MARK: So what's the answer? Did the fish get away or not? *(Laughter)*

RICHARD: *(Laughter)* That really blew me out of the water, that we had remembered that differently!

MARK: Yeah . . . Well I think you're probably right because my memory is vague enough that I don't really have the sense that, you know . . .

RICHARD: Well, we might go around and ask. . . . Margaret says she wasn't there; in fact, I didn't share much of it with her, just because I didn't want to corrupt my memory much, but I think as far as your remembering of the sermon, which I did not remember . . .

MARK: That was the other thing I was going to ask you about.

RICHARD: I did not remember that; it's you who remembered that pretty distinctly, and you've got the younger mind. Obviously we don't have to reconcile this.

MARK: No, no. Absolutely not. It's interesting though.

RICHARD: It is interesting to me that we have often referred to this event, but I guess we haven't broken it apart.

MARK: That's right.

RICHARD: Therefore it's been a sort of a whole, and —

MARK: A whole, meaning . . . ?

RICHARD: Meaning we talked about the fish and our being together and my scrambling after, et cetera, but I guess we rarely if ever talked about the final end.

MARK: Right, right. You're saying as we talked about this over the years, we talked about the event as a whole, without going into all the details. It was just kind of something that stood for something else, without going into the details of it.

RICHARD: That's the same for me, too. . . . So I don't worry about it, but I think it is very interesting.

MARK: Well, I mean for me, really what struck me so much, you know, was you going into the water and kind of throwing all caution to the wind, and that's what has stayed with me, and whether or not the fish was caught or not. . . . I was trying to think, is there any way I can think more clearly about that? And that's just not part of what I remember, that there was a fish. I mean, that you came up with the fish. I do remember cleaning fish in the bathroom, so I know that we caught some, now whether it was the fish that got away or not I don't know, but I do remember that we did have some fish at the end of the day. And then the other part, for me, is your talking about it the next day. I was going to ask you whether you had any memory of that or what you said or what that would have been?

RICHARD: In fact, I've saved a lot of junk over the years, and I don't have any file for 1963 for some reason, and I don't think I would have written it out anyhow; it was more spontaneous. But I don't doubt that I helped with the morning service. I'm sure that there was a little chapel there, or maybe an outside amphitheater, and I'm sure we had a little worship service. No doubt I participated in it, and I would not doubt that I said something about that, but I probably used it, I don't exactly know, but I'm sure I was trying just to relate to what we were doing, and I guess generally I would have been trying to talk about the beauty of nature and God's creation and things like that—

MARK: Fathers and sons, or something like that.

RICHARD: So then I probably talked about we're here together as father and son, to get acquainted, and how important that is, whatever.

MARK: Well, it's funny. I really do think that that reference to it, as I tried to say, sort of solidified it or something for me. I mean talking about it publicly or sharing it again in a way that sort of made it clear to me that you'd been thinking about it too, or something. Again, I think what a six-year-old makes of all this is part of this; it's sort of hard to go back to that. But there was something about you talking about it the next day that I have always remembered, too, as sort of important to the story.

RICHARD: Well, the way you remember it and what you've made of it, and obviously so many of these things, who knows. The quality of the original incident compared to how we reminisce about it and the value of it to us later on, it all gets added together. I think it has meant something to both of us over the years and it's meant especially something to me because you have remembered it and I guess it has been interwoven into our lives.

MARK: Are there any other things that struck you in reading my piece that we should talk about?

RICHARD: Well, let's see. I was moved by the reflection of the importance of my action in your life. A matter of this being something of a revelation to you, my love and concern for you. And it was certainly done instinctively, not done with premeditation. Diving into the pool, making a fool of myself, and it probably wasn't just fatherly instinct, it was self-preservation, all kinds of stuff. But anyhow, what it meant to you, even in your memory, is an interesting thing.

MARK: Yeah, it's been interesting trying to put it down, as it's existed as a sort of amorphous and vague memory, but meaningful—emotionally meaningful, but literally vague memory. I don't want to overanalyze it, though, because I don't want to change it too much; I just want to preserve it. But it's helpful just even to try to do that, I think. And when I do try to think about it more objectively, I do think that it's tied to being six and sort of just kind of coming into a more general awareness of the world around me—"waking up," as Annie Dillard says. It's not as if you hadn't been around or we hadn't done a whole lot of things together, but it's something about that age and sort of waking up and here was a very immediate, concrete, and kind of shocking example of your love and concern, and your willingness to sacrifice your own well-being for me that struck me. And if it had happened a year earlier it might not have struck me nearly as much and a year later or two years later, the moment might have passed. So I do think for me it had something to do with that particular moment in my own developmental history, that I was sort of ripe for that, suddenly just being aware of this, and here was a very clear example, for a six-year-old, of what a father's love means.

RICHARD: Well, I think it needs to be said too, probably, though my memories are vague, that you were living in a woman's world up to this point. You did not have a father, like you are a father, in terms of spending a lot of time with you daily, evenings some, yes, but I had to go out for meetings, and certainly weekends as much as we could. But this was a man's event, a boy's event, and it probably had a unique power for you because of that, too. It was also a unique event for you partially because it was outdoors; it always heightens things, camping out, but also we'd not done a lot of things together in terms of just daily puttering around.

MARK: Or outings like this.

RICHARD: That's right, so, it had, no doubt, additional meaning.

MARK: That's not really part of my memory, but I'll take your word for it, I guess!

RICHARD: One other thing, for me, is that this incident, and our attempt to recapture it really illustrates the value of parents going over incidents of childhood in detail, not just "oh you remember that," "yeah I remember that," going onto something else. Maybe not parents . . . Children would be as interested as we are. But it's been a fascinating experience for me just to do that, and to have as a core of that the fact that we have different memories of it would have been interesting to trace long ago. But it's interesting, too, that it's come out now.

MARK: Yeah, it is. I'm glad that we didn't talk about it beforehand, but to see that . . . It's such a major difference in a way but it just doesn't matter, it's not a difference that matters at all, in the end, but —

RICHARD: But that could have been the end of it, if you'd just said, "Oh, you don't remember that, you don't remember that right." If you start at that point, that would have been unfortunate, if one of us had said that . . . but I don't think we would have, anyway.

MARK: One last thing. There is this distinction that Donald Spence and others have talked about between "narrative truth" and "historical truth."

RICHARD: Yes.

MARK: So there is, you know, a historical truth of what happens in people's lives; there are "true" events that happen, and somehow you might be able to get back to that, but in the end it's not really nearly as important as the narrative truth that people construct as they think about and retell their life stories and make meaning out of their experience for themselves and others over the years. I think this is an interesting example of that, that there is a historical truth of whether or not that fish got away, but the narrative truth of the story we both tell is what matters. And you could take that even further to say that your narrative, ending with the fish being caught, has meaning for you in a certain way, and my narrative, ending with the fish getting away, has meaning for me.

RICHARD: I was thinking about that, not in those terms, exactly, but I asked myself, "Would I have revised that story to protect my pride a bit?"

MARK: Uh-huh.

RICHARD: And I have no idea. *(Laughter)*. Especially at this distance. I guess it's just going to be an "unsolved mystery," unless somebody remembers for sure.

Chapter 10

Learning to Appreciate the Sublime: Don't Knock the Rock

Frank J. Barrett

Jung and Adler both claimed that one's earliest memory is luminous. My first concrete memory surrounds an event that occurred on December 25, 1958, when I was six years old. It was Christmas at my maternal grandparents' house. I recall the living room as a warm, familiar place where aunts, uncles, and cousins would gather around the piano and sing spirited songs to my grandfather's syncopated ragtime. How he could play the piano. My grandfather and his music brought such joy. I was small enough to sit under the piano bench, to watch Gramp's right foot beat time on the damper pedal. I fit snug under the spinet ledge. I could feel the pulse reverberating through the sound board. This particular holiday, perhaps because I was so enthralled, Gramp decided it was time for me to learn to play the piano, an experience that would change my life. He taught me the left-hand accompaniment to "Chopsticks."

I would learn later that this was an initiation: "Chopsticks" was the first tinkering of many others, including my grandfather himself, my mother, and my uncles. It was fortuitous that I would begin by learning the single bass note in the left hand and three-note chords in the right hand with an oompapa-oompapa pulse instead of the two-fingered right-hand melody that most learned. Perhaps it was here that I first developed the capacity to hear harmonies and overtones (a mixed blessing when listening to older, out-of-tune pianos). My grandfather penciled Xs on the keys that make up the G chord and Os on the keys that make up the C chord so my fingers, which could barely reach, knew where to land. I played the chords over and over until I could hear the differences deeply. Since we were the first family to arrive there, my grandfather had what seemed like hours of free attention just for me. He leaned over my back and gently directed my awkward hands to the right beat. I barely noticed my father—or anyone else—for most of that afternoon; I was so engaged. I remember the moment when my grandfather added the melody in the high keys. Suddenly we were making music. And it was beautiful.

It was dark by the time my uncle and his family walked up the porch bearing pies and gifts. My dad quickly placed me back on the piano bench and beckoned us to play again. He pointed at me as the guests entered. I pretended not to notice them noticing. This was my first performance. My father swelled with pride. He watched the faces of the new arrivals as they appropriately and politely nodded before moving into the dining room to exchange greetings. The traces of that vignette that linger involve the image of my dad proudly directing my cousins to notice the accomplishments of his son. I didn't care if they noticed. But I loved that he did.

* * *

It's a long fly ball. I run with my back to the plate, full speed, diving through the air, parallel to the ground. *How did he cover so much territory?* I stretch my mitt and the ball barely settles into the very edge of the web as I belly flop over the grass, stopping just short of the fence. I remain frozen for a moment, framing my catch for all spectators still incredulous. That's right; I caught it. Then I slowly uncoil my body and jog back to the infield, glancing at the ground—nonchalant, composed, grass-stained, carefully indifferent to the cheers of the crowd. *Don't let them see you notice the cheers.* Except for the only one whose cheers you really relish.

Of course this was all fantasy. I only remember my father coming to watch one Little League game. Each time I came to bat, he came out of the stands and stood behind the backstop, less than ten feet from me. He didn't say much, but I knew he was there. "Stand in there. . . . Don't bail out of the box." I struck out three times.

I suppose every boy wants his father to watch him excel at sports. But for me there was something extra. My dad was a giant. In pictures of him from that period he is an imposing, large, muscular man in his early thirties. He was the biggest father in the neighborhood. This was not a fantasy. He stood 6'2" and he was in terrific shape in those days. He looked important. My uncle said that when my dad returned home from the Army he would run five miles every morning, lift weights, and then go to church.

Back then he was active and vibrant. Shortly after I was born, my parents moved into a new Catholic parish and my dad started the sports programs for the parish school. He coached football, baseball, and basketball. On Saturday afternoons, I held my mother's hand and watched seventh and eighth grade titans in blue and gold uniforms encircle my dad as he directed and encouraged. Girls would hover around the players and the players would hover around my dad. He was the center of their universe too. I was so proud of him. The popular players would come over to the house, sit in our living room, drink Cokes, and call my dad Mr. Barrett. Tommy Cochrane, the star quarterback, visited. So did Bob Ivony, the giant offensive lineman who would later become a high school star and a standout at the Naval Academy. My dad called everyone "son." But in those days there was really only one who deserved that title.

When I entered the fifth grade and was finally old enough to play football, my dad mysteriously quit coaching. It was puzzling at first. I wondered if I disappointed him in some way. But his work was consuming more of his time. He and his brothers had started their own business and he could no longer take off early for afternoon practices. I was convinced, however, that the men who were our coaches learned everything they knew from my dad. I went out for quarterback and although I made the team, I was fourth string and only played in one game. My dad wasn't at that game, or any others for that matter. I never got to throw a pass. I handed the ball off three times and one of those times I gave it to the halfback instead of the fullback. My quarterback career ended on that play.

One evening that summer my dad and I were watching the all-star game on TV together. My dad made us popcorn. He put a stick of butter on top of the popcorn and the kernels stuck to the sides of it. I wouldn't dare tell him that I didn't like it this way or that there are ways to melt the butter over the corn. I ate around the butter stick. It was a mess. As usual, he said very little as we watched the game. Then I had a brilliant idea. I could make hamburgers for both of us. That would impress him. I had happened to see a TV show the previous day that showed how to make hamburgers taste good. The secret ingredient was in the salt. They said that it's good to put salt in the meat as you make the patty. I had made one for myself that afternoon and it tasted good. When I offered to make one for my dad that night, he was surprised. "Can you?" he asked. He always thought of me as small and this was clearly a big person's job. Hamburgers for me and Dad. I dug out the electric frying pan and tried my new recipe. "Do you want lettuce and tomato on it?" That must have impressed him. I even toasted the bread. We watched most of the game in silence. "Did you put salt on this?" he asked after a few bites. Oh good, he likes it. Juice dripping between his fingers as he took another bite. Without looking up from the TV, he said, "Too much salt."

My childhood hero was a baseball player named Rocky Colavito. Some called him the Rock, and it was an apt name. He was even the subject of a book titled *Don't Knock the Rock*. He was a handsome, strong right fielder who hit clutch home runs for the Cleveland Indians. Every Saturday afternoon I would put on my baseball uniform, get my mitt, sit in front of the TV, and watch the Tribe. But I was really watching for Rocky. He would take the bat, lift it over his head, and extend it behind his back. The famous Rocky stretch. All the kids in the neighborhood used to inflate themselves into the Rocky stretch when it was their turn to bat. But no one could do it like me. When Rocky was up I watched intently. I studied how he walked slowly to the plate, gazing at the pitcher—he looked confident, but quite respectful as if he really liked everyone, even this guy who was trying to mow him down with fastballs. He would make a sign of the cross with his bat—the secret signal that only a few of us understood. He was a Catholic, like me. He went to Mass and Communion every Sunday in an Italian parish in the southern suburbs of Cleveland. Something great would happen when he came to the plate.

One morning I woke up to breakfast to find a baseball on the kitchen sink. My mother said Dad brought it home for me last night. Really? It looked like a brand new baseball except for one scuff mark. As I turned it over I noticed there was something written on it. That looks like an R. Sound it out. "R-O-C . . . Rocky? Rocky Colavito? . . . Is this ball signed by Rocky Colavito? No. Really? How did he get this?" Maybe my dad knew someone important who knew Rocky Colavito and went into the dugout after the game to get his signature. Maybe my dad knows the Rock himself. Of course. He is a baseball and football coach after all. Why wouldn't Rocky be friends with my dad? Everybody in the neighborhood loved him. My heart raced. I picked up my mitt and ran outside. Out in the front yard I tossed the ball into the air and caught it, mouthing the cadence of Casey Coleman, the Indians' announcer: "And now Harmon Killebrew is up to bat. Bases loaded. It's a long fly ball to left field. Colavito is racing back, back, back. He dives and pulls the ball down. Indians win! What a catch by the Rock!" I ran toward the dugout that was a front porch, jaunted into the locker room that was our living room as the crowd cheered.

I called three friends and told them to meet me in the backyard. When I showed them the ball, they were impressed all right. One side was stamped:

> Regulation league
> Cleveland Indians

It was clearly an official ball of some kind. We even smelled it. It had that special smell of a brand new ball. My dad got it for me. He got it at the game last night. Rocky Colavito hit a home run with this ball. My dad got it. He got Rocky Colavito's signature. He knows him. They're friends. I was very popular that day. Word spread around the neighborhood quickly. I brought it to school to show my best friend Bobby Kubacki. I loved having the ball. The kids wanted to play catch with it, but I wanted to protect it. Finally I agreed, but only after I carefully covered Rocky's signature with Scotch tape.

One day later that summer Greg Gottschalk, who was five years older than me, stared at the ball for a long time. "It's spelled wrong." What's spelled wrong? "This isn't real. This ball says C-A-L-A-V-I-T-O. That's not the way he spells his name. It's C-*O*-L-A-V-I-T-O." I looked at the ball. Nope, he spells his name C-A-L, I insisted. What's he getting at? Why would he say that about my ball? The next day I read a story about the Indians in the paper and was shocked that Rocky's name was misspelled in the newspaper too.

A few days later Greg came over and brought two of our friends. "Show them the ball." I handed it over. "See? It's definitely misspelled. This ball can't be real." They stared at it and they too agreed that it was a fraud. Then they began to tease me. I took a long hard look at the ball. Finally, I conceded that maybe Rocky spelled his name with an "o," but as I kept looking at it, I could see that this really was an "o." That's exactly what the ball said. Yes. That was it. Of course. Look how round that letter is. It's an "o." I was convinced.

They pointed out that the second and fourth letter of this signature looked similar—they were both "a"s; they were not round but flattened out on the side, and neither looked like the round "o" at the end of the signature. Nope, I insisted. It's definitely round. It's definitely an "o." Why would Rocky misspell his own name? He's not a some kind of jerk.

I put the ball in a shoe box in my closet and never took it out to play catch again. Finally, years later when I was in my twenties, I asked my mother how dad got that ball. I just couldn't ask my father, not even then. She confirmed what I already knew. He was drinking at Mitchell's, the neighborhood beer joint, and one night somebody came in who had been at the game and caught a foul ball. Dad paid him five dollars for it. I still have that ball. It's become a family joke. When I look at it now, I can recognize that it's my father's handwriting. It's more valuable to me now. My dad signed this ball.

He grew up in a different era. I have felt guilty, and still often do, because my life seems so easy compared to his. I can change jobs to improve my quality of life, or to have a schedule that affords more research time so that I can read and write and "make a living with my mind." Sixty years ago my father, then a teenager, spent high school afternoons and evenings loading ore on Lake Erie ships for fifty cents a day, money he himself never spent or I should say could not spend because "it never got into [his] pocket" but went to his father to pay the family bills. The day after graduating from high school I took a summer job cutting weeds while I waited to start my college career. The day after his graduation, my father was drafted into the Army. World War II was raging. The day he was to report to the Army Federal Building, his mother served him the usual breakfast of tea and toast. When he stood up from the table, she took his cup still containing the grounds, steaming with a spot of tea, and she set it in the cupboard. Every morning she opened this shrine, held the cup that last touched his lips, and prayed for my father. The relic would remain just the way he left it until the day he safely walked back through the kitchen door three years later. It was part of that old Irish belief in spirits: As I keep this memory alive, God is keeping my son alive.

I can't help but imagine that the Army changed him. He rarely talked about it and when he did it he always finished with "I'll never sleep outside again." And indeed he didn't. When my Cub Scout troop went on weekend camping trips, my dad was never one of the accompanying counselors. Other fathers came along, showed us how to set up tents, how to start fires, how to cook, and stalk. My dad stayed home. I always remember my first camping trip in the Pennsylvania mountains. It was my first time away from home. As we drove away from Cleveland I couldn't understand why my stomach began to hurt. This was supposed to be fun. One of the other dads noticed I looked forlorn while the other kids were active and setting up camp. He took me into town so I could call home. I just wanted to hear his voice.

Yes, the Army changed him. I would later read something that Heidegger wrote: Philosophy is a form of homesickness. If we felt comfortable and secure, we wouldn't have to search for the meaning behind everything. I would eventually quit the Scouts and become a philosopher. I guess the Army changed me too.

It was probably from his mother that he picked up the habit of worrying about people he cared about. I was not allowed to have a morning paper route because the cars might not see me in the dark. I was not allowed to play tackle football because I could break a leg. (Of course I played anyway, but somehow with the background awareness that I was flirting with trouble.) My father had the uncanny ability to anticipate breakdowns and problems. "You have to protect your own" he would say. Life for my father was an obstacle course. He had trouble navigating through hurdles, having come from a long line of Irish male firstborns who had faced a century of adversity. He told the stories about the Irish famine, the Great Depression, and widespread prejudice: "No Irish or Dogs allowed" read signs on corner stores and taverns.

I remember once when I was twenty-two years old, at home from graduate school for a vacation, I used the family car to drive to a local health club to play racquetball. I was surprised when someone knocked on the door, interrupting the game, and asked if anyone answered to what I recognized as my own name. He said there was a phone call for me. My heart pounded; my stomach felt heavy. I knew there must have been some emergency; perhaps one of my grandparents died, or someone in my family had a serious accident. As I walked to the phone at the end of the hall, I remember thinking that I wasn't sure I wanted to hear about the urgency that had already changed my mood. I immediately recognized my dad's voice. Then the sentence that I will always remember: "Don't forget to get gas. I didn't leave much gas in the car. You're likely to run out." My skin was cold and clammy and he had to repeat the message before I acknowledged I heard him. I walked back to the racquetball court and then broke into laughter. How long had he been worrying about that?

Worrying was one of his core disciplines. Once when I was in my thirties and studying for my doctorate, I received a rare call from my father. He wanted to know if I had remembered that it was time to renew the registration for my car. I answered his questions and said little more. What a stupid question, I thought. He's still treating me like a child. When my mother came to the phone, I told her what Dad had wanted and how silly I thought it was. Then she reminded me why third parties are so important for sustaining interaction: "He was just looking for an excuse to call you. He wanted to talk to you. Don't you know that by now?" I immediately knew what she meant. He would never call just to talk or see how I was doing, to say he had been thinking about me, to ask if I wanted to meet for lunch sometime. In those days a large part of our relationship was built upon platitudes and long silences. It kept us going.

As I grew older, my father began to look less heroic. Partly because of failed business ventures, and an overall sense that work was not rewarding, he looked increasingly drawn and haggard. His face was often blurred behind a haze of cigarette smoke. I can still see him sitting resigned in our living room chair, encircled by rumpled foil and cellophane packets, cigarette butts, and ashes, his banter laced with tease and sarcasm. He became increasingly withdrawn, except when entrapped in an alcoholic fog. Then his displays were blunt and exaggerated—he laughed loudly at comments others did not find funny; he condemned and criticized with misdirected indignation; unprovoked sadness swelled into tears. It was painful, sometimes embarrassing, to witness these bungled, vulgar attempts to relate. When directed toward me, they were unbearable. Alcohol does that. It became hard to predict when he would be agitated and restless. Something changed: As a child I could not get enough of him. As a teenager and young adult I shunned him more than I want to remember.

My father rarely expressed approval or love. I now know that he simply couldn't. I also know that these emotions were swarming in him. I knew that he was happy that I chose to attend that Irish Catholic bastion, The University of Notre Dame. Not that he ever said it directly. When my acceptance letter came he couldn't stop himself from opening and reading it before I got home. From the time I entered as a freshman until he died twenty years later, he followed Notre Dame football each Saturday. For Christmas and birthdays my brothers and I would give him memorabilia with the ND insignia. He is wearing Notre Dame hats, sweatshirts, or jackets in virtually every picture I have of him over the last twenty years of his life. When I would run into relatives or family friends, they always seemed to know what I was doing and what projects I was involved in. Frequently I would meet someone who knew my father and they would say, "Oh you're the piano player who went to Notre Dame." When I would bring friends over for holiday meals, they would inevitably huddle with my father, talking intently. And they seemed to enjoy it. That always puzzled me. "Your father is such a nice guy. Boy he's proud of you. He's not the way you described him at all." They would later tell me that he was waxing philosophical about my accomplishments and asking them about theirs. Or confiding in them about how he's concerned that I was working too hard, that I was too serious for my young age and not enjoying myself enough. My father, it turns out, talked about me endlessly to virtually anyone who would listen. But why were there so many awkward silences, instances of small talk, and clichés between him and me?

I wish I could have seen then what seems so obvious now. He was brimming with love and pride; other than a generalized anxiety about my safety, he had no words to contain his yearnings. I remember the day that I passed my doctoral defense. It was official: I was now a PhD headed for an academic career. I was so exhausted that I didn't notice that this was a big day for him too. Who could have imagined that one of his sons would have this kind of chance? My father had spent his early life in a very poor Irish neighborhood; had heard stories about ancestors leaving school prematurely to work long hours in potato fields; watched his own father physically fight to defend his fragile working-class pride; witnessed his people suffer from abuse, misfortune, shame, and guilt. Now his son would be a college professor.

A few hours after my dissertation defense, my family and friends gathered to celebrate my graduation. Suddenly, my father stood up from the table and asked for attention. The moment is carved into my personal storybook. First he joked that since I was slow in a number of areas he was not surprised that it took so long to finish graduate school. Everyone laughed. He loved to tease. Then he raised his glass and said, "But seriously, we're all . . . very . . . pro . . . " He couldn't continue. His throat clogged and he barely mouthed the last word. Did I just hear my father say he was proud? He never got the word out and he never looked at me. He sat down immediately and his eyes misted with tears. It was the only time I ever heard him try to be direct. And in front of all my friends.

My father was probably more proud of me and my brothers than he was of himself. I wish that during his life he could have been as proud of himself as I am of him now. Love like my father's insinuates into unlikely crevices; it is elusive, wily, convoluted. It's a good story to tell: Maybe we all want more of each other but just haven't learned to recognize the invitations. I hope I will be able to appreciate the sublime gestures next time: the furtive catch of the eye, the curious questions, the teasing, and above all—the listening. Even now I can almost hear my father hearing me.

And just now I think I heard him say, "Don't be so hard on yourself. Why are you writing about a stupid goddamn baseball? . . . Have you checked your oil lately?"

I recall that early Christmas memory, when he stood over my left shoulder, at the periphery of my sight, almost imperceptible, blessing me with approval. If I had looked at him directly, it would all evaporate.

Chapter 11

Remembering My Father

Ernest Keen

Remembering the past always happens in a present, which supplies a context for the content and shape of that remembering. Therefore, my understanding of my father, and my relation to him, occurs in the context of my relationships to my sons. But in addition to this context, I have an entire ensemble of current relationships, which reflect and express our current culture. These too contextualize the content and shape of my memories of my father, as well as my sense of my current relationship with him. Most notably, I have a daughter, and so does he. I have a wife, and so does he. And we all share the changes of the early twenty-first century, which includes multiple layers of memory of the past into which I insert, and from which I extract, my memories of my father.

It is futile to try to cleanse my recollections of my father of these contexts. I cannot experience the present in any other way. Therefore, it serves the truth of what I recall to reflect explicitly on these contexts and their definitive role in my memory. There are, of course, many layers. I must select. This selection was done for me in an interaction I had with my wife. This interaction made it clear that one of several important cultural changes from the 1940s to the 2000s has been the emergence and pervasiveness of feminism since the 1960s. In fact, in an interaction with my wife, which was also an interaction between me and feminism, I discovered myself remembering my father in a certain way. In part this recollection was a self-serving defense against feminist encroachment upon traditional masculine culture, but its occurrence also makes inescapable how the present always informs our memory of the past, and how the content of that memory will be misapprehended unless that context is taken into account.

In the memory I am about to report, therefore, it would be easy to accept virtues and vices implicit in the story at face value, without seeing how they have been determined by current moral struggles. Such a memory of my father, for example, as enacting masculine virtues may accurately depict him as having done so, but our interpretation of them as virtues is not free, and cannot be free, of a current struggle with feminist interpretations of them. I shall therefore proceed in the following way. First, I will describe the context (an interaction with my wife) of this memory of my father. Then I will quote from a note I wrote to her, which contains that memory. Then I will elaborate the memory with both further data and some analytic exploration of some of the layers of meaning that are reflectively visible to me.

CONTEXT

It was an argument about how men refuse to "read the directions," as if doing so is a confession of masculine failure. I had insisted on upholstering some chairs without reading the directions on a box of staples and, I must admit, I displayed a certain contempt for doing so. My wife naturally understood my behavior in her terms and proceeded to explain to me my masculinist bias and its various vices. The most aggressive version of the feminist argument points out that men not only presume that they are writers of (as opposed to readers of) directions, and that women are those who need directions, but finally the masculine tradition assumes that to read the directions is to confess to being less than masculine, weak, not in charge, some kind of "weak sister" (to quote a masculinist put-down). I did not succeed, at the time, in either refuting this feminist argument (which may be impossible) or establishing it as irrelevant to the controversy with my wife.

I did, however, write this note to my wife:

Dear Teresa

On the matter of our thirty minute discussion Sunday morning on the trip from Laporte to Lewisburg, which can be stated as whether I should agree with you to use small staples on the remaining upholstery we will do on the dining room chairs: I have come to the conclusion that you are perhaps right—that our disagreement is an enactment of a gendered conversation that is going on nationwide, one way or another, as men and women overcome traditions of domination and role definition, traditions that leave males feeling that their special position places them beyond the need to "read the directions." Your vehemence surprised me at first and I simply wanted to escape the discussion, partly because I had a vague sense that your analysis of the character of the dispute was correct, and I did not like arguing the classical male position. I believe I even said or implied (I certainly thought) that I was not enacting that masculinist script.

I have thought about this further and now believe you are right about me and my argument. My history as a male, and especially my training in the 1950s, was as you say. At a manifest level males had to do the maintenance of the home, and they combined materials bought at lumberyards and hardware stores with ingenuity and hard work to avoid paying plumbers, electricians, and auto mechanics. Part of that was as foolish as you made it sound, but another part was not foolish. Such specialists were not only expensive then (as opposed to doing it yourself), but often unavailable. I remember my father supervising the whole family's effort to "pull the pump," which extracted from the well six or seven poles of fifteen feet each, the last of which had "leathers" which wear out and must be periodically replaced. Plumbers would take a week to get there and in the meantime we had to flush the toilet, so we did it ourselves. It was a family ritual, and my dad spoke of the homestead in North Dakota as we did it . . . spoke sentimentally.

I tell this story to verify that there is real merit to your interpretation of my attitude. The story itself is a part of a "masculinist tradition," which includes features of domination I explicitly reject. But as you say, my enactment, understood this way, is exactly gendered. Of course, taken in its fuller meaning, it has to do with a tradition richer than the single experience of domination, and a tradition not very well represented in the famous dislike of "reading the directions." That it is sentimental and realistically out of date are certainly likely arguments, but the cryptic "directions" one got on a container at a hardware store were not, in the 1950s, either respected or respectable. One had to add one's own common sense and hands-on experience to such directions whenever one used anything bought at a store.

I write all this down partly because I want to acknowledge the truth in your attitude about the discussion. I also want to try to answer your question about how I could "think X when the directions clearly say Y." It involves the arrogance of a tradition you dislike intensely, and for that arrogance I am sorry. But this tradition, like all traditions, lives at the fringe of the consciousness of us who were raised in it, and our job is to separate the foolishness from the wisdom and the power-laden from the merely industrious. I did not, in our discussion, get very far in this task, but I've gotten a bit further here.

I certainly understand at least some of your attitude about this tradition, and yet I can't reject it all as simply as you can. I confess to valuing selected parts of it and hope you too can see that even if that confession is mere sentimentality, it is not an attack on you in the gender wars.

ELABORATING THE MEMORY

I am sure pulling the pump happened several times during my childhood. Remembering it now doubtlessly confounds them. The following details may therefore be more telling of my remembering than of the incident as a simple *ding an sich*. The atmosphere was, for example, tense. The stakes were high. Once a joint in the 100-foot shaft was reached, the protruding fifteen or eighteen feet of pole had to be unscrewed from the one beneath it. At risk here was not only damaging the threads or breaking the pole itself, but the remaining shaft, still in the well, was holding up a certain amount of water. To let go of it would be to lose it permanently to the depths, and a new well would have to be dug. Therefore, it was necessary to secure the bottom of a screw joint both to unscrew the protruding pole and to prevent losing the remaining poles. The screw joints were metal but the poles themselves were wood, which, of course, was wet and slimy. My father improvised an ingenious combination of metal plates and C-clamps to secure the lower pole while we carefully turned the towering upper one, balancing it carefully so as not to jar the C-clamps loose.

Once free, I remember laying the poles in the grass. They are cold; the sky is grey; my hands are numb; but my job is important. The entire shaft must be reassembled in the exact same order after the leathers at the bottom have been replaced. My father is clearly in charge, with my mother second in command of my sister and me (and sometimes a neighbor). My father coordinated the routine, creating an order, getting from each his or her best contribution, giving each a sense of importance. I look back now recalling how we enjoyed the task, in spite of its wet, cold, dirty, and tense atmosphere. It makes me recall other similar routines that I will also report here.

My father had been a sign painter, and after he left that trade, he still made Christmas cards every year. That too was a family production, with linoleum block or screen process dictating who did what. As the youngest, like in the case of pulling the pump, my job was to distribute the pieces, this time freshly printed cards, by laying over a hundred of them carefully across the couch and living room rug to dry. At an early age, I was part of the crew. This sense of teamwork was also present in a two-year project, indulged maybe one Saturday or Sunday afternoon a month for many months. The four of us would let ourselves into a factory, deserted on the weekend, weave our way through mysterious machines, some enormous in my ten-year-old eyes, to a storeroom where hundreds of boxes, a foot square by three feet long, stood against the wall. Inside each was a thirty-inch road grader, made as a toy, weighing seven or eight pounds, painted bright orange, and bearing the logo of J. D. Adams and Company, in black.

Our job was to add black trim: selected rungs of the grill, the steering wheel and floorboard, and most important of all, the predominant grading blade that bisected the machine at an angle so as to scrape the road. From packed graders without trim to packed graders with trim involved many steps. Unpacking yielded empty boxes that were stacked to create our work space. Each person had a job in the actual painting, then stacking to dry. Every trip to the deserted factory began by repacking the graders we had trimmed the week before, which, as I recall, did look much more striking than the solid orange ones we then unpacked to paint.

Ingenuity in coordinating four people, work space, drying space, the actual painting of those selected details, coordinated temporally so every grader was treated the same way . . . the design of this process was entirely my father's. Only now do I call it "ingenuity." Then it was merely teamwork and maintaining a civil cheerfulness until the job was done. While it is a long way from the North Dakota homestead where he grew up, this atmosphere created by my father must have been central to his experience of surviving the long winters of vast fields and close quarters of homemade safety, where my father, with his parents and three brothers (he was the youngest), lasted for ten years early in the twentieth century.

My fathering, in the 1960s and 1970s, bears resemblances to and differences from this family culture amidst the Indiana of the 1940s and 1950s, which was more individualistic but no less achievement-oriented. The cooperative teamwork of the family appeared a generation later in the 1960s only in some camping trips with my wife and children, which also imitated memories of my family camping during my childhood.

ON FATHERS AND SONS

This topic is crucial now because the existence of father-son traditions is disappearing in the current redefinition of gender roles in this culture. In fact, such traditions are part of a larger gendered life that is being revised, and that revision may not only correct the ways of male domination and privilege relative to females; that revision may also be the occasion of a forgetting of more benign and sentimentally attractive aspects of a tradition that characterized rural and homestead America half a century and a century ago.

Fathers passed on to sons many attitudes, only some of which belittled, subordinated, and insulted wives, mothers, and daughters. I certainly do not want to let my sentimentality spread to traditions of male domination, and it is very difficult to retain any father-son traditions without eventually becoming a part of male reaction to feminism. I would give up the effort except for my belief that some aspects of the father-son tradition are interesting, at least, if not valuable. And they are a part of my identity. They are increasingly not a part of my son's identities, I see, assessing the generations in my family. My father spent a decade of his youth on a homestead in North Dakota in the early decades of this century. I did not.

I really can't know what it meant to my father when his father took the family to North Dakota. Homesteading was surely not an easy life, as they must have known. And there was nothing in Ohio to escape from. But in 1907 Edward Keen took his wife and four sons to scores of acres of treeless prairie, where the winters were cold and hard. They built a house, dug a well, established a farm, and lived there for ten years, until my father was sixteen. He likes to tell the story of his mother leaving the train station in 1918 to return to Ohio.

"I know I am supposed to cry," she said. "I've tried to cry. But I've never been so happy in my life."

I can see some, at least, of what my grandmother thought. I never met her, and her story also remains untold except for this comment. Ten years. Mother, father, and three older brothers, in a small house on windswept plains. What can I know of that experience beyond the snapshots my father offers from time to time? At ninety-six, he still remembers, of course, but we tend to recall together our common experiences more than his more radical and unique one.

I have often been impressed with how much, and especially how quickly, he reads. His explanation is that with three older brothers, who all read the same book at the same time, he had either to learn to read quickly or he was left behind. Competition must have happened too, of course, but my impression is, from how he later ran his family, that this setting included a spirit of "We are all in this together," yielding a sense of teamwork and cooperative effort. It is this theme I have inherited.

In contrast to my father, I spent my formative years in a quasi-rural but well-established neighborhood in Indiana in the 1940s. My sons grew up in the 1960s and 1970s in a small town in Pennsylvania. My father had to be self-reliant in important ways that I did not, and even less did my sons. And yet there remains hints of this as a father-son tradition, and even as a definition of masculinity. As a term, "self-reliance" was defined by Thoreau, whom I never read but my father did. Curiously, one of my sons found *Walden* very meaningful. I had attributed that simply to his curiosity, but I have discovered that this notion permeates the father-son tradition in my life.

THE TWENTY-FIRST CENTURY

It is now possible to discern several features of this father-son tradition and how it is changing. First, it is currently perceived as a part of patriarchal domination. As that aspect of the tradition recedes, as it must, self-reliance in its traditional masculinist sense is also disappearing. It is clear to me neither that it could be salvaged, nor that it should be salvaged. Second, that version of self-reliance was embedded in a family structure that concentrated power centrally in the father. Such a family structure may have been useful in times of homesteading and other nineteenth-century conditions, for it created familial teamwork in an efficient but hierarchical way.

Third and finally, the conditions of family life have changed as the infrastructural uncertainties have disappeared with increasingly efficient technology. Going to the hardware store now, I notice that packaging has in fact gotten better, and instructions are more necessary and helpful. The increased complexity of home repair technology is making the instructions more useful. But this change also bespeaks the disappearance of the tradition of self-reliance. Technology inevitably produces specialization; specialization inevitably requires networks of integration. These in turn are increasingly codified legally and formally into organizations that replace the intensely personal one of the family.

ANCHORING ACROSS

Thinking of myself across generations, I realize I am more than myself. I was a part of my parents' narrative construction of themselves, and of my grandparents' constructions. I was a presence for the generations that preceded mine. Those constructions and that presence that I was remain a part of my constructions of myself. Similarly, my narrative construction of my sons' lives are present in their lives, so I am also a presence in the generation that follows mine. And there are grandchildren. The self for most of us continues to be anchored in both the preceding and succeeding generations.

The perspective from which I can see all this is that of myself, in my generation. But that perspective inevitably includes more than my generation. I am a continuation of my forebear's perspective, and my sons and grandsons are a continuation of mine. The "me" that I am is thus grounded not only in my experience, but also in how I experience their experience of me. I have control over only part of that complex. I can change what I think of myself, but I can't necessarily change what they think of me (nor what I know they think or thought of me). Similarly, my sons and grandsons can change themselves, but what I want for them, hope for them, and expect of them remains up to me.

This is an experience of myself as multiply anchored, across at least three generations, if not more. The "anchoring across" is an important part of everyone's personal history, and it is integral to family history. And yet this "anchoring across" is nearly mute. It has little language in which to be what it is. I remember my father's injunctions and his expectations; I can see them still. I hope my sons know my expectations, but I do not know how they code them. I can only be who I am, and somehow that says who I think they are, which codes my view of them. But like my father's view of me, it seems nearly mute. Unlike Willy Loman, my family has fortunately lacked the tragic intensity of "Be a success," of fathers judging themselves through their fathers' and their sons' eyes.

One of the goals of my thinking about this now is to try to see more clearly the medium of this anchoring across generations. If it is not worded in slogans such as "Be a success," then how is it coded, and what is its content? My approach is to ask questions such as: What do I want and not want to pass on to my sons? What am I glad and sorry my father taught me? To be able to articulate these things is to specify my own "anchoring across generations." It is the definition of myself in that anchoring. It writes the narrative of my life in its presence beyond the terminals of my birth and death dates.

CODA

The content of any memory will be misapprehended unless the context of remembering is taken into account. Such a current context shapes and even dictates the meaning of the memory itself. In what I have written, I am using a cultural respect for the tradition of self-reliance to cope with attacks on masculinist traditions that include male domination and privilege, which I too wish to destroy. I am also using feminism to help me select from that masculinist tradition what I currently understand as valuable, and to cleanse such valuables of their historic accompaniments that I currently reject.

Such a dialectic, between present and past, happens all the time. Recognizing it amounts to no more nor less than appreciating the fact that consciousness is always situated in a particular historical niche. I cannot remember but from the perspective of myself in my present. There is no such thing as an objective history.

Chapter 12

Blessed Be the Name of the Father: Generational Echoes

Kenneth J. Gergen
J. Stanford Gergen
Chase Martini

Centuries of accumulated myth, legend, fiction, and folklore freight the contemporary relationship between fathers and sons with deep significance—high drama can lie buried beneath the slightest nuance of demeanor. It is also clear that these dramas are scarcely confined to the moment of their occurrence. Their effects spring out of time and place and echo through the lives of the participants. They function as a forestructure through which the remainder of life makes sense (or not) and action becomes significant. Yet these are not simple effects—indelibly stamped into the psyche of the participants. Rather, they are more like voices insinuated into a dialogue. They participate, but in the ensuing interchange they give rise to new forms of intelligibility and action. Further, this process may be carried on into other relations—into succeeding relations between fathers and sons, and more. Echoes of relatedness reverberate through the centuries.

It is within this context that the present contribution emerges. Essentially we shall attempt to trace the echoes of father-son relationships across four generations. First Ken Gergen will write about a critical aspect of his relationship with his father, John J. Gergen, and of the ways in which this relationship has entered into his own actions as a father. Then, his son, Stan Gergen, will respond with a meditation on how this preceding relationship has entered into his own life, favoring certain ways of being as opposed to others. Finally, Stan's son, Chase (nine years old at this writing) will speak about his relationship with his father. Therein we shall locate echoes, evolutions, and silences that span an entire century.

KENNETH GERGEN:
ON RELATIONS WITH MY FATHER

It is difficult to write in any simple way about relations with my father, John Jay Gergen. He was a very complex man, and I have my own share of quirks and convolutions. We lived together for almost twenty years, and shared a life together for many more; both of us were always in transition. So there is scarcely one voice that is adequate, an appropriate fixing of the man and our relationship within a structure of words. I can only tell stories, and in this be guided by the demands of narrative itself. But given our propensity to live our lives in stories, there should be some resonance between what I write and "the way we were." I shall select only a single theme that pervaded our life together, but it is one with which I have continuously wrestled, and which also entered importantly into my relationships with my own son, Stan.

The theme is that of silence—not action but inaction, or rather, action far more consequential by virtue of its very impenetrability as action. I am not speaking here of a general aversion to speaking. My father was, in fact, a highly articulate man, one of the finest mathematics professors I have ever heard lecture, and a winner of a Presidential Medal of Honor for his efforts on behalf of military research and education after World War II. Language—whether displayed in the infinite production of symbolic scribbles in his mathematical work or at his weekly conversations at Rotary club—was not his problem. Rather, the silence was highly selective, and in this selection of sites formidable in its consequences. The sites were typically those in which I had erred in some way, and the silence for me was an expression of profound disapproval. It was not an instructive disapproval, the kind that points to promising routes toward improvement; nor did it seem a charitable disapproval, the kind that otherwise suggests understanding and sympathy for the errant action. Rather, those silences seemed to bespeak a disgust; the depths of which I could not fathom. Judgment day had arrived, and there could be no words of extenuation or mitigation. The evil was pure and I must live (and perish) with it—alone.

I am not speaking here of a single, critical incident but rather a form of relating that pervaded our relationship from my earliest recollections onward. A few examples will illustrate:

—I had just learned to swim, and my father had taken us for a Saturday morning faculty swimming hour at the Duke gymnasium. Toward the end of the hour, my father went to take a shower. My older brother John decided that this was an appropriate time to demonstrate what he knew (or didn't know) about lifesaving. In the deep water he approached me from behind, leaped on my shoulders, locked his arms around me, and carried me toward the bottom of the pool. I couldn't free myself, couldn't breathe, and began taking water into my lungs. Panic! When I was loosed from his grasp and reached the surface I was frightened, furious, and in tears. I went tearing into the dressing room after my father to enlist sympathy and a force of retribution. I tearfully poured out my story, looking desperately for signs of commiseration. None were forthcoming. Instead there was an icy stare. What kind of weakling was I, the silence seemed to say; why was I disturbing the peace of faculty swimming hour; why couldn't I stand up for myself like a man?

—Delivering my report card was always a moment of great weight and few words. Perfect grades went without remark. An A− or God forbid, a B+ stimulated either questions such as, "What's the matter here," "What's this all about," or brief orders to "Get that grade up." During one grading period, however, I "fell in with the wrong lot," and managed to be caught for several prankish outbursts—disturbing an auditorium service with merrymaking, publicly making fun of my music teacher, and spearing a sack of lunchroom potatoes with a makeshift sword from shop class. Sheepishly I brought home a grade of C for "comportment." My other grades that month demanded but slight comment. The grade of C, however, elicited a bellowing "Good God! . . . " And then silence . . . for days . . . I had desecrated my home and family.

—Adolescent dating was always suffused with desire and doubt, desire for romance and all its wonders and doubt that my father approved of my expanding interests beyond the rigors of school and athletics. Before I was able to drive, there were dance nights on which I desperately needed a ride home—typically from the house of a date where my friends and I would be partying. On these nights my father would arrive earlier than the appointed time in our large, black Buick, and sit there sullenly with his overcoat and hat generating a forbidding silhouette that we could spy from the window. The ride home typically proceeded in silence. My male companions, whom we occasionally dropped off at their homes, nicknamed my father "the bear." Worse still were the later periods of my adolescence when I could drive. It was difficult enough to generate the courage to ask for the family car, but when I did receive the green light, I was given strict orders for the time of return. And my father would inevitably wait up for me. One cannot always end an evening's relationship at precisely the appointed hour. Girls seemed gifted in creating relational complexity, and it would be rude beyond repair suddenly to insert a "well, gotta go!" into an otherwise delicate *engagement*. Thus, I was not always on time; on occasion I was egregiously late. And inevitably, there he would be, sitting alone in his bathrobe in an otherwise dark room, a single light over his chair, not reading—just waiting. When I entered I confronted only that stern and silent stare. He shuffled off; I took the guilt to bed with me.

—In one critical instance I was forced to rethink the meaning of silence. I was on summer vacation from Yale; I needed the car for a date with a very special girl who lived across town. My father was hesitant. He had fancied going to see the Durham Bulls baseball game that night. After some tense and understated negotiation, we agreed that I could drop him at the game and pick him up after it was over. We set out for the evening, I behind the driver's wheel. I turned the car in the direction of the stadium. He asked me where I was going. "I'm dropping you by the game," I replied. Silence . . . anguished silence . . . why? . . . Suddenly he shouted, "Let me out!" "Why, what's the matter?" I cried. "Just let me out. . . . I'm taking a bus!" he bellowed. Shocked and perplexed, I began to slow the car. He didn't wait for me to stop; he leaped from the car and strode toward the curb. "Dad, Dad. . . ." I beseeched. He turned away. . . . no answer. It was a very long and difficult evening for me. No one waited up. He left for the office early Saturday morning so there was no opportunity to talk. Finally, I could approach my mother. She had served as the major conduit of emotional exchange between my father and me for many years. She related to me that my father was deeply wounded by my choice to drive him to the game before picking up my girlfriend. He saw this as a sign that I would be embarrassed by having to present him as my father. This was totally unbelievable to me. Embarrassed?

How was this possible? The silence was sustained for days. But during this time my reveries turned to questions of interpretation. Could I have been mistaken all these years in reading his silence as profound rejection? Is it possible that my errors were actually his wounds, that behind the seeming anger was a flood of tears? I will never know.

The repercussions of the silent treatment are many and complex. In many respects the internal dialogue that they created continues to haunt my daily actions: "What am I doing wrong; how am I failing; am I being silly or stupid. . . ." With this dialogue a pervasive fixture, I can scarcely disconnect it from an unflagging penchant for productivity on the one hand, and an enormous rebellion against the dominant order on the other. My social constructionist writings were scarcely accidental; they are both numerous and rebellious. Yet, it is not my professional life I wish to address in this case, but my life as a father. How did these critical incidents in my life with my father enter into my relationship with my own son? Was I destined to duplicate the pattern, as developmental specialists so often describe, or were other possibilities open to me?

Here I tend to see the emerging pattern primarily in a dialogic light. That is, the pain created by my father's distance called forth a countertext: I was determined not to repeat this pattern with my own children. Rather, my hope was to explore its opposite, a warm, spontaneous openness. I wanted to open my arms, understand, accept wherever possible. My general sense is that this determination entered importantly into my relationships with both my son and daughter. I recall raucous play together in their younger years—jumping, running, hiding, wrestling, screaming, chortling, faking, and inevitably laughing—always laughing. Later there were weekend outings, sports of every variety, movies, hamburgers, Baskin-Robbins®, and travels, where a sense of light camaraderie prevailed. I found it very difficult to correct these children, very difficult to say anything that would hurt them. An intense sense of closeness was there for me; their pain would be my pain.

Was I being too lenient, a pushover with spoiled brats to show for it? I don't think so. What seemed so ironic to me in all this was that neither Stan nor Laura seemed prone to . . . I want to say "disobedience" here, but it is not quite the word. I didn't lay down the kind of strong rules, I felt, that one could disobey. Let us say that their actions seldom needed correcting. Perhaps Carl Rogers had it right!

But then a critical deviation: Stan was typically an enthusiastic boy; his interests were often passionate. Unfortunately, high school classes had lost their allure; his grades were excellent but his interest only passing. Like many teenagers, his circle of friends were his muse, full of mirth, innovation, curiosity, and mutual care. Unfortunately, however, this same group shared Stan's alienation from school and from the "goody-good" culture that seemed its ally. They were eager to explore the limits. As I slowly and sorrowfully learned, much of this exploration was in the direction of alcohol and drugs. These were difficult times for all of us. And my father was there perched on my shoulder. I tried to shake him, and to locate sympathy, concern, and understanding. But at times I would snap; I was too burned. Yet, stony silence still seemed the wrong way to go. I struggled then to find ways of articulating my anger, to speak and be heard, to find my "command voice" (a phrase my veterinarian taught me, as she saw my inability to control my unruly dog). I wasn't very successful, a result that was perhaps favored by the fact that Stan and Laura now largely resided nearby with their mother. My marriage had not been a success and I was trying desperately to blend together the two families—Mary and her teenage children with Stan and Laura. Harmony and goodwill were my chief aims. How was I to integrate "angry words" into the mix?

This struggle came to an excruciating head when Mary and I returned from a weekend away from home. Teenagers in Swarthmore, as in other suburban areas, were given to the practice of finding homes where parents were away for the weekend and using them as sites for "high" festivities. Stories of unfortunate consequences abounded, and we earnestly warned our offspring "not to have parties" while we were away. Our return on Sunday afternoon surpassed even our worst fantasies. We were welcomed by alcohol and vomit stains across the floors; the door to the liquor cabinet was gashed and torn from its hinges; not only had windows on the porch been shattered, but the window frames were ripped away. Contents of the room were strewn in the yard below. As we slowly learned, Stan and his friends—along with their invitees—had descended. Intense partying had ensued—alcohol, drugs, and rock 'n' roll—until the fighting broke out. No one had remained, literally, to pick up the pieces. Nor had Stan returned on Sunday before our arrival.

At that moment the father on my shoulder screamed into my ear. Not only was there a deep anger, what I suspected my father had always felt, but as I had also come to see, there was also the wounding—"If he loved me how could he . . . " And there was more: How now were the families to blend? How could Stan and I ever rekindle the intimacy we had once enjoyed? Had he now gone so far in his rebellious exploration that he could never return? All was turmoil, and I lapsed into silence. That silence remained for six weeks. I never called or visited Stan; he was content to remain "out of harm's way." The intimacy was now between my father and me.

Stan and I did slowly pick up the pieces, mend the tatters of the relationship (as well as the house), and renew moments of spontaneous joy. And, fortunately, Stan discovered a new passion: girls. The previous explorations could be pushed aside; there was time for schooling again; the "upward track" toward the future was again reasserted (the same track to which my father had been steadfastly dedicated, which had been all I ever knew). The inner dialogue with my father is now largely put to rest—he is enjoying me more and vice versa; I can now see in him characteristics to which I was blind. And for Stan and me, I feel the silences we do share are most frequently in the mutual realization of our deep connection and its significance to us. There are no adequate words.

JOHN STANFORD GERGEN: LIFE WITH MY FATHER

For some (and perhaps many) sons, writing about their relationship with their father would be a daunting, even threatening, task. I believe that it speaks to the relationship that I have with my father that I'm able to avoid the silence and approach this subject with a sense of warmth and adventure. In fact, it is with a high sense of exploration that I have always seen my dad experiencing his life, and this has manifested itself in my behavior.

From my earliest memories, the times that my father shared with my sister and me were indeed full of dynamic activity, warmth, and laughter. Perhaps some of this was due to the nature of our visits—an effort to condense as much love and action into our biweekly interactions as possible to compensate for the time lost by Dad's absence in our home. But I believe that there was more to it than this. Dad's natural warmth was a shelter from the storm that had enveloped our life due to the divorce. In addition to his warmth, his encouragement of curiosity and constant exploration was ever present during these visits.

He even made eating lunch an adventure. One day, I went over to his house for lunch and was surprised by a plate full of orange food. While eating, I remember Dad and I speculating about what other uniquely colored plates of food would be possible—green (certainly), yellow (possibly), but what about blue? Dad eased my doubts by saying that even a plate of blue food would be possible.

A trip to visit Dad in Japan turned out to be a week-long journey to the Inland Sea. Forgoing typical Western accommodations, we stayed in Japanese ryokans at every stop—sleeping on tatami mats and eating (or attempting to swallow) the local cuisine. Yes, it was difficult to acquire a taste for sushi and less identifiable edibles at age twelve, but it was the exploration of this "new world" that nourished me.

Even though our time spent together was intermittent, I believe that I absorbed Dad's sense of adventure, which pushed beyond the typical societal restraints and conventions to explore even further. Unfortunately, my sense of adventure took me down a path of drug use in high school that ended up being quite a dark period of my life. I knew exactly what Dad's silence meant during this time. It was painful to know that I had hurt him, and his silence was an effective conduit to my guilt. Had he spoken up and lambasted me, however, I would have been crushed. Based upon our past, I knew that in his silence there would eventually be forgiveness. He rarely raised his voice to me, and when this had occurred, its effect had been devastating. In a sense, the silence was a more graceful and effective way of punishing my behavior.

It took me a while to learn my limits and, fortunately, Dad was there to encourage my new interest in the opposite sex. One evening, after my girlfriend and I were "caught in the act" at my mother's house, I remember Dad telling me that I was free to use his spare bedroom anytime to be with my girlfriend.

Dad mentioned silence as a recurring theme with his father, and I feel that there was a great deal of silence in his relationship to me, albeit of a different nature. Dad's eligibility for academic sabbaticals and his acceptance in the international community took him overseas frequently. The difficult part of this for my sister and me was that he was often gone for long periods of time and, when he was home, our time together was relatively short. I can't remember seeing Dad at any of my Little League baseball games. My contact with him was often limited to long-distance phone calls, care packages, letters, or cassette tapes. From a distance, Dad's sense of adventure, warmth, and humor was still present. One time I received a canister of sand from the Sahara Desert from him, but instead of a live voice it seemed more like an echo, and could only do so much toward nurturing our relationship. There clearly was silence in his absence from my daily world.

I think the most painful absence was on the eve of my second heart surgery. Dad was in Australia, and it was difficult to hear him on the phone. After a short conversation, I mumbled "I love you." After a brief silence on the other line, I heard the words "OK" and then "bye." I doubt that Dad heard me, but it was a difficult moment. Although Dad was very affectionate, we hadn't often (ever?) expressed our love for each other, and I was trying to reach out. Subsequently, it took some time to heal and, fortunately, we are now able to communicate our feelings more directly.

As I have grown older, and Dad has continued to travel, his pace seems frenetic. My sister and I have often been challenged to remember which hemisphere he is in, let alone which country. What has amazed me is that not only does he have tremendous energy for his craft, but also time to fit in a whole lot of living as well: skiing in Switzerland, doing the tango in Buenos Aires, or living on an island in Greece. However, his globetrotting, carpe diem approach can be exhausting to the outsider, and I sometimes sense that there is a restlessness in Dad that is unsettling. He doesn't seem to take much time to relax. All his days seem so filled with activity—whether at home or on the road.

In some ways I'm treading the same path. Last year, I took six business trips overseas along with a holiday in Europe. As I write these words, I'm traveling back to the United States after a week's stay in Brussels. Like Dad, whenever traveling to a foreign city, I make the most of it. Last Sunday, after a sleepless night on the plane and a 7 a.m. arrival in Brussels, I bypassed the bed for a train ride to Gent. In Gent, I thought of Dad as I explored the town's sites and sampled the favorite local dish, waterzooi, because "I just had to do it." It may have been a push, but it was my Dad's pace that I believe was driving me.

As I follow my father's passion for travel and new experiences, I try to do so with restraint. I need to constantly remind myself not to overdo it and to set aside time for my family and relaxation. For me, the frenetic pace can lack spirituality and often doesn't allow much time to be reflective. So, whenever possible, I take time to "cool down"—playing my guitar, reading, or watching TV. In my relationship with my son Chase, I try to encourage his exploration of new adventures as much as possible, while also trying to ensure that he realizes the importance of relaxing or taking it easy.

Chase is a very active, social boy who embraces new adventures; whether participating in different sports (baseball, soccer, karate), acquiring a new pet (he has had ferrets, guinea pigs, fish, cats, and dogs), moving to a new city (Chase has attended four different schools in the past five years), or traveling to Europe. In the midst of all of this activity, however, I try to encourage him to take time out to relax and be reflective. We often spend hours on a Sunday afternoon watching football or videos. We used to attend church regularly, and are now seeking a new place of worship. By encouraging these less active tasks, I'm hoping that he will be able to achieve a balance in his life that I sometimes see as lacking in my father's (and mine).

The other important aspect of my relationship with Chase is that I try very hard to be there for him, despite my hectic schedule. A few years ago, I was an assistant coach for his Little League team. My wife and I never miss his soccer games. I have assisted him on class assignments and have regularly taken him downtown for sporting and cultural events. I don't want him to experience the silence in absence that I had with my father.

The biggest challenge I have now with my relationship to Chase is my inability to express my love and appreciation directly to him. I was not able to have a child with my first wife, and Chase literally arrived on my doorstep one day with his mother—one of my life's miracles. I am grateful for the opportunity to be a father to him, but I lack the sense of warmth that my father showed toward me while growing up. It is a challenge for me to express myself in this way, and my silence often shows. It is difficult to attribute this to any particular influence, but perhaps it is partially due to the fact that, while my father was very affectionate, he was often not there.

There is no silence, however, in these words that I have written. Their echoes will undoubtedly shape our future interactions. As my relationship with my father and my son continues to evolve, I look forward to this future with a sense of warmth and adventure.

CHASE MARTINI: ON RELATIONS WITH MY FATHER

I* met my stepfather, Stan (who I call "Poppy") when I was four years old. My mother had gone through a really bad divorce with my dad about a year before so I was kind of scared of grown men being with my mom. One of my first memories of Stan is how quiet and nice he was. When we came to see Stan's house as a possible place to live I was kind of nervous, excited, and hyper at the same time. In my excitement during my mom's interview with Stan, I broke several lightbulbs in his basement. I was scared knowing how angry my own father would have been. I was really surprised when I didn't receive anything more than a smile and "that's okay; accidents happen." I felt as though I was going to be able to trust this man with my mother and, maybe, I'd even get to like him.

My mom soon became more than just a roommate with Stan and they announced they were dating. Stan was gentle with my mom and me and was always very patient with my wild behavior. I will never forget the first time Poppy yelled at me. It was terrible. I was kicking a tennis racket against the wall, for no reason of course, when Stan turned from the football game he was watching and started yelling at me. Although I deserved it, my feelings were hurt. I was confused about what turned a usually quiet man into an angry person.

My own father really didn't participate much in my academics or sports. He has never sent me to any camps or signed me up for sports. Poppy, along with his cousin, Chris, were the people who taught me how to ride a bike and how to throw a good spiral with a football.

When Stan got transferred to Florida I was afraid my mom would be very unhappy, but I knew we would see him again so I was fine. When Stan told me my mom and I would be moving to be with him in Florida I was very excited, but I was also confused on how I was go-

---

*As related to and edited by his mother, Lisa Gergen.

ing to feel about being away from my own dad for such long periods of time.

When we were living in Florida I begged my mom and Stan for a pet of my own. Stan sat me down and educated me about the responsibilities involved with taking care of pets. Stan is a real animal lover just like I am. Although Stan didn't really like my guinea pig, Rusty, all that much, he was very kind and sympathetic when Rusty died while I was visiting with my dad over spring break. I couldn't believe it happened! Especially since I felt my parents would blame me for not taking good care of him. They were always yelling at me about keeping his cage clean, etc. While I was gone, Stan made a coffin for Rusty out of a shoebox, wrote his name on it, and placed a rose in the coffin with Rusty. He then made a cross out of some Popsicle sticks for his grave site. He buried Rusty in front of our house and had a little funeral for him. I remember making Stan tell me every detail. He was very sad, too, but most of all he took especially good care of my Rusty for me, even in death. That means a lot.

Only two years after moving from Georgia to Florida, Stan had taken a new job in Virginia. He traveled to Mexico and South America a lot and he had found a better job where he could visit Europe. Stan liked to travel and he promised we would all go away some time. He has always brought me back cool things from the places he visits. Moving to Virginia meant a new school and new friends again. Poppy made me feel better about another move by telling me all about the good and fun things we would be doing when we moved. He even promised to buy me a sled. Stan has always kept his promises.

Like a lot of other children these days, I am from a divorced family. Although I love my biological father very much, I am proud to be Poppy's son. He always refers to me as his son, not his stepson. He is more strict than my mother and tells her she is too lenient with me at times. But he's usually fair in his punishments. I truly love him, too, but it's hard for me to express it sometimes.

I plan on following in Stan's steps and attending Duke University or Clemson University. Stan consistently encourages me to study hard and get good grades so this dream can become a reality. He emphasizes the importance of being educated and he believes I can be anything I want to be. He is a wonderful role model and I'm glad we answered the "Roommate Needed" ad five years ago.

SPANNING THE GENERATIONS: BEYOND THE SILENCE

What do these stories tell us of the relations between fathers and sons, and of their echoes across the generations? At the outset it seems clear that no relationship is self-contained. Whatever of significance passes between father and son is likely to spill over the boundaries of their relationship and into others. In the present exploration we gain some sense of this diffusion as the relationship between Kenneth and his father establishes the contours for Kenneth's relationship with his son, Stan; and then in turn, this relationship becomes a fashioning agent in Stan's relationship with his son, Chase. In a broad sense, then, no relationship is a closed circle; the here-and-now of any relationship always bears the traces of myriad other relationships. We are always swimming in a sea of complex crosscurrents; the here-and-now is always there-and-then. There is much in this way of seeing things that militates against individual blame—for fathers of sons and vice versa. Each father and son brings to the relationship traces of still other relationships—commitments, standards, ideals, rationalities. And whatever we find "problematic" about the individual father or the individual son is inevitably the manifestation of yet other relationships.

However, as the present accounts suggest, the metaphor of the cross-generational "echo" is limited; likewise problematic is the metaphor of the multigeneration "reverberation." That is, what we seem to find in these accounts is not so much a trend, habit, or orientation that persists across the generations, but a process more akin to "corrective compensation." The contours of one relationship often seem to establish grounds for critical reflection. With each generation we seem to find the question raised, "What is happening here that I do not wish to duplicate in my relationship with my own son?" Thus, Kenneth attempts to avoid repeating his father's critical silence in his relations with Stan. However, because of the pain experienced at his father's absence, Stan tries to avoid this pattern in his relationship with Chase.

If corrective compensation were all that took place, we might anticipate a continuous movement toward the ideal father-son relationship. Each successive generation would correct for the faults of the preceding until we would all approach perfection. Clearly, however, we do not live in such a Panglossian world. In part this is because few forms of action (perhaps none at all) represent universal or transituational goods. What is good, proper, and even ideal in one setting or era may be counterproductive, irritating, or noxious in another. For example, Kenneth did emulate his father's highly active, achievement-oriented lifestyle. There was no compensatory correction here but, rather, an admiration that entered into his own way of life. Yet, this same lifestyle, from his son's perspective, was the cause of deep pain. It functioned as a wedge between them. And even though Stan also took on this style for himself, he continues to fight against its all-consuming potentials as he works out a mode of fathering his son, Chase. In the same way, there are individuals who feel they were smothered and crippled by too much parental affection and involvement in their lives, others who feel that their parents' high standards have created in them a lifetime of self-scorn, and so on.

It is partially because the goods in one context are evils in another that we also find any action open to multiple interpretations. The process of interpretation is never principally closed; fathers and sons may continuously interrogate each others' actions (as well as their own) to find new, different, and sometimes contradictory features. Kenneth finds that his mother's interpretation of his father's silence casts it in terms of his "father's pain"; suddenly the long-standing understanding of "silence as rejection" is unsettled. All that seemed rejecting could be refigured as love. Similarly, Stan is torn between an admiration for his father's adventuresome lifestyle and an antipathy at its divisive repercussions. Chase finds his father given to silence, yet, unlike Kenneth, he doesn't interpret this silence as uncaring or critical.

As a final contribution to the unpredictable character of cross-generational movement, we find that the players are seldom unified and consistent beings. Possibly because of the multiple relationships in which we are all immersed, we carry with us an assortment of disparate and often incoherent tendencies, tastes, desires, and the like. There is little, then, that is so solid and unmitigated in its presence within a relationship, that either compensation or emulation are wholly embraced. Nowhere in his account does Kenneth describe the enormous sacrifices made by his father on his behalf, sacrifices that complicate considerably the ways in which his relationship with his father influences his ways of fathering. Stan finds in his father manifestations of deep love and simultaneously, of distance. Chase finds in

Stan enormous warmth and caring but cannot comprehend his bursts of anger.

In these ways, development across the generations seems not so much like an echoing, a reverberating, or a dialectic so much as a transformative conversation. Each action, like an entry into the conversation, sets the context for what follows, but is also refigured in that following. New voices continuously enter the conversation, again unsettling the patterns, the recollections, the interpretations, and the trajectories. John, Kenneth, Stan, Chase—their conversation continues even now to reshape them, not in predetermined ways but as they, and the many who are closely connected to them, now contribute. They have the resources—the vocabularies of relationship—that will enable them to sustain a warm, loving, and bonded future, but the conversation is never complete. We must care for each and every word.

Chapter 13

Their Way

Robert J. Pellegrini

Memories of my childhood have been surfacing more frequently than ever for me in the past few months. Not always memories of major things, mind you, but all sorts of things. In these reminiscences I can envision, with impressive clarity and detail, apparently trivial things that happened decades ago. I've wondered about what might be stirring up the occasionally quite vivid imagery associated with such recollections, especially since my characteristic obliviousness to mundane matters of the here and now (e.g., where I left my keys, my eyeglasses, my wallet, my car, etc.) seems to be solidly intact.

In what I suspect is more than just coincidence, these reawakenings typically occur to me during or after events that remind me how quickly life is passing, and how little time is left to do whatever there is to do. Celebrating the birthday that qualified me for senior discounts; learning of grave illnesses, retirements, deaths, births of children and grandchildren happening in the lives of family members, friends, colleagues, neighbors, and other people I've known for many years; and most of all, the unparalleled luxury of time spent with my children and grandchildren. These are the kinds of experiences that often seem to serve as mortality markers preceding resurrection of long-lost episodes in *my* life story.

The story behind the childhood memory of this sort that I will relate here begins one chokingly hot August day on the high chaparral dirt trails of the rugged Pah Rah Mountains, about sixty miles north of Reno. The road names like Ax Handle Canyon, Pony Canyon, Broken Spur, Wrangler, Stirrup, Stallion, Crazy Horse, Piute Creek, and Chieftain, aptly convey the Wild West quality of this region, reminiscent of scenes from a John Ford movie. Not uncommonly, locals here still carry hip-holstered six-shooters on mounted rides over these sometimes treacherously narrow trails along precipitous cliffs, bordered by an infinitely textured landscape featuring outcroppings of rock to which the eye is drawn magnetically. Silence, except for the wind whistling through the ubiquitous sagebrush, or howling through jagged ravines. A flock of chukar roused from the thicket by horses that still run wild here, and for which the surrounding Palomino Valley is named. Red-tailed hawks soaring the air currents as if surveying a domain that is ultimately their own. And from the heights of its mountain peaks, a panorama spanned by the silver blue serenity of Pyramid Lake.

The vast, unspoiled natural grandeur of this area stirs a very special passion in those of us who have learned to love it. But my son and I also learned years ago that what we have come to see and feel as the compelling majesty of this desert mountain wilderness, where one can spend several days in midsummer without encountering even a trace of human life, is not reliably so appreciated by others. Admittedly, enjoyment of its natural wonders can be diminished some by the realities of poisonous snakes, bloodthirsty insects, scorching sun, and occasional sandblasting by windborn dirt, all of which sometimes seem to be conspiring to suck the life out of anyone foolish enough to tread on these grounds that were once totally the province of Native American tribes. But none of these ecological challenges ever bothered us nearly as much as the whiny complaints they evoked from people we brought up here to share in the beauty of our secret paradise retreat. We had long since decided to avoid having any more of our visits to this place cut short because a newcomer was overwhelmed by its liabilities, which we accept as part of the price of admission to the show. This trip was just the two of us.

As planned, we left San Jose right after the full-contact martial arts contest in which Bob competed for the heavyweight open division championship. His loss in the finals dampened the mood of our drive for the first hour or so, during which there were almost no verbal exchanges between us. His coach, teammates, friends, students, and fans (including his mother and me) had all told him how proud we were of him for having fought such a great match against a magnificently skilled incumbent champion. I guess all that helped some. As we drove, I thought about trying to console him with more of the same and by reminding him that he'd still finish the year with a not-so-shabby third place statewide ranking.

But I said nothing. I've come to accept the fact that the less anyone says to my son in such moments, the better. It's usually not long before something triggers his irrepressible sense of the ridiculous, and he's doing an improv sketch that runs until he decides he's milked it dry. This comedic thing worked well for him in road gigs. He played drums and occasionally rhythm guitar for a rock band that self-destructed of internal conflict soon after getting a contract from a major recording company. Ironically, this same style of humor, which so many of his public school teachers and counselors tried so hard to extinguish in Bob, is clearly integral now to his professional effectiveness in the field of juvenile probation. By the time we'd reached Sacramento, he was back into that more accustomed form, dialects and all, and we were having a good time.

The scenery, the banter, the anticipation, and just being together on our way to something that we both truly love to do helped the time go by painlessly. It was well past noon now, and we were almost there. I sat in the passenger's seat while Bob drove until not even the lowest gear of his semi-monster, four-wheel drive pickup truck would take us any farther over the increasingly unpassable "roads." From that point on, we'd unload the Yamaha YZs we were trailering, and ride with backpacks the rest of the way to camp and hike for a few days.

I guess it was the surrealistic remoteness of all of this from anything I could ever have imagined doing with *my* father that aroused in me a collection of images that resolved to a moment in the hot summer sun, at the other end of this continent, a lifetime and a culture ago. The setting for this recollection was summertime Saturday afternoons at the small tailoring shop my dad and his brother ran for almost forty years in Worcester, Massachusetts. My mother, father, sister, and I lived in a tenement flat right above the ground floor where the business was located. Just behind the store was a sparsely graveled driveway, where the south wall of the building provided a perfect "bounce back" against which a kid who had dreams of pitching for the Red Sox could throw a tennis ball for hour after hour, fine-tuning his curve, his slider, and his someday-to-be legendary fastball. There was an extra measure of suspense and even a little danger in these practice sessions, because the strike zone was between two windows, the panes of which were as thick and durable as potato chips. But hey, if a guy couldn't stand the pressure of such relatively insignificant catastrophes as might follow an errant throw here, he'd *never* make it in the majors.

Some of the other boys in the neighborhood were playing organized junior competition. But not me. I wasn't going to Little League tryouts until I was thoroughly certain I was good enough. Yes, my personal insecurity tree was already quite well-established, with deep roots and an impressively strong fear of rejection branch.

It didn't matter that I wasn't playing in real games anyway. My fantasies on those sweltering New England afternoons were so fulfilling that I probably wouldn't have traded them even for a chance to wear a team's uniform—the kind with the sponsor's name in big black letters across the front of the shirt. All I needed for *my* game was a T-shirt, Keds, and jeans—only sissies wore shorts in those days regardless of how hot it was. When I first came on in my relief role though, despite the oppressive heat, I also sported a kind of warm-up jacket that was several sizes too large for me but pretty good for its purpose all the same. In place of an actual warm-up jacket, which I didn't actually have, I substituted a dark brown, woolen sweater that I had found in a throwaway box behind the foot pedal-powered sewing machine my dad and uncle used to alter clothing and occasionally make exquisitely crafted, custom-tailored suits for some of Worcester's wealthiest and most prominent people. I pretended that grizzled, button-up-the-front sweater was the shiny, zipper-up-the front jacket that Frank Sullivan wore when he strode slowly and resolutely out to the mound from the Boston bullpen. I never really understood why, no matter how wretchedly hot and humid it may have been, pitchers always seemed to need that warm-up jacket. Nonetheless, hot and sweaty as I was, I wore mine too.

The only other component of my game attire was a Red Sox cap that my cousin Domenic had given me. A combat veteran of World War II, Dom had gotten Purple Hearts and other medals for heroic service during the allied invasion of Normandy. He had also gotten a piece of shrapnel in his head that affected the way he talked, and lost his left leg in the actions acknowledged by those awards. I thought he was terrific and would often mimic his halting speech impediment because I thought it sounded neat. But I never did so when he was around. I guess I knew that what was loving role modeling for me, might be mistaken as mocking by him or others.

And so, on Saturday afternoons from June until late August, I knew where I was going to be. Right there in that driveway, saving a game for the Bosox in a brilliant performance that play-by-play announcer Curt Gowdy (simulated by me) described in every superlative detail to a spellbound radio audience, while the crowd at the ballpark (also simulated by me) roared with each pitch. All too often though, the spell was broken with the bases loaded and the count at three balls and two strikes on somebody like Bobby Avila, Harvey Kuenn, Ray Boone, Nellie Fox, or Minnie Minoso, when one of my trademark fastballs went wilder than the imagination that made this activity so engaging to me. Fast as the ball was moving, it seemed to hang suspended in time for an eternal moment just before impact—not unlike the home run balls I occasionally gave up to sluggers such as Vic Wertz, Al Kaline, or even Stan Musial, all of whom I almost always struck out.

In the grotesque instant that a well-worn ball made its fatal contact with the uncompromising laws of physics, it wasn't just glass that broke, but the enacted daydream by means of which a solitary little boy escaped momentarily from a dismal, lower-than-middle-class reality. The personification of life as it really was appeared almost immediately in a doorway about fifteen feet to the right of what was home plate just a few seconds ago. In that rear entrance to the dimly lit, poorly ventilated, creaky-floored place where they worked from early morning to late at night, six and often seven days a week to earn a living for their families and to give their American-born children a better life than they had, stood my father Felice ("Felix") and my Uncle Nicola ("Nick"), dripping with sweat born of toil not play.

Within seconds after hearing the unmistakable sound that punctuated the destructive results of one of my wild pitches, Nick and Felix walked to that back door as deliberately as any big league manager ever walked that walk from the dugout to send a pitcher to the showers. But they spoke no words. They didn't have to. Instead, these two masters of nonverbal communication just glared at me with that aura of exasperated bewilderment I had come to know so well. They could say more by saying nothing than anyone else I've ever known. And they did it with what my sister, my cousins, and I called "The Look." The Look said it all. In this case it said, "Good God, Bob! How many times do we have to tell you that our work here is hard enough without having to listen to the endless whacking of that ball?" They couldn't hear the play-by-play announcer or the crowd noises. I mostly whispered those to myself. But that wasn't all The Look said. It said, "Worst of all, you've given us still more work to do, because now we have to fix another window, and that's going to cost us time and money—for the third time this month!" They didn't say any of that out loud. They didn't have to. And I didn't say anything out loud either. I just sort of stood there, looking at them as they looked at me.

I wonder if my look conveyed to them what I was feeling.

"I'm sorry, Dad. I'm sorry, Uncle Nick. I know I've never told you. You never taught me how to tell you. But you must know that I love you, that I know how hard you work for us, that I appreciate all that you do for us and don't want to make life harder for you than it already is. The pitch slipped. I'll sweep up around the shop, run errands, and do other stuff to make up for it."

But I articulated none of this. Maybe it had all been said. Maybe I had learned something about the art of nonverbal communication from the masters. Maybe their frustration dissipated some as they saw me standing there in that stupid, moth-eaten old brown sweater, staring back at them with my own Look of silent guilt. And maybe I'm just beginning to understand what those interminable silences really meant.

Among many other things, my mentor and friend Ted Sarbin has taught me to be mindful of the context of thought, feeling, and action in analyses of human experience. Well, there was one more contextual factor in these imaginary game-saving episodes of my childhood. It was the sound of opera that filled the dingy back room of the Highland Tailoring Co., along with the hiss and steam of pressing machines. Most of that sound came through the static of a little white plastic Philco radio tuned to the Saturday afternoon broadcast from the Metropolitan Opera House in New York City. And as the featured artists in those productions gave virtuoso renditions of arias from *Carmen, La Tosca, Rigoletto,* or *The Barber of Seville,* they were accompanied in Worcester by the mellow tenor of my father Felice, and the rich baritone of his brother. Nick's and Felix's passionate intensity more than made up for whatever vocal skills they may have lacked. Notes they missed here and there, but the libretto they knew "by heart," in the most human sense of that term.

These two mostly self-educated sons of an indigent shoemaker in the small town of Bisceglia, Italy, had fought successfully to fulfill *their* father's dream by getting themselves to this country and becoming American citizens. And now, at least implicitly in my construction of the situation, it was up to us, their children and the first native-born American generation in their family, to give meaning to fulfillment of that dream by becoming productive members of this society. Complex as each of our lives has been, there are some key respects in which my father's and my uncle's ideals are reflected in what all of us have done with our own lives.

First, there is my exquisitely compassionate and elegantly effective sister Eleanor, who got all of the pragmatic intelligence from our mother and father, leaving none for me. Eleanor went to medical-secretarial school and soon afterward worked for Drs. Ralph Dorfman and Gregory Pincus, whose research at the Worcester Foundation for Experimental Biology became renowned (or infamous, depending upon one's attitudes toward birth control) for its central role in development of "the Pill." After that, in addition to raising her son, Michael, she became the executive administrator of a private medical office center. She is one of those people whose sense of social conscience and responsibility is acted out in quiet, anonymous ways, every day of her life, in real contributions to real people in real need of emotional and/or economic support, in all kinds of circumstances.

My Uncle Nick's (and Aunt Mary's) daughter Helena was the first member of our family to go to a four-year college. The tears of joy my dad and my uncle shed on the day Helena graduated with honors from Radcliffe must have been mixed with a profound feeling of incompleteness for the absence of their deceased father from that grand moment. Surely, the symbolic significance of this milestone achievement in the cultural evolution of their family was not lost on these two immigrants who valued education with a reverence. In addition to raising three children, Helena earned her PhD at Tufts University. Her research on male-female differences in communication constituted the core of what subsequently became an area of highly publicized popular as well as scientific attention. After a distinguished career working in community mental health settings, she is now a clinical psychologist in private practice whose personal growth workshops, known as "The Gathering," have been conducted throughout the world.

In the summer of 1996, the sweetness of our family's joy was again blunted somewhat for not being able to share with Felice, who died at the age of eighty-four in 1991, the pride and joy we all felt for Nick and Mary's son Gerry (Helena's brother and my cousin). After nearly thirty years of relentless, materially uncompensated, and often even scorned efforts, Gerry finally gained the attention of scientists and the media throughout the world for his arguments (published in the *American Journal of Physics*) challenging key inferences drawn from one of the major experiments invoked as empirical foundation for Einstein's theory of relativity. If the latter work serves to stimulate a mini or even a major revolution in the world of science, and most of all a whole new line of research and discovery, it would fit the essence of Nick's and Felix's true legacy to us, established through the work and way of their lives.

As critical aspects of our development, Eleanor's, Helena's, Gerry's, and mine, were inaccessible to our fathers' parents, so were many critical aspects of our fathers' development unknown to us. Dad and Uncle Nick communicated to us very little about their own immigrant experience. Not because they were ashamed of it, but more, I think, because they felt it was irrelevant—just part of what they accepted as the process or the price of becoming Americans. Only in their most senior years did my father and my Uncle Nick, who died at the age of eighty-seven the week before the Christmas of 1996, begin to share with us some fragments of information about their early years here. What little they told us revealed all too poignantly the kinds of prejudicial hatred against "greenhorn foreigners" they encountered in the economic despair that swept this country during the 1920s, a time when recent immigrants were seen by established immigrants and their progeny as the enemy in a war of competition over very scarce jobs and even scarcer resources. Social welfare programs simply did not exist. There was no availability of food stamps, unemployment compensation, etc., no matter how needy a family might have been.

Characteristic of what was happening throughout America in the Great Depression, real-life horror stories scripted out of poverty abounded in the Italian settlement around Worcester's Shrewsbury Street. Concerned by an ever-worsening epidemic of such personal tragedies that threatened to engulf a whole community, Felice, Nicola, and a few courageous friends created in 1928 the Coloniale Bisceg-liese Societa Di Mutuo Soccorso. With Felice as its first president, the Biscegliese Society's main purpose was to aid its member families in times of special hardships such as joblessness, illness, or death.

Fundamental to its philosophy was the idea that those who can will help those who cannot, with each individual expected to contribute according to his or her own particular skills, talents, knowledge, and abilities. This exemplary prototype of grassroots self-help organizations in America, so quintessentially American in its longevous tradition of proud independence, was founded and has thrived for a whole generation without any public funding whatsoever.

Our fathers told us very little about this part of their lives. In fact, much of what we know of their young life we learned from friends of the family. The part about their struggle to survive and make a place for themselves and their families in a country where they were anything but welcomed warmly was the very least of what they shared with us. The indignities and privations they endured from their first moments at Ellis Island. The pennies they were paid for laboring dawn to midnight shifts in New York City's garment industry. Apparently their sense of personal responsibility involved taking all of this for granted, as something equivalent to a necessary rite of passage on the way to citizenship.

They were Americans now—not hyphenated Americans—just Americans. And as little as they disclosed to us about the challenges they confronted in becoming Americans, they never let us forget how much they loved this country, how deeply honored and thoroughly blessed they felt to be Americans, and how lucky *we* were to grow up as Americans. Looking back through the lenses of my own reconstructed imagery, implicit but dominant in all of this was the idea that as first-generation Americans, we owed a huge debt of gratitude that could only be repaid by contributing, each in our own way, to making what our fathers saw as this "great land of opportunity" even greater. If there was an unambiguous and uncompromising message here, it was the expectation that we would dedicate *our* lives to leaving this world a better place than it would have been had we never existed in it and, ultimately, to having a substantively beneficial impact on the lives of others.

Nowhere in either their overt or covert messages to us, however, do I recall anything even vaguely approaching a self-pitying complaint about their having been exploited or victimized by anyone. This is not intended to deny, demean, or trivialize the validity of alternative ways of constructing and expressing the painful history of one's own personal, ethnic, racial, or national identity. It's just a factual statement of how two men lived their lives.

Although far less factual than the foregoing observation, I know something else now that I didn't know until very recently. On those sultry, midsummer Saturday afternoons while my imagination carried me to play alongside Ted Williams, Clyde Vollmer, Mel Parnell, and Jimmy Piersall at Fenway Park, through the magic of radio, Dad and Uncle Nick were right there at "The Met" with the likes of Richard Tucker, Robert Merrill, Giorgio Tozzi, Leontyne Price, Lauritz Melchior, and Renata Tebaldi. In the piercing moment as one of my wild pitches missed its stucco target, a treasured fantasy was smashed for them too. When that window shattered, so did *their* escape. My father, my uncle, and I were probably never closer than when we stared in mutual silence at one another over the shards of glass that lay as tangible elements of a mutually rude awakening.

Chapter 14

In Absentia

Genaro Gonzalez

At the start of 1968, despite the uncertainties plaguing the rest of the world, two outcomes were almost a given in my own small corner of deep south Texas. First, in a matter of months I would graduate from high school. Second, unless I went on to college, I would soon add to the already large number of Chicanos in Vietnam.

I was not too concerned about the latter since my grades through high school were almost all As. The one exception was a history class where a friend and I, sitting in back, had scribbled dialogue bubbles on World War I photos posted on a bulletin board. Our teacher was a young, laid-back Anglo, but he went berserk when he discovered our captions.

"Christ!" he exploded after class. "Rosemary's father lent us those magazine photos! And you guys had to mark them with pens! Christ!"

That was how I ended up with my only B. My friend, who came from another barrio on the outskirts of town, was not fazed. He once showed me a clipping from a Mexican police gazette on his father's troubles with the law across the Rio Grande, about fifteen miles from our town. In a sense he was simply following in his father's footsteps.

Given my grades, I had my own plans for the future. Gilbert, an older Chicano from the predominantly Anglo side of town, had offered to help with my college applications. One Sunday afternoon, while typing out a statement of purpose, he paused abruptly. "I hate to bring up the matter of money, but . . . "

Misinterpreting the statement, I promised to pay him from my weekend job at a supermarket. It was his turn to look perplexed, until my misunderstanding made sense.

"I don't mean paying me! I mean your education! You think they'll let you in for free?"

I knew better, just as I knew better than to ask for assistance from my stepfather, who never tired of reminding me that he barely made ends meet on his grease monkey's wages. Yet he never linked his meager earnings to his limited schooling in Mexico. According to his lights a high school diploma was more than sufficient to ensure one's future.

My alternative for financial support, my father, was not much of a choice either. He lived some 700 miles away—about as far as one could go from our border town and still be in Texas. Although the family grapevine claimed he was quite well off, I had come to expect little support from his corner. Since the divorce twelve years ago I saw him about twice a year, and lately his visits had become more infrequent and brief. His sporadic letters during the past year groused about the sixty dollars a month he sent for child support even though, to hear his side of the family, this was spare change for him. Perhaps he resented that his checks were covering the mortgage on my stepfather's modest house in the barrio. Still, it was a small price to pay for being relieved of the day-to-day work of raising a son. His last check upon my turning eighteen the previous month was accompanied by a letter reiterating an earlier vow to "yank away the teat."

So now, with Gilbert forcing me to review my options, I realized that my only resources for college were financial aid plus whatever earnings I could muster.

"Didn't you once say I could apply for grants and loans?"

He nodded but pointed out I still needed a financial report from my parents verifying their earnings. "You said your father runs some packing sheds in the panhandle."

"Here, too, depending on the season. I even heard he's in town, setting up for the upcoming onion harvest."

"Perfect. Just show up with the paperwork and have him fill out his earnings. That way he can't say the forms were lost in the mail."

"But he made it clear he won't help me anymore."

"And you make it clear it won't cost him a cent. The schools just need some figures as a formality. Besides, once he sees you're motivated he might have a change of heart."

I rolled my eyes to show I neither expected nor cared for his help. Yet another part of me wished otherwise—that he'd reward my efforts with a helping hand. In fact the offer need only be symbolic, since financial aid and my summer earnings should cover my costs. The thought was what counted.

Although he had not contacted me, I knew he was staying at his sister's house, so I took over the paperwork he needed to complete. A part of me wondered whether he was as well off as his relatives said, since his frugal habits did not betray a clue. I suspected their admiration was biased by his having provided jobs for several family members—before the divorce, as a crew boss during our years as migrant workers, then afterward as a packing shed foreman. He was the youngest sibling, yet the family's precocious patriarch.

My Aunt Lila, with whom he was staying, was the matriarch and had been our go-between after my grandmother's death. She never tired of stressing two things. First, although my father now had a second family, I had the honor of being his firstborn. Second, despite my poverty I should bask in his reflected affluence as the rest of the family did. However, she always added in the next breath that his recent finances were not going well—crop failures or labor problems. Perhaps the caveat was meant to nip any expectations that might end up dashed.

When I showed up with the financial forms she apologized for his not having seen me, adding that as soon as he finalized plans to run a local packing shed he was returning home for a few weeks. Since there was no telling when I could see him—or even if I would—I left the forms with her, stressing that his income statements were merely a formality for loans and scholarships.

When I returned the following week Aunt Lila handed me the uncompleted forms and added that my father had already left town. At first I assumed he had not had a chance to look them over, until she relayed the reason for his refusal: his earnings might jeopardize my chances for financial assistance.

I wanted to ask why, despite her assurances about how much he cared for me, he not only did not lift a finger to help but actually did his best to keep me down. But protesting the matter made as much sense as arguing with a ghost. The decision had been his alone and he had disappeared, leaving me holding the incomplete forms.

I returned home and talked things over with my mother, who suggested I ask my stepfather for help. "Perhaps it's better this way," she added, trying to put a more positive spin on the rebuff. "You said your family's need might help your case. Well, you can't get much needier than us."

That evening I sought out my stepfather and braced myself for a lecture on how I should have asked him in the first place. He was sitting at the dinner table, waiting to be served—first the placemat, then the first plate served, and finally his pick from the stack of tortillas. I had never cared for the ritual and deference but, then again, I was not the breadwinner. He stared hard at the financial forms, taking slow, deliberate chews, as though carefully masticating my vows of full responsibility for any loans I incurred.

"Then why do they want my signature?" he interrupted. Without waiting for an answer, he tossed it back on the table. "I'm not signing this." He shook his head indignantly, as though I had tried to trick him. My mother tried to rephrase my assurance, but he cut her off too, adding that I only approached him when I wanted something.

I went to wait in the living room, upset yet hopeful he would reconsider. Often his obstinacy was only a reminder that he had the final word. But after dinner he sat before the TV without a word, as though the matter had never come up.

Coming so soon after the blow from my father, it seemed I had turned the other cheek only to be struck a second time. Everything that evening had the surreal feeling that my father and stepfather had entered into a sinister complicity. Later my mother came to my room and explained, "I think it hurts his pride, your having to turn to your father."

"Then how come he took the child support checks for all those years?"

"Because he had to. That's the only way we could make ends meet."

I suspected he also resented the slight autonomy that the child support had given me, but I did not mention it to my mother.

The following morning I walked the two or three miles to Gilbert's house, numb to the winter drizzle lashing my face. I kept my eyes half shut the entire way, and although it blurred the road before me it also gave my inner turmoil a melodramatic vividness. I felt at once vanquished yet invincible, inert yet brutally alive. Rather than ending up sobered by the long walk, I arrived at Gilbert's house seething with self-pity.

I quickly blurted out my back-to-back rejections and ended with a suicidal flourish: I had decided to withdraw my college applications. "So I won't go to college," I said, interrupting Gilbert's protests. "It's not the end of the world."

"You're the one acting like it's the end of the world." His smile only upset me more.

He was right, but my statement also had some truth to it. The main reason I had applied was because several teachers had encouraged me. At home, however, no one had ever brought up the topic, while my paternal grandfather was outright opposed to the idea.

"So you don't end up going to college. And after that? They'll draft you."

I shook my head. "They won't draft me. I'm enlisting."

He pinched my cheek, already raw from the cold. "There's a war going on! If the Vietcong don't get you, the Army life will. Guys like you end up squashed under Uncle Sam's thumb."

Actually I was not anxious to enlist, at least not for the usual clichés. I simply wanted to get back at my stepfather and father, and a scenario involving death or dismemberment had a perverse, martyr's appeal.

Gilbert, sensing my despair, even offered to forge my stepfather's signature on the forms. "But not your father's." He added that anyone willing to send his flesh and blood to die in such an uncertain cause was not a man to mess with.

Back home I mulled over his plan which, while risky, seemed infinitely more sober than mine. But within days my mother's work behind the scenes made the scheme unnecessary. She persuaded my stepfather's cousins to shame him into cooperating. Afterward I thanked him to keep the peace in the household, but the damage had been done.

The estrangement from my father continued, while his motives remained a mystery. I tried to fathom his indifference over the past few years, but my only explanation was the same one as my mother's. Four years earlier, during a summer job at a produce shed he supervised, I had turned down an offer to live with his family.

That summer was actually my only memory of quotidian contact between us. My Uncle Virgilio, his right-hand man at the packing sheds, had taken one of my cousins and me to work in the fields and sheds where my father was a foreman. But even as we reached the

Texas panhandle I already sensed a world where I was not quite welcome. Halfway there we had truck trouble and stopped at a service
station, where an Anglo in charge waved us away. It went that way
until our fourth stop.

Once there, things were not that different. Although race relations
back home were hardly harmonious, Chicanos were so omnipresent
and Mexico so close that Anglos were forced to rein in the racism
somewhat. In my father's town, though, we were outnumbered and
relegated to stoop labor. After my first week I walked into a downtown barbershop and waited my turn for what seemed an eternity. My
cousin, who had worked there the previous summer, finally called me
outside and explained that our facilities were a few blocks down.

Downtown was not the only place where I felt like an unwelcome
outsider, a necessary evil. I sensed a similar strain in my father's
house. While my stepmother treated me decently, especially considering how I had moved in from one day to the next, a few of her relatives also staying at the house minded my presence. Although I was
only there for the summer, perhaps they feared I might stay.

My father's young brother-in-law, one of several kin working for
him, especially resented my father's child support payments, despite
his own parasitic presence in the house and despite our otherwise fast
friendship. Once, during a lunch break at the shed, he boasted of an
expensive watch my father had given him. It reminded me how my father had once taken me to buy a watch and had steered me toward the
cheapest brands.

Yet ultimately this sort of psychic sniping came to rest at my father's doorstep. He either overheard and condoned the conduct or else
was too busy running two sheds and supervising field workers to
bother with my adjustment.

Halfway through that summer my mother was diagnosed with tuberculosis—a lifetime of work in packing sheds and agricultural
fields had taken their toll—and she wanted to see me before entering
a state hospital in another city. My father, perhaps seeing his chance,
suggested I visit her then return with him. I gave him a roundabout refusal, adding that I already felt comfortable with my stepfather and
his family. That was true. Winning over my first extended stepfamily
had not been easy. I did not look forward to leaving it behind to start
on a new one, especially knowing that my father worked away from
home for most of the year.

Now, four years later, my mother put that decision in retrospective perspective, as an affront to my father's efforts to win me over and away from my stepfather's poverty. For her this explained his remoteness, and perhaps she was right. After all she had known him longer than I had.

In spring, my father started the onion harvest in my hometown. But instead of the anticipation I had once felt at his arrival, I realized that his refusal to fill out the college forms still gnawed at me. I considered boycotting our meeting altogether, but with graduation expenses around the corner, I could earn much more as a shed worker than as a supermarket bagboy. My cousin, also graduating and already working after school at the shed, said my father was asking why I had not showed up.

I finally did, evasive and unapologetic. My father, his five o'clock shadow already grizzled with gray, took me with barely a word to a conveyer chute to replace the large sacks as they filled. I was already acquainted with part of the stag crew, which included some familiar faces from the panhandle, and I was also acquainted with their initiation rite for novices, commenting on my tears from the overwhelming smell of onions.

Toward the end of each workweek my father sent me home to figure out the workers' wages, sparing me briefly from what my Uncle Virgilio called men's work. "There's work," he liked to point out, "and then there's men's work."

By the final week, and with graduation approaching, my father asked whether I owned a sport coat. I did not, so his graduation gift was cash for a modest one, with the implicit understanding that I make up the difference.

The following month our school counselor called me to her office to inform me that in our graduating class of 500 I had the highest grade point average among the males. She seemed as surprised as I, since everyone had assumed the anointed one would be one of the affluent Anglos we always heard about. After a few complained that I should have taken major work courses each semester, the administration took steps to close that loophole for future seniors. In truth my major work classes, which I preferred because I had friends there, had seemed easier than the college prep courses.

Senior scholarships were announced shortly before graduation, with the usual white suspects sweeping the gym ceremony. The racist charade spilled over into graduation night, when I was asked to utter a brief invocation prayer, while the real speeches went to Anglos with lower grades. I savored the irony both as a fledgling activist and as an evolving atheist. The recent turns in my life had not merely eroded my faith in my father and stepfather, but in the social order as well. Moreover I was losing my faith in a metaphysical father. The world seemed less absurd without a God than with an ineffectual, unjust one.

Eventually I received a small scholarship for a charter honors program at our regional college. By then I had set aside my interest in medicine and psychiatry. It was not just because our counselor had done nothing to encourage my attending a university. The financial hurdles of a protracted education, to say nothing of bankrolling a practice afterward, seemed overly daunting without moral or monetary support from either father. I opted for psychology, the poor man's psychiatry. It might even teach me a thing or two about dealing with life's difficult episodes.

At our local college I continued to question life's injustices and joined a small group of Chicano activists. By the end of my first semester, with my father in town for the holidays, I felt it was time to put my militant ideology into practice at a more personal level. I returned to my earlier plot to sabotage our annual reunion.

For the past few Christmases he would have my Aunt Lila arrange a meeting on the last hour of the last day of his two-week stay, after he had visited family and friends. This time, after my aunt called to confirm his dropping by, I decided to boycott our get-togethers, which had become as ritualistic and hollow as most holidays. I rehearsed the scenario like a battle plan, anticipating moves and counterattacks. For instance, if he honked his horn from the curb, should I ask him to leave? And if I did so by stepping out in the open to tell him, was that already capitulation? Yet if I stayed inside, was that cowardice? For that matter would he even wonder whether I had heard, or would it serve as a convenient excuse to get out of an onerous obligation?

When his truck finally pulled up and he sent my Uncle Virgilio to get me, I momentarily lost my nerve. I retreated to the rear of the house, fearing my uncle might walk in before I could work up the will. A volley of sharp knocks at the front door felt as stark as my pounding heart. There followed a long silence, until I told myself that the terrible decision had been settled indirectly, or at least delayed, by my father's departure.

Suddenly the contours of my uncle's face pressed against the rear screen door. Saying simply that my father was there to see me, he began to walk back. Then, perhaps wondering why I had not followed, he paused and turned. "Your father is here. He wants to see you."

"I don't want to see him." The sentence felt like someone else had said it, or else it was uttered of its own accord. Then, to prove I had not imagined the words, I repeated them.

For a moment my uncle stood his own ground, until something inside him seemed to sag. "Bueno," he said—not as in "good," but as a more resigned "all right, then"—and walked back to my father.

That evening I told my stepfather about the incident. While he agreed that my father needed to be taught a lesson, he added I had gone too far. Perhaps he reasoned that if I could turn my back on my flesh-and-blood father, I would not hesitate doing the same to him.

A similar reaction occurred when I gave my maternal grandfather the news. I even expected some congratulations, since he still held my father responsible for the divorce, after alleged affairs with our maid and the proverbial young widow next door.

My grandfather, though, admonished me that a son should not censure his father. Perhaps the conflict struck too close to home. His own incorrigible son Yeyo, who shared their shack, not only burned his candle at both ends of the border but never tired of pointing out that he was merely following in the old man's footsteps. The difference, Uncle Yeyo explained, was that he was still a bachelor, while my grandfather had squandered his children's fieldwork earnings in cantinas, treating his drinking friends to generous rounds until he spent himself into a shack.

In the end, in fact, the only male relative who backed me was Uncle Yeyo. Our bond went back to the divorce, when my mother and I had moved into my grandfather's house. Uncle Yeyo could be downright dangerous when drunk or stoned, which was often, but even after I had moved out of my grandfather's house I could count on him for an occasional helping hand.

After telling him what I had done, he turned pensive for a moment, then related his own run-in with my father. The account took me by surprise. Although after the divorce the barrio had predicted trouble if the two crossed paths, any bad blood between my uncle and father had remained unspilled. My father, impressed by Uncle Yeyo's stamina and strength, had even hired him as a packer. That was the time my uncle now referred to. "Remember some years back, when I worked for him in west Texas?"

He added that my father had also hired a character who, before becoming a packer, had been a *brazo fuerte,* a strong-arm enforcer. The man's love of a no-holds brawl impressed even Uncle Yeyo, who gave him a wide berth despite my father's attempts to goad them into a *mano a mano.*

One idle afternoon, while they waited in the shed for a shipment from the fields, my father succeeded in getting them to lock horns. The man took the bait at once, but my uncle, anticipating the inevitable, already had a strategy. Gesturing the thug to follow him out the back door, he waylaid him on the other side and slammed the door in his face. He then took a chain he had spied earlier and proceeded to flog the man into absolute submission, paying special attention to the strong arm.

Even taking into account Uncle Yeyo's tendency to embellish his exploits, the story sounded plausible. The thought that my own father would egg on a man to beat up my uncle bothered me, yet the episode was consistent with other disturbing accounts I had heard through the years. I was uncovering unexpected pieces of a puzzle that I was barely putting into place, pieces that made the larger picture more complete yet also more complicated.

Over the next few days several family members on my father's side began to recast my actions, claiming I had been reluctant to face him with my long hair and radical ideas. But explaining away my quarrel as social rebellion diminished the issue of his injustice. Indeed, one could also argue that my quarrel with society was simply a projection of my family drama, yet this would have detracted from the moral arguments of my activism.

In truth both realms were interrelated. My father's rebuff had sensitized me to the plight of others. At the same time my growing awareness of social inequality had forced me to confront conflicts closer to home.

Yet the two spheres—ideological and interpersonal—occasionally collided. Thus, while the Chicano movement sought to validate our cultural heritage by framing our family as an emotional sanctuary, especially against racism, my own experience with both fathers had been anything but exemplary.

I refused to see or talk to my father for the next six years. At the end of that time we agreed to discuss our differences in a meeting brokered by one of Uncle Virgilio's daughters. But the exchange, which took place in a packing shed he was running, lasted less than a minute. In the end we each turned and walked away in opposite directions, staying out of each other's path for another six years.

During those years I found out about my father's complex relationship with his own Mexican father who, days after his wife died in labor, allowed a married sister in the United States to raise the newborn as her own. My father remained in the dark about the arrangement until his enlistment during the war led to a bureaucratic background check that unlocked the family closet and brought to light two disquieting truths. First, he had been living in the United States illegally. Second, the uncle living across the border was actually his father. Their relationship remained distant to the end, but how that experience affected him—and perhaps prefigured our own—remains a mystery, another odd piece of that paternal puzzle that I finally decided was best left unsolved.

I came to realize that while the need to retrace our steps, including our pratfalls, may be human nature, a father and son must perforce look back differently on the mutual path they took. Nature put us on disparate footing, since a son has but one father, while a father may have several sons, each one an opportunity to wipe clean the messy slate with his mistakes and reconfigure his role. He is permitted the fiction of starting on the path of fatherhood afresh, returning to the start if he loses heart or tires along the way.

A son, however, cannot start anew. He can only revisit the scene of the crime and scour the terrain for old, overlooked clues. And if the father's presence was minimal—more implied than actual—that very absence makes him even more pervasive. So in the absence of his father's hands-on fingerprints, the son is left to interpret the relationship as a vague Rorschach of his own uncertainties. When the father is not there to corroborate or contradict those speculations, the circumference necessary for closure grows wider, and the search for answers merely uncovers more questions.

These days my father and I are on cordial speaking terms, an emotional detente in a relationship which, while no longer a cold war, never fully thawed either. He pays my family a visit whenever he's in town and we make small talk, but we soon find ourselves unable or unwilling to move beyond an awkward exchange that is more civil than intimate. And yet considering what had come before that, it nevertheless can be seen as progress.

Shortly after our fragile truce, he asked me to encourage one of his sons to enter college. I did not bother to point out the irony in his request, but neither did I do much to motivate my half brother, whose indifference to the idea made it evident that his interests lay elsewhere.

Last year my father called to wish me a happy birthday, something he had never done. After expressing my appreciation I pointed out that my birthday was still a full month away. Afterward my wife commented that my candor must have made him uncomfortable. I agreed, but added that his gaffe had bothered me too.

Time may indeed heal wounds, but not even optimists who swear by the cliché would argue that one ends up as good as new. Often scar tissue remains, to remind one of a past battle's ugliness and to harden thin skin against future blows. On the odd occasion when my father and I meet, I am grateful to see him alive and well, given the dying among his generation—including my stepfather—and the beginning decimation of my own. And yet at times his visits resemble those of an uncle paying me a brief, nostalgic visit. It is then that I accept what our bond has come to, as Father Time dims the burning, blinding light that was once my father into a warm, avuncular glow.

SECTION III:
STORIES
OF SELF-UNDERSTANDING

Chapter 15

The Presence of What Is Missing: Memory, Poetry, and the Ride Home

Mark Freeman

I

My father could scarcely have imagined that I would someday be writing essays such as this one. To be honest, he may very well have had no idea whatsoever *what* I would do in this world. In fact, there was a sizable span of time during which the distinct possibility must have been raised that, whatever it would be, it would be precious little. I don't want to create the wrong impression here. It's not as if I was condemned or considered a disappointment or a blot on the family name or anything else of that sort; I was loved, cared for, played with, and all the rest. But my dad died very suddenly when I was quite young; I'd just turned twenty. And at that particular time, given the kind of life I seemed most interested in living, it simply wasn't clear how everything would pan out.

Part of the problem was my age. I have two older brothers, one of whom is eight years older and one of whom is six. By the time I graduated from high school, they were each married, beginning to build their own families, and, in general, were well on their way to becoming "established." The oldest one had graduated from Georgetown and NYU Law and, despite some serious tension with my father—he had been something of a radical in college, which occasionally made for some rather heated exchanges at the dinner table—had eventually gotten it together. When he and his wife produced a beautiful baby girl early in July of 1975, in the bloom of summer, all of that tension seemed to melt away. At age fifty-five, my dad had become a grandfather,[1] the first girl had entered the family healthy and happy, and the future promised more and more deliverances, more and more abundance. As for my other brother, who had been valedictorian of his high school class, who had graduated something-or-other cum laude from Yale, who had gotten married to a Wonderful Girl from a Good Family at age twenty-one, who had gone on to Harvard Business School, only to land shortly thereafter at Procter & Gamble, where he would market diapers for the nation's young and helpless; the only thing he was missing was a Purple Heart or a Presidential Medal of Honor. He was a dutiful son too. Not too long after I was appointed an assistant professor, he told me that he'd have sooner thought I would be in jail than in a classroom. He said it with a smile, but on some level he probably meant it. Not only was I the baby of the family, who had been spoiled, "got away with murder," and so on, but in his eyes, at least, I'd been something of a wild man, who'd already done some things that he himself would never have *dreamed* of doing, particularly given the much-mythicized wrath of my father.

The myth goes something like this: My two older brothers, living under my dad's reign of terror, had been forced to live the straight and narrow path. When they were my age, there had been no room for shenanigans, backtalk, broken curfews, or anything else that gave the slightest hints of disobedience or disrespect. By the time I came along, though, my dad had mellowed a bit, the times were a-changing, and, by my brothers' account (particularly the Procter & Gamble exec), my life had been one great big fun fest, in which I had been able to do everything they had not. In any case, set in contrast to the clean-shaven family men my brothers had become, there's no doubt that I must have seemed like a different kind of creature altogether. There is a picture of my father and me, taken when I was around eighteen, in which we're standing outside on a sunny winter day. He's in a woolen coat, strong and serious, with a thick mustache, gazing sternly at the camera. I'm standing apart from him, in a two-tone suede jacket, hair halfway down my chest, with just the tiniest smirk on my face. In some ways, we were worlds apart.

I fear I might be giving the wrong impression again. It is true that my dad had an incredible temper. He never, ever laid a hand on any of us, but the way he would sometimes yell at us, like he was ready to boil over with rage, would actually lead us to wish he would just whack us and get it over with. I can remember one time when we were cruising along the highway on (what had appeared to be) a pleasant family outing when, due to some jockeying in traffic, a guy in the car next to us wound up giving my dad the finger. Not wise. I won't pretend to remember every last detail of the incident, but I know that we both pulled off the road; my dad had gotten out of our car and the other guy had remained in his, no doubt shaking with fear. Suffice it to say that he was lucky to keep that finger. One other time, my first serious girlfriend, a sweet and kind girl from upstate New York, was visiting from college. My dad had been nothing short of delightful with her; at his best, he too was sweet and kind. Anyway, one night we decided to have pizza for dinner; he would go pick it up at the local pizzeria. Well, they didn't tape one of the pizza boxes together like they usually did. And when my dad slammed on his brakes on the way home, one of the pizzas slid right out of the box and all over his spotlessly clean car. Not good. He did have enough self-control not to go completely berserk around my new girlfriend. But it was a long time before he could utter a word to anyone. And he absolutely refused to eat any of the pizza, even from one of the intact boxes. It was a real meal to remember.

So there's no denying that he could be a pretty tough character. But he was also funny and charming, passionately in love with my mother, warm and affectionate with his children, playful with the family dog, greatly enamored of food and drink and nice clothes and traveling and dancing and many other things besides. For all of his rage and occasional sullenness, he was also a favorite of lots of people. He'd been called "Sonny" when he was younger; in the way people dealt with him, you got the sense that he was special somehow, larger than life. He loved to imitate newborns' faces. We would visit proud parents who would ooh and aah over their new babies, *kvelling* (as they say in Yiddish), gushing over how cute they were or how much they look liked so-and-so; as soon as we were out the door, he'd be making a dopey baby face, poking fun at how sappy and deluded everyone was about their wondrous offspring. "For Chrissake, they all look the same!" And he kissed me, or I kissed him, each and every night before bed, for as long as our lives intersected. There was tenderness and the smell of shaving lotion and a sense of real—albeit unspoken—connection. *Damn it*. It was so long ago: twenty-two years. My God, why did it have to be? *Why?* The death of a parent can leave wounds that never fully heal.

II

For a while, during my youth, everything no doubt seemed kind of touch-and-go to my parents. When I was in tenth grade, an able but not exactly driven student, I became a member of a "gang" of sorts— not a chain-wielding, black leather jacket gang of the sort that "hoods" or "tree-boys" (tough boys, with greasy hair, who counted "one, two, tree") formed but a good-time gang, a bunch of guys who became bonded together in friendship and, every now and then, mayhem. We called ourselves the "Misty Mountain Maulers," Misty Mountain having been taken from the pages of Tolkien's *The Hobbit*. We had special shirts made up (I still have mine) and commenced what we called a "Viking Feast," which, as it turns out, we have held every year but two since 1971. It was, and still is, great fun. We were a ragged bunch, to say the least. We had contests to see who could grow their hair the longest and in turn annoy our parents the most. My good friend Lew, whose hair eventually reached his waist, when it was wet at least, was the winner. I wasn't far behind. We also loved basketball; a few of us played lacrosse. We communicated mainly through sarcastic jokes and what we then thought were intellectually penetrating commentaries on the absurdities of the New York suburban life we were all leading. Everything we did was filled with irony; despite our profound closeness, it was the only way we knew how to talk with one another. I also shouldn't neglect to mention the fact that we were bonded by books as well, especially roguish adventure stories such as Kerouac's *On the Road* and heavy existentialist novels by Sartre and Camus and Kafka. We fancied ourselves as being living contradictions; we were madcap, literary jock good-old-boys, shuttling between parties and poetry.

There were a few serious crises. I, for instance, was almost killed in a car accident the summer after eleventh grade—intensive care unit, critical condition, lots of broken bones, the whole bit. My dad passed out cold the moment he saw me. I wouldn't wish it upon anyone, but some good actually came of it. For one, some of the incessant squabbles my parents and I were accustomed to having, over topics ranging from my hair to my politics, vanished for a while. Needless to say, having seen their baby boy looking like a piece of raw meat, lying motionless in a hospital bed with tubes everywhere, they could only count their blessings that I had come out of the whole thing alive.

For another, I myself learned a lesson, a very painful lesson, about death and life; knocking on the door of the grim reaper does give you some new things to think about. The second crisis happened at the end of the next year, my senior year, when the founder of the Misty Mountain Maulers, who had gone on to MIT where he became a basketball star, prankster, and budding intellectual in good standing, died, wasted, from cancer. The five remaining Maulers were thrown for a loop. We would still have our Viking Feasts, still play ball into the night, still drop sarcastic lines, and so on. But things were different. One of us became a frantic party animal, his main goal in life being to be numb, to stop the pain. Another became world-weary, as if everything that was to happen from that point on would be poisoned, a long and steady fall downhill, with no prospect of ever fully returning. Another engaged in simple denial. It didn't really happen; things were basically all right; you move on. As for me, I was somewhat aimless, a kind of wanderer or nomad, moving through people and places and things without quite being there. Much of that period is difficult to recall.

I am not about to tell you that I didn't have any fun after all this or that I spent my time grieving ceaselessly or that I was living in utter desolation; it wasn't that way at all. When I got to college, I took a few interesting courses, made some new friends, had a couple of short-lived but entertaining relationships, and spent a great deal of time listening to extremely loud music in the poster-strewn dorm I lived in with my frazzled roommate, who, rumor had it, had ingested so many powerful mind-altering substances that his hair and beard had just plain stopped growing. He did eventually go on to graduate school at Harvard to study architecture, so apparently he managed to retain some functioning brain cells beneath all that hair, frozen in its tracks. But he was quite a piece of work. In any case, things were okay back then, but as I can see now, in hindsight, just okay. I missed too many classes, which was a big mistake. I got so-so grades and was actually relieved about it, and I really didn't connect at all to what I was learning. Part of the problem had to do with the courses I was taking. As a fledgling psychology major, eager to plumb the depths of the human condition and perhaps give some form to the strange and confusing world within me, I was disappointed to find myself in classes with hundreds of people, often reading tedious textbooks, taught by boring professors or inexperienced graduate assistants who seemed more interested in playing with their laboratory toys than they were in exploring the inner recesses of being. But another part of the problem was me. The D– I received on my first college essay had put some fear into me, and it was a bit disconcerting to try to learn the contents of an entire course in a night or two. But none of this had been enough to shock me into getting serious about school. So the first year was okay, but again, just okay. Something was missing, and I could feel it in my gut even then.

Sophomore year was different. First, I had met someone—a free-thinking but serious anthropology major, interested in poetry and dance (the one from upstate New York who probably has bad associations to pizza dinners)—who helped me get some of my priorities straight. She could apparently see that I was a worthwhile cause, a bit out of kilter about some things but, in some way or other, promising. In addition, I found myself gravitating toward an intellectual crowd, for whom Eastern philosophy and modern fiction were often the topics of the day. A group of us moved off campus the second semester of that year; as far as we were concerned, we had exhausted the dormitory scene and decided that living in a house together, communally, was a far more cool thing to do. We were all remarkably proud of that house, and this despite the fact that it was a dump. I, in particular, was so proud that I immediately invited my parents up for the weekend so they could behold their independent, intellectually cutting-edge son's wonderful new abode. My mother remained quiet, in a "This is nice, dear" sort of mode. My father, on the other hand, who was bigger on comfort and cleanliness than I had assumed, was horrified. Sleeping on an old mattress on the floor of my bedroom, which I had (unconsciously) painted the color of Howard Johnson's—orange ceiling, turquoise walls—was one thing. The living room furniture ("Oh, the people down the street were throwing it out, Dad") was another. My bearded, shoeless, yogi-like housemates, wafting about like so much vapor, were another still. My parents fled as soon as they possibly could. So much for pride in one's new abode.

But something strange and wonderful happened that spring when my dad picked me up at school to take me home for summer vacation. The two of us were alone in a car for four hours—something that had never happened before. And he and I *talked* with one another, about college, about life, about ourselves, two men, father and son, making up for the strains and silences of a lifetime. He didn't tell me straightaway—he was never given to that sort of direct disclosure—but right then and there he let me know, as best he could, that I was all right, even with my shaggy mane, weird friends, and dilapidated house. He could tell, I suppose, that I was in the process of heading somewhere and that I would probably turn out all right. When I was off working at a camp that summer—it was the summer my niece, his first grandchild,[2] was born—I even received a letter from him, in which he basically said that it had been a pleasure to meet me and that he was confident that things were, in their own way, progressing nicely. Once again, he couldn't possibly have had any idea at all about what I would do in the world, concretely. I didn't either. But there were hints that it might be *something*. I do wish that he could have seen what; not unlike my brother with the jailbird fantasy of my future, he probably would have been quite surprised. It was only a brief while after receiving that letter, that seal of approval as it were, that I received a call in the camp's kitchen from my oldest brother, the father of a new girl, telling me that dad was gone. He had been at my uncle's pool, swimming, and his heart had seized on him and wrenched his life away, just like that. Oh, my God. No. *No*.

III

Twenty-two years ago, this man I loved and in some ways barely knew, my father, had just yesterday, or what seemed like it, sat and talked with me for the first time, had uttered words that would echo through the years, speaking the presence of what is missing. That ride home, this "incident," such as it was, may appear entirely too fleeting and undefined to serve as a focal point for my relationship with my father. I cannot recall the details of our conversation, formative though it seems to have been. I cannot remember which car we drove or which route we took home or, more telling still, where we stopped to eat. It is all a blur; there is almost nothing. And what I do recall is, in a certain sense, impossible. As I look back, I can see the two of us in the front seat; I can see myself turning my head his way, leaning toward him. He doesn't quite look back; his eyes remain on the road, but he's fully there, doing what he can. It's as if this picture is taken from the backseat, off to the side, or somewhere near there. There's the steady hum of the road underneath, and the scenery flashes by, like time.

There is something condensed in this scene, something unspeakable, that has raised it to the level of a kind of mythic moment. It's become a founding moment, though what it has founded, I cannot say. There is an important qualification that ought to be offered here, however. I have little doubt that had my dad not died, suddenly and inexplicably, two months later, this incident I have been at pains to recount would have had far less power and privilege in my history. It may simply have been a nice ride home, surprising and gratifying for the talk that took place, but not much more. That's because there probably would have been lots of other events following in its wake, fresher and clearer maybe. Life would have simply gone on, like the flashing scenery, and that ride home would have receded like so many other scenes, falling backward into the past. But life didn't simply go on; it came to a screaming halt. And as a result, the ride home, in and through its very fleetingness, its lack of definition and clarity, its *absence,* has come to loom large in my memory.

It has become common knowledge in the narrative approach to exploring human lives that memory, far from reproducing past experience as it was, is constructive and imaginative, maybe even fictive, in its workings. Along these lines, it might therefore be suggested that I myself have created a fiction of sorts surrounding that ride home, transforming what might otherwise have been just another event into something extra important and meaningful—foundational, as I called it. In one sense, this is quite right: without my own imaginative reworking of what happened that fine spring day, without my desire to tell it this way rather than that, it would indeed have been just another event. For all I know, mothers and fathers and their college children were all around us, littering the highways, talking with one another, making contact. Isn't that all we were doing?

Interpretations proliferate at this point. It could be that, in order for me to fend off the grim reality of my father having died without our ever really having the opportunity to make contact, I had to somehow convince myself that we did. After twenty years, something had happened, a breakthrough; boy, was I lucky. In this case, of course, much of what I have told you would deserve to be called illusory, the product more of a wish than a reality. Similarly, perhaps I have merely devised a means, through this yarn, to assuage some of my guilt and shame over the fact that, at the time of his death, I had done decidedly less than my brothers to make him proud. Maybe I had to convince myself that he could see that I was finally getting it together, that I had some promise and potential. To admit that he had seen nothing of the sort would have been too painful, too wasteful. Each of these interpretations presume that I had somehow foisted meaning onto that car ride, using it as a means to ensure that there was—or that there *appeared* to be—some redeeming value to our lives together. I could have chosen any one of a number of things to serve in this role. Not unlike the way dreams seem to work, according to Freud at any rate, maybe I just latched onto to this particular scene because it somehow allowed me to do what was necessary to carry on with some measure of self-affirmation: I think I can make something of that car ride . . .

All this is possible. But there is another way entirely of understanding what's been done here. In all honesty, I don't really take much solace from that ride home. I'm certainly glad it happened, and in that sense I do feel "lucky." But that incident, as I suggested a short while ago, is as much about what was, and is, missing as anything else. It is about what was missing from our relationship. There could have been so much—in a way, we proved it in that car—and yet there wasn't nearly enough. I can still feel the presence of what we missed together. It is also about what is missing now. It's been twenty-two years since that car ride home, and in nearly everything I've done since that time, particularly those things I might have been able to share with him or that might have made him proud or happy, he is right there, missing. Strictly speaking, it's not so much *him* I miss, in the sense of a present being. Rather, I feel the presence of his absence. This in itself might serve to correct the idea that memory deals only with what's happened, with "events," once there, now gone. It also deals with what didn't happen and what couldn't happen.

There is another way still of fleshing out this idea of the presence of what is missing. It is sometimes said that poetry seeks to make present what is absent in our ordinary, everyday encounters with the world. Or, to put the matter more philosophically, it is a making-present of the world in its absence. It is thus seen to provide a kind of "supplement" to ordinary experience, serving to draw out features of the world that would otherwise go unnoticed. But there is a kind of puzzle at work here. If it is assumed that these features go *totally* unnoticed and that absence is essentially complete, then poetry can be nothing more than the fashioning of illusions, replacing absence with presence. Not unlike what was said earlier regarding the view of memory that speaks of foisting meanings onto the past, it would have to be considered one more defensive maneuver, one more attempt to fend off meaninglessness. This is possible too: it could be that the meaning of poems, like the meaning of my ride home with my dad, is merely a matter of wishes, that things could be other than the way they are.

But it could also be that absence is *not* complete and that the world of ordinary experience bears within its absence a certain presence, a limited presence, which the poet, in turn, must try to bring to light. Seamus Heaney (1995) has spoken of the "redressing" effect of poetry in this context, which "comes from its being a glimpsed alternative, a revelation of potential that is denied or constantly threatened by circumstances" (p. 4). In a sense, you could say that poetry deals with what's not there and there at the same time. From one angle, it's about what is absent in presence; it's about what's often missing from our ordinary experience of things by virtue of its being "denied" or "threatened by circumstances." From another angle, it's about what's present in absence, the existence of a certain potential, "waiting" to be disclosed. Along the lines being drawn here, it should be emphasized, there is nothing intrinsically defensive or illusory at all about poems. Quite the contrary: they may very well serve as vehicles of disclosure and revelation, not so much "giving" meaning to experience as "allowing" it to emerge. And the same basic thing may be said, I suggest, about memory. A short while ago, you'll recall, I flirted with the possibility that the ride home with my dad, ordinary as it was in many ways, might simply be serving as an occasion for me to do some psychic patch-up work. I also acknowledged that, had that ride home not been followed by death, its story might have been told quite differently. Indeed, it may not have been told at all. But what my dad's death seemed to do was activate the poetic function of memory, such that I would return to that ride home and try to disclose what was there, waiting. The incident itself, as a historical event, was filled with a kind of diffuse, unspecified potential. It could have been played out in a wide variety of different ways, from the most ordinary and unmemorable all the way to the most extraordinary and memorable; it all depends on what follows. The reason the balance has in this case been tipped to the latter is clear enough. If only that ride could have remained in its ordinariness, pleasant and good, father and son, going home for the summer.

But it has become filled with an urgency that will always remain. This urgency is not something I put there. Rather, it's something that exists in the very fabric of this story I have been trying to tell you. Writing of this sort can be strange; even though I have tried here to "create" something—an image, you could call it, of a significant incident—there is no feeling at all that this image is merely a weakened replica of the real or that it is merely imaginary: "This world which cuts itself off from the world," Bonnefoy (1989) has written, "seems to the person who creates it not only more satisfying than the first but also more real" (p. 164). The situation is a fragile and delicate one. "In the very heart of writing, there is a questioning of writing. In the midst of this absence, something like a voice which persists" (p. 167). The ride home, etched first in memory, now in writing, speaks in this voice. There is nothing more real.

IV

The story continues. As fate would have it, the very next year there was a complete turnaround in my college experience. There was one course in psychology, another in philosophy; they were about fundamental questions of meaning and value in life and in art. And suddenly, the world of ideas seized me, took me by storm. The power and the beauty of what could be thought and said and written and painted let me know for the first time that there were some truly worthwhile things to do. I had finally become a student. How ironic that it should have happened within months of that awful summer day. Or maybe not. It is difficult to say.

V

Given the way my father died, at poolside, it is strange that my memory of him often turns to our times together in the water, in the ocean especially, playing in the waves. He somehow seemed more at home there than anywhere else and he seemed closer to us too.

People say that my dad and I have a great deal in common. I look more like him than either of my brothers do. When I went to a memorial service recently and encountered some long lost relatives, several

were taken aback, in shock almost: "Oh my God, it's Bernie . . . "
"You look more and more like your father . . . " "He's the spitting image; only he has a neck and Bernie didn't . . . " (When my father was
at his heaviest, his head rested squarely on his shoulders.) I also share
his moods and mood swings; there are lots of good times and lots of
laughs, but rage and sullenness are always a short step away. I also
like good food and drink and nice clothes and a number of other
things my father had been drawn to. Who knows? Maybe in the absence of his being there, I took in what I could of his desires and made
them my own. I also love playing in the water with my two daughters.
They dive off my shoulders and glide through my legs. I swim under-
water, unseen and unheard, and take them by surprise. "Don't!" they
scream. "More." Sometimes we just hold one another, gathering as
much warmth as we can. They are moments of fullness and presence
and, at the same time, sadness and brevity. Nothing lasts forever.

Oh, if he could have known those two girls, his granddaughters,
playing in the water, glistening in the sun like jewels. Oh, if he could
have known us all.

NOTES

1. After sending a draft of the present article to one of my brothers (the former
marketing exec), who proceeded to share it with his sons, I was reminded by the
older son that *he,* in fact, had been the first grandchild and that my father, in turn,
had been fifty-four upon the event of his becoming a grandfather. This sort of factual information is unquestionably important; hence my including it here. I nevertheless decided to leave the body of the text as it was. The reasons are many.

2. Make that second.

REFERENCES

Bonnefoy, Y. (1989). *The act and the place of poetry.* Chicago, IL: University of
    Chicago Press.
Heaney, S. (1995). *The redress of poetry.* New York: The Noonday Press.

Chapter 16

Paternal Role Slippage Across Cultures

Ki-Taek Chun

When my older son Stephen was in his early teens, he and I would become involved in conflict situations. When they occurred, these incidents usually ended up in an impasse. Each of us was convinced of being in the right, and felt hopeless at the seeming blockheadedness of the other. It was not uncommon for these incidents to end with manifestations of utter frustration.

The incidents had to do with the aggravation and confusion caused by my unwitting change of the rules of the game. My story deals with the situation where, due to the weight of the moment, a father and a son are unknowingly thrust into different cultural orbits. Writing this essay provides me with an occasion to make an interpretive sense of what had happened and draw some implications. Although this essay is being sent to the editors without Stephen's corroboration, narrative fidelity has been my goal. A faithful account is most essential for readers who may find my experience germane to their endeavor as a father, a son, or a counselor dealing with clients from different cultural backgrounds.

CRITICAL INCIDENT

A typical episode could have started with or without me as a contributing participant. For example, an interaction between Stephen and his mother would reach an impasse with no sign of resolution. Stephen would claim how unreasonable or misled his mother was, while his mother was equally adamant that Stephen was describing not her, but himself. Harsh words were traded, further irritating both actors. By then, the registered decibel level may have been a few notches too high for general comfort, upsetting the routine calm in the household. At such a moment of seeming impasse or escalating exacerbation, I would intervene thinking that I could ameliorate the conflict.

In volunteering as the mediator, I was interjecting myself without invitation directly into the situation rather than gliding into it by humoring either Stephen or his mother. I must have been as welcome an intruder as a social worker or a police officer who decides to intervene as an unsolicited mediator upon hearing a heated marital argument while passing through the neighborhood. I used to believe strongly, though implicitly, that it was only proper for the father to set a tone for the family and the entire household regarding standards of propriety, concerning not only the content of what is said but also the manner of expression.

Having forced myself into the situation, I would start analyzing the dynamics involved in the ongoing drama, identifying faults and distributing blame to each of them as appropriate. In this phase, it often was the case that I required Stephen to acknowledge his share of fault and offer due apology to his mother. Sometimes he would find fault with my analysis or distributive calculation, not accepting my arbitration plan. His critique often had merits, but he would go on extrapolating his criticism to invalidate the entire arbitration effort, removing any responsibility on his part. He would insist that he would not apologize unless his mother apologized for her part and I for my part. Insistence would sometimes become a demand.

Not only did he not appear interested in having an uninvited mediator tell him to apologize, but also he seemed to resent the intrusion. At that point I seemed more interested in enforcing the basic premise that the father has a duty and even a right to settle family disputes and set an overall disciplinary tone. Stephen's seeming negation of my effort at resolution was received by me as a challenge to my role as a father. Viewed from my notion of a father's role, a son demanding an apology from his mother or father was simply outlandish. Furthermore, when the demand was presented as a condition for enunciating his share of apology, his behavior seemed plain unthinkable, setting off a confrontation between Stephen and me that served as the proverbial "straw that broke . . . "

Other times the episode would start innocently between Stephen and me. Although things may be moving along smoothly, they would veer into an unpaved road when I directed attention to what seemed to be misguided, ill-advised, or faulty reasoning, planning, or manner of presentation. My corrective effort would then meet Stephen's counter-moves. He might point out errors in my logic or some faults in what I was doing. What he pointed out used to strike me as nonsubstantive. Though he might be correct in a limited context, he appeared insensitive about the core issue of the moment. He seemed intent on scoring a point against his old man, the bully. Mutual insistence often led to an impasse. Concerned that Stephen's insistence on a seemingly trivial point, while refusing to acknowledge the larger picture, might undermine household discipline and parental authority, I would persist with my argument. By this time, tempo and decibel level would have risen above the ordinary, and Stephen was likely to have made statements and gestures that to me were unacceptable. I was then drawn to shift focus to these misbehaviors, an action that infuriated Stephen because in his mind I was getting off the topic. He would accuse me of unilateral, evasive switching. The more he became vocal about his feeling of my inconsistency and shiftiness, the more I tended to dwell on his misbehavior, which only reinforced his belief that I was being unreasonable. Thus, we again set up a situation that promised further escalation of the confrontation.

By the time we reached this stage, our positions were locked in and things became quite explosive and sometimes even ugly. The tone of exchange was more like shouting. Harsh things were said; excessive expressions were used. I was persistent in pointing out his defiant insolence, and insisted on his acknowledgment of misbehavior as a son. Not comprehending my seeming preoccupation with propriety concerns, Stephen was pushed to the end of his wit, often throwing up his hands in utter desperation. He wanted to return to the main issue that was the starting point, but to me that issue was secondary at best to the emergent crisis of open filial attack. There was pounding on the table and hands thrown up in despair. Unable to get anywhere, one of us would suggest taking a break and coming back to the issue some other time, or one of us would walk away from the scene in utter disgust.

The critical incidents had two themes in common. From Stephen's point of view, the issue we started out with was pushed to the margin, almost becoming a nonissue; instead the blunders he allegedly made during the course of interaction became the focal issue that he was pressured to acknowledge. This arbitrary switching of focus away from the substantive issue to a preoccupation with proper manners both infuriated and at the same time perplexed Stephen. To Stephen it seemed like an evasion, needless harping, and harassment.

From my standpoint, Stephen's manners and expression of angry frustration appeared abusively defiant, presenting an open challenge to the father, the head of the household. His demand for an apology from his father or mother was more than a negation of, but an attack on, the family. Believing that such misbehavior was not permissible and, if condoned, would mark the beginning of a disintegration of family discipline, I decided that a line had to be drawn, and was bent on forcing an on-the-spot resolution.

Each episode was a source of private consternation afterward. The fact that I was having these episodes was painful in itself. And when I recalled Stephen's expression of exacerbating desperation, I felt sad and also plain ashamed. I knew that he, too, was not relishing these incidents. Why should I be causing this pain to him? I would ask myself. With the passage of time the felt intensity of these incidents would diminish, but a similar episode would occur. During one of the recurring episodes, Stephen said, "Here we go again!" Then I knew it was time to do something about it. In this utterance, I saw a clear sign of resentful anguish for having to endure the ordeal again, but I thought I also heard a plaintive request.

I began to ponder the situation, probing for a way out. During this period of reflective searching, initially I was dwelling on Stephen's misbehavior such as insolence, defiance, and disrespect, saying to myself, "How could he?" Gradually I was able to make allowance for his age-specific characteristics like assertive independence, ambivalence toward authority figures, clamoring for self-defining territory, etc. This tolerant perspective gradually replaced my earlier feeling of indignation, though it was not easy. Soon thereafter, it dawned on me that he and I were talking to each other across a deep divide and that this divide was filtering out signs of good intentions, replacing them with miscues or at best confounding cues. I came to realize that Stephen had no understanding of where and how I grew up as a boy and of the consequences that upbringing had on me. He could not have any comprehension of how my peers or I acted toward our fathers when we were boys and as a result what my cohorts or I would reflexively expect from our sons as proper behavior. After all, I spent my teen years in Korea, whereas Stephen was born and raised in the United States.

FATHER-SON RELATIONSHIP AS CULTURE-BOUND

The father-son relationship in Korea, as it is in Japan and China, requires a few background commentaries. Although the tide of Westernization has steadily affected the father-son relationship in Korea since the mid-twentieth century, the modal norm still seems distinctly different from its U.S. counterpart. Constituents of this relationship are lasting absolute terms: It is a permanently binding relationship, consisting of unconditional obedience, loyalty, caring, and deference.

Some illustrations might convey this flavor. Parents do sacrifice their personal comfort and interest for their sons, and indeed the norm is to go to any length for the sake of their sons. In return, sons are to hold their parents in unquestioned absolute terms.

It is common that a son offers a "big bow"[1] to his father not only at special occasions such as the father's birthday or the New Year, but also visiting him after absence. The big bow is a gesture of respect and devotion. When it is offered by a subordinate to one's superior as in a Japanese samurai movie, it connotes a declaration of surrender, obedience, and preparedness for ensuing followership. In the 1990s my friends' sons visited me from Korea on several occasions. Some asked me to receive their big bow. When I explained that it would not be necessary though I much appreciated the gesture, some would hesitantly withdraw but others persisted. They were placing me in the same rank as their fathers; thus their gesture of respect. The point is that this occurred in the 1990s.

I personally know many families in Korea where the grown-up sons routinely offer 10 to 20 percent of their monthly earnings to their parents for spending money. If the son lives with his parents in the same household, the son would offer his entire salary every month to his parents who then exercise the option of giving allowance, keeping the rest, or returning the entire amount after proper acknowledgment. Of course, when parents give an allowance to their sons out of the sons' earnings, parents put the remainder in a special savings account for the sons' future. This ritualistic practice probably has the implied meaning: "I am what I am as a result of all your sacrifice, and I offer this salary as a gesture of appreciation."

Talking back to one's father in his face is considered an extreme form of disrespect and misbehavior. During our boyhood days, getting slapped or whipped for such disrespectful behavior was not uncommon. One did not, and dared not, argue or debate with his father. Doing so was also considered a dumb move, not only because of the risk of incurring parental wrath, but because there were more effective means of registering one's disagreement. A smart, proper thing was to remember available alternatives. One could plead his case or convey his disagreement through his uncle or mother who in turn could talk to his father at a receptive moment. If you truly had to say something or protest to your father directly, you first let your "old man" vent his displeasure and indict your misbehavior as long as he could last, and then, and only then, would you meekly ask for his permission to speak.[2] Endurance often paid off because by the time your father came around to granting you permission to speak, he was likely to be more reasonable because he had vented his displeasure.

In a father-son exchange, particularly when the interactive dynamic temperature is above the usual comfort level, a son does not look directly into his father's eyes. Direct gaze at an authority figure, let alone staring or glaring, is construed as a sign of rudeness and defiance. Focused eye contact is a risky move, unless it is a passing one shadowed by a soft, friendly touch. When combined with talking back, glaring could be suicidal.[3]

These are illustrations of a few role-defined behavioral particulars. The father-son relationship, as with other relationships such as mother-daughter, husband-wife, and teacher-pupil, embodies a host of reciprocal obligations, duties, and expectations. Most of these relational reciprocity obligations are uncodified and unwritten, but within each operative culture they are understood as shared norms. Though implicit, they serve as a normative yardstick. The father-son relationship is also defined by the embedded role script. What is embodied in the role script could vary from one operative culture to another, making the role script culture specific. The acquisition of these unwritten, implicit normative role scripts is the key ingredient of acculturation and proper upbringing. Discordance or conflict is a natural outcome when a father and a son enact different cultural versions of the father-son script.[4]

RESOLUTION

Suppose a father is planning to take his family to visit Japan for the first time. He would surely make every effort to prime everyone in the family for a host of things Japanese, including mannerisms, body language, customs, etc., so that by the time they land at the Narita airport, everyone would have adopted a mind-set that is open to adventure, alert to differences, and ready to adapt. The father is unlikely to pluck his family up one night without prior notice and land them in Japan. Such a move would be inconceivable. Yet, something like this occurred when I enacted the Korean version of the father script, utterly confounding Stephen.

With the passage of time, critical incidents became less frequent. Two things seem to have contributed. On one hand, Stephen became less confrontational. Perhaps he taught himself the meaning of futility, thinking that the mountain may be moved, but not "this paternal wall." He started using the phrase "Yes, Dad" in a slow deliberate tone as if to mean "Please, let us not continue." He injected into his tone a shade of implied obedience, as if he caught on to what had in the past riled me into paternal fury. Sometimes, he even added an extra phrase to his trademark "Yes, Dad," saying, "Yes, Dad, I understand." When he added that supplement, I knew then that the traffic light was changing from yellow to red. It was time to stop.

On my part, I realized that we were on different pages of the father-son script. To be more exact, he and I were enacting father and son roles, but our role scripts came from different plays authored by different playwrights. I had to stick to the play Stephen was relying on. It was not easy for me. After all, I had to persuade myself that Stephen's objectionable acts were not a frontal challenge to the very core of what framed for me a father-son relation. I had to admit my oversight in not having introduced or sensitized Stephen at an early age to the Korean version of the father-son script. I also had to realize that at moments of perceived challenge to my sense of fatherhood and, by extension, to my self-identity, I was prone to revert to the submerged, unrehearsed portion of the father script that had not been adapted to the North American setting. In role-theory idioms, I slipped deeper into the engrossed level of organismic involvement when I felt the premise of father-son relationship was being negated.[5] As I slipped deeper, I was responding more reflexively and viscerally. This awareness placed me on guard to watch out for those moments when I was vulnerable to trip across the cultural divide, switching from one text to another.

Over time I have learned to welcome that affectionate, jestful "Yes, Dad" drawl in place of a big bow. When I am about to launch on an escalation course with Michael, Stephen's younger brother, Stephen says in a deliberate low voice, "Michael, you say 'Yes, Dad.'" Whenever I hear that distinct "Yes . . . " drawl, I usually get the message. Even to this day, whenever Stephen pulls that "Michael, you say . . . " line, every one in the family seems to look at me (or so I feel) although it is to his brother he is imparting his prudence gained from father-taming. I get ever slightly embarrassed and then bemused, realizing that it is their way of complimenting me; in their eyes I changed for the better. Such has been the reward of learning from the critical incidents of paternal role slippage.

NOTES

1. "Big bow" refers to a bow in which you put the back of your hands in front of your forehead while standing erect, slowly bend forward, and kneel down until your hands touch the floor.

2. Some psychologists and commentators find this practice a matter of concern because of its probable consequences not only for the psychological development of such traits as assertiveness, independence, expressive ability, etc., but also on democracy building in Korea.

A dramatic illustration of how this ingrained trait could be a powerful variable in real life is that in August 1997, Korean Air flight 801 slammed into a hilltop as it approached the Agana airport, Guam, killing 228 of the 354 people aboard. A *Washington Post* article reports that "the question haunting investigators is why the copilot and flight engineer failed to challenge the captain. Specifically, some investigators are wondering whether cultural factors—in this case, a traditional Korean deference to command authority—may have played a role in the crash." Phillips, D. Is Culture a Factor in Air Crashes? *The Washington Post,* March 18, 1998, A1. It is significant that in a subsequent investigative hearing, a Korean Air spokesperson said, "Since the crash, training procedures have been revised. . . . More important, the training [now] emphasizes that first officers and flight engineers must speak out forcefully to 'make all necessary advice' to the captain. After the second advice, if there is no response, he will simply take over the control." Phillips, D. Korean Air Denies Culture Played Role in Crash that Killed 228. *The Washington Post,* March 26, 1998, A10.

3. There is a Korean expression, which in translation means, "to talk back with glare." To incur this characterization is like uttering four-letter words to one's high school principal in front of other students.

4. This idea opens up a possibility that complications of cross-cultural communication could be explored as instances in which participants are enacting different cultural versions of role scripts.

5. Social psychologists will recognize that I am referring to ideas more fully developed elsewhere. See Sarbin, T.R. (1995). Emotional Life, Rhetoric, and Roles. *Journal of Narrative and Personal History, 43*(3), 163-183; Sarbin, T.R. and Allen, V.L. (1968). Role theory. In Lindzey, G. and Aronson, E. (Eds.), *The handbook of social psychology* (pp. 488-567). Reading, MA: Addison-Wesley.

Chapter 17

To Tell the Secrets of My Prison-House

Joseph B. Juhasz

> *Ghost:* I am thy father's spirit,
> Doomed for a certain term to walk the night;
> And for the day confined to fast in fires,
> Till the foul crimes done in my days of Nature
> Are burnt and purged away? But that I am forbid
> To tell the secrets of my Prison-House;
> I could a Tale unfold, whose lightest word
> Would harrow up thy soul, freeze thy young blood,
> Make thy two eyes like stars, start from their Spheres,
> Thy knotty and combined locks to part,
> And each particular hair to stand an end,
> Like Quills upon the fretful Porpentine:
> But this eternal blason must not be
> To ears of flesh and blood; list Hamlet, O list,
> If thou didst ever thy dear Father love.
>
> *Hamlet,* Act I, Scene 5

If I am in the audience, and for a moment suspend my "Juhasz" identity, and if the actor playing the ghost speaks the above lines, then, in saying "I am *thy* father's spirit," Hamlet's ghost identifies himself as *my* father's spirit. As a member of the audience I just had an encounter with my father's ghost. Encounters with ghosts are known to be tricky.

May 26, 2000. I have reread this text today. It seems to stand on its own feet despite all the predictable and unpredictable events that have happened in the meantime. I have resisted the temptation to revise.

Like Hamlet, my father's ghost haunts me. The ghost of the father, whether my father or Hamlet's, appears as an expression of a longing for continuity. Indeed, between my father and me, now that he is dead and mourned, all conversations are such expressions of a longing for continuity. I am building links to my past and to my future. The foundation of this building is my father's ghost.

Hamlet is a revenge play: Revenge upon the uncle at the bidding of the father's ghost. The ghost's revenge, Hamlet's revenge, Shakespeare's revenge—as a member of the audience, also in the sense that I have submerged my identity into that of the protagonist, my revenge. In many ways I identify with Hamlet. That is why I have chosen the ghost's speech as my prologue. So, when I say that I am using this text as a way to build a link to the past and the future, indirectly I am stating a theme of revenge. The "building," which is the object of the longing for continuity, can thus have the flavor of an "architecture of revenge" much as Shakespeare's playwriting builds his own architecture of revenge. I wonder: Is the object of his and my longing for continuity the building of an architecture of revenge?

Hamlet is also a play about evil, about conscience, about unnatural acts. In Hamlet's solitary reflection, "Thus, conscience makes cowards of us all," conscience in that sense is the antidote (albeit an "unnatural" one) to an architecture of revenge. In doing the bidding of the ghost, Hamlet acts against his conscience and seals the doom of his house. The architecture of revenge has made the house of Hamlet into a prison that confines and dooms both father and son.

In Hamlet's case, the ghost is a "projection" of the prince into the king, son into father. They are namesakes; on stage, in the frame of the play, both father and son are known simply as Hamlet. It is Hamlet's uncle, the stepfather, who has the alien name. The secrets of the Hamlets' prison-house arise from identity and betrayal, the ethics and ends of violence, power, forgiveness, conscience, and revenge.

In my case, the tale is even more complex and more ambiguous than Hamlet's. My father and I have different names—his name is the same name as the birth name of my two elder brothers. I was the first of my blood to be named Juhász (Shepherd). They were all born Haas. Juhász had been his pen name. I was either a piece of fiction or a documentary—I am not sure which—but he disconnected me from my blood, from my German-Jewishness (as I imagine his father had disconnected himself from Hassidism [or Haas-id-ism] as well as from the lurking "Spanish" [Sephardic] blood in *his* veins). When Dad "Hungaricized" his name, the judge said Juhászi (something like a *von Juhász*, however really a nonexistent name—and a name-change-marker). This is the name that appears on my baptismal and birth certificates. He preferred Juhász—how I am still known, despite all the tortuous turns—legally now after the judge assented at my naturalization hearing.

I have been naturalized Juhasz—my brother changed his name to Shepard. A couple of years ago we started to publish a series of articles in Hungarian in *Liget*. The authors are Joseph Juhasz and Lester Shepard. Shepard, with the "English" name, has the better Hungarian. We are clarifying issues in ethics that had haunted my father into his death: the problem of power and conscience in ethics; the *Deus Absconditus* as against the Christus *Rex*. My father's Hungarian writings on that subject were never published and are our legacy. This paper itself is struggling with those same issues: identity, power, ethics, conscience, revenge.

Fictional names; real names; pen names; Christian names. Truth and lies. Falsification in the face of oppression. Fiction perilously close to fact, as Nixon said.

My mother's maiden name: Mary Christianus (Mary the Christian). As to the first of my Christian names—it's Hebrew—it's the name of a prince, the youngest of his brothers; it's the name of Mary's consort, the putative, earthly father (or stepfather?) of Emmanuel—Jesus. I was born on January 30, in 1938, in Budapest, Hungary, and I am a Holocaust survivor.

I have five daughters. My two marriages have ended in divorce. I have one granddaughter; her name is Emma Sadie Juhasz Schwartz. My five daughters are Alexandra Juhasz, Jenny Schwartz, Antonia Juhasz, Christina Juhasz-Wood and Linda Juhasz-Wood. The confusion continues. Narratives are about a longing for continuity.

My father having been a Jewish convert, and my mother Christian (at least by name and by legal papers)[1] —to the Gentiles, I was a Jew, and to the Jews a Gentile. All the loony anti-Jewish propaganda on the radio and the other media as I grew into the Age of Reason, and the shooting, looting, bombing, shelling, raping, pillaging, hunger and starvation, bombings, fires, floods, and all the plagues and abominations of war left me mighty confused. What cipher on the door would save me?

The Germans and the Hungarian Arrow-Cross were out to get me.[2]

I was destined to become a social psychologist, apprenticed to an undercover Jew; to become a specialist in role theory, and then to become a professor of architecture.[3] The story of my life would not cohere without these events, so they happened. And so I have become what I am. The foundations of my house are confused. Has the object of this longing been a Shakespearean "architecture of revenge"? "Thus, conscience makes cowards of us all."

In actual truth I have never taken a class in architecture, nor in any even distantly related discipline or profession. I have not taken many psychology classes either. Mostly, I didn't go to school at all, I think, except for bits and pieces now and then. I don't think I am or was very well socialized—but then Harrison Gough says that Berkeley psych graduate students have the next lowest socialization scores to San Quentin inmates.

I feel as if I am somewhat of a fraud, spy, double agent, ghost . . .

My father disappeared now and again. He would walk through a wall and be gone; he would walk through a wall and reappear. I would say build a lodge for yourself here or maybe I will build you one, or I would try to palpate his side wondering about the fleshiness of his wounds. He was not really into domesticity, I think.

He went to Belgium in 1936, leaving my brothers and mother behind. He returned unaccountably to Hungary in 1937 (going in the wrong direction for sure even for an ex-Jew; wrong way, like a runaway slave rafting down the Mississippi). I was the outcome of a reconciliation; I never thought I looked anything at all like my brothers.

He went undercover in 1944. I didn't actually know where he was. He appeared once for a night, I remember. My mother and brothers and I were in our apartment that was in my mother's people's house. Seventeen Vadász (Hunter) Street, second floor, apartment nine. Later, during the siege, I was in the cellar with my mother. My brothers were sometimes in the cellar, sometimes in the apartment. The apartment was protected by a scarlet fever quarantine sign so they didn't have to worry about being shanghaied to war or a camp by the Germans or the Arrow-Cross; on the other hand, upstairs there were the bombs from the American and British planes or Russian shells. We were starving. One day my mother went into the street danger zone to fight with the other mothers for bits of a horse that had just been killed by a stray bullet. The meat of this cavalry steed tasted luscious.

In the Spring of 1945 my father reappeared. He had walked across the (frozen) Danube.

> I was at couple's therapy Monday; I am somehow trying to "work things out" with Jill, my lady friend. We have some form of companionship, not conventional marriage nor a "relationship," but something "absolute" not in the line of children. It seems a huge puzzle; I feel haunted by my father and mother and all the subsequent parents.
>
> Jill told me of a dream of hers in which my mother assures her that I need not fear her (Jill) because I had eaten horse meat as a child and I am "inoculated."
>> One day my mother went into the street danger zone to fight with the other mothers for bits of a horse that had just been killed by a stray bullet. The meat of this cavalry-beast tasted luscious.
>
> I had written that bit about an hour before.

In 1948 my father disappeared again, to reappear when two months later my second brother and I and my mother clambered out, in Vienna, from the boot of a 1947 Plymouth (we were smuggled there by the Americans). It was Graham Greene, it was Orson Welles, it was Anton Karas, it was Kim Philby, it was "The Third Man Theme";[4] spies, double agents, living-off-the-mold-war-miracle, black market penicillin.

I had imagined that he spied for the Vatican, for Israel, and for the Americans. After we came to America in 1951, he nominally worked for Free Europe Press and broke my mother's heart when he followed the American line in 1956. He manufactured American propaganda to keep the revolution going. He had thus "disappeared underground" yet again in New York.

When I went to the Holocaust Museum in DC, I discovered that the German race laws were all based on American Reconstruction-era precedents.[5] When those laws are applied to my children: more confusion. That Suzanne Juhasz, my first wife, is Jewish (but not observant) and still lives here in Boulder makes Alex, Jenny, and Antonia Jewish, by a hair, though they were all baptized Catholic. The second wife never took my name; Christina and Linda were never baptized either. I went to the Holocaust Museum with Antonia[6] and Christina and Linda. I found out that according to the German race laws I was (and I suppose, I still am) a *mischling* (a little of this, a little of that—the result of mixing things that aren't meant to be mixed).

I have a whole string of Christian names: József Borisz Brúnó Béla Arnold Frigyes; in Hungarian, these precede the surname. Emma Sadie Juhasz Schwartz, my granddaughter, is Jewish; she is just one and a half. She can say Menorah, Sábesz, and a bunch of other stuff; she calls me "Pa."[7]

At the moment of catharsis, the longing for continuity that narrative is about transforms into desire. The object of that desire is a silver bullet in the heart. The cleansing of catharsis involves a death of the self, a rebirth, a new identity. Who or what is killed? What ghost? In American iconology the silver bullet of the Lone Ranger is the Masked Man's signature, his calling card, his identity. If you receive the silver bullet (waiting for you—inscribed with your name) then, within the story, the source is the Lone Ranger's pistol; but the Ranger himself is masked. The audience members are the only ones who are in on who he is; within the story he is the Invisible Man. Or is the silver bullet a reference to the vampire who longs for a release from its own hellish earthly immortality?

The work turns on the maker; the House is its own undoing. Architecture become siege machinery.

One of my earliest memories is of a dream. I am in our summer place in Máriaremete (Mary the hermit) *and I walk to the store. There are tall shelves as in a shoe shop. Actually it is a grocery. There are the owner and his wife. The owner laughs at me; he tells me that my so-called father is not my actual (real) father. In the dream I call my mother to bring the "billy."*[8] *I wake up in a pool of urine.*

My mother's brother—my Uncle Otto—had been an officer in World War I. He fought on the Italian front and got tuberculosis.[9] I think my mother was very attached to my uncle. Shades of *Hamlet.* Otto died before I was born. His daughter went to an orphanage. Mom kept his rusty, bloody sword under her bed with the chamber pot. I would examine it as an enigma, a cipher; I looked for its code. The maid slept in the pantry; my mother in the small room; my father in the middle room; my brothers and I in the big room. My mother's father died when she was nine. Another *Pater Absconditus.* Her stepfather was a seed wholesaler. He was very rich. He used to fart at the dinner table to piss off my grandmother who was very ladylike and who had married beneath her.

Later, I became an American naval officer and I had a sword. I had top secret clearance. I was "regular Navy." I resigned my commission to go to grad school for psychology at Berkeley.[10] When I "reported for duty" to Ted, he said, *"Lófasz a segedbe!"* He had learned some Hungarian in Cleveland as a boy.

Ted Sarbin has my Navy sword hanging in his study—I gave it to him, of course. I was a willing Aeneas to his Dido.

When I was a psychologist he and I made a name for ourselves debunking hallucinations (believed-in imaginings; ghosts taken for real; fictions become facts) and mental illness. My father died the year I left Berkeley for Bennington—my first teaching job—and on his death I passed my sword to Ted. My cavalry saber and my Sam Browne belt are still in my office, witness to my officer-dom at Xavier High School—the Jesuit Military Academy in Greenwich Village where I was a debating champion and whence I graduated in 1957.

In another early memory, I am listening to the radio on the "gang" (the airborne walkway outside our apartment), and they are announcing that the Arrow-Cross have taken over the government and that Admiral Horthy—the Regent—has been arrested. There is the Arrow-Cross anthem:

> One rabbi
> Two rabbis
> The head-rabbi has "croaked."
> Courage,
> Long live Szálasi![11]

And there is a warm, patriotic spirit in my heart as I feel at one with the new Hungarian nation—wishing the deserved, already earned death upon my father, my brothers, and me. My six-year-old self is explaining to the sixty-year-old now writing this: looky here, Haas deserves death; hopefully he'll croak too, dad and rabbi, and with them your Haas identity. You're Juhász; Haas has croaked; *I* am back on the scene in Budapest as Juhász(i?) József, son of the Hungarian soil, Szálasi's blood brother, a corporeal emanation of the Hungarian bloodline. On the psychological map: in my own eyes I am totally deserving of self annihilation, self-ghost-making; my identification with the aggressor is absolute. Then as now.

I'm this, I'm that; I'm no thing; I can't return to my own past; I can't be converted; the sin is too original all together.

> But that I am forbid
> To tell the secrets of my Prison-House;
> I could a Tale unfold,

My first marriage was breaking up. My wife and kids were in Boulder. I was in Aspen; sitting next to me was the future wife, the mother-to-be of Christina and Linda, my last two daughters. We were at a funky movie house watching *The Tin Drum*—it was in German with English subtitles. The story is of a boy who remains a dwarf growing up in Germany during the war. I am following the German and I am following the English—the two melding together as in a dream as I submerge into the make-believe, the hypnosis, the role-taking, the believe-making of the story. The war has ended and the Russians have come in. The Germans are in the cellar. The trap door opens; a pair of boots is descending the staircase.

I squinch my face and shut my eyes closed with an exaggerated grimace. A voice orders me in Hungarian: *"Ezt nem szabad nekik megmutatni."* This pronouncement, although it is unambiguous in Hungarian (it is a prohibition and an abomination) is ambiguous in English. It could be, "These people cannot be shown this." Or, it could be, "These people are not allowed to show this."

An English voice intervenes. "It is just a movie, and these people are merely actors; they are simply playing a well-rehearsed role." I open my eyes; my face relaxes. Shakespeare's Hamlet's ghost has worked his revenge—I'm a dwarf yet.

> It seems to me I am trying to tell you a dream—making a vain attempt, because no relation of a dream can convey the dream-sensation, that commingling of absurdity, surprise, and bewilderment in a tremor of struggling revolt, that notion of being captured by the incredible which is of the very essence of dreams . . .[12]

Have you ever wondered who is the narrator of *Heart of Darkness*?

More to the point: Have you wondered who is Ophelia's mother, Laertes' mother, and Polonius' wife? Have you ever thought about the question of whether Ophelia and Hamlet may have been brother and sister, or that Laertes and Hamlet may have been brothers, or that Polonius may also have been Hamlet's uncle? All the uncertainties surrounding blood and marriage, identity, and the architecture of one's identity, fold fiction into a mythic reality. We are always haunted by them: especially sons, I think. These kinds of familiar relationships are spooky; they make you think of haunted houses.

Toward the end of his life, my father told me many times how he had become very attached to Conrad. I was probably in my fifties before *Heart of Darkness* really became staple reading for my courses. This spring, in the studio cum seminar that I snuck through the censors (Tom, Huck, Jim, and Becky), *Heart of Darkness* is coming second, just following Huck.

Heart of Darkness, Hamlet, Huck, the Lone Ranger, Dracula ... all are connected in the complex links established in the reader by the narrative devices, which the author employs. Shakespeare and Conrad and Twain (Clemens) create ambiguities of identification when you as reader, as audience, become an as-if protagonist. Who are you? The situation is not unlike the multiple identities one acquires when, for example, one identifies with the aggressor, and the self splits; in "hypnosis" when role enactment, role-taking and role-playing fold into a "multiple self"; make-believe becomes believe-making. The way that the characters in *Hamlet* are haunted by their complex parentage is reminiscent of the way the narrator of *Heart of Darkness* or the narrator of *Huck Finn* is haunted by the ghosts of other(s') (?) experience(s) and memory(ies). Each hypnosis in each story, each break in the story, is another stored identity, a disjunction point in the narrative.

Back at Berkeley we in Ted's group were teased by being called "belletristic psychologists." I think that Ted and I were at once irritated and titillated by the teasing; somehow we were both wanting to assimilate to literature, play, drama. We must have been ahead of our times.

There is something quite familiar and quite strange, almost surreal or dreamlike, in looking at texts and analyzing literature. After all, it was what my father did and what I wanted to escape from.

I flew to Atlanta for Emma's naming ceremony. Paul, my son-in-law, and the lady rabbi had cooked up this ceremony—something like a *bris* without foreskins—and the grandparents passed Emma along, and spoke to her. I wore the white yarmulke that I had worn to Jenny's wedding; I faced the audience; the trees were behind me; I stood on a deck. All my forefathers stood behind *me* as I blessed my grand-daughter; I enfolded the silver bullet in my heart, and for an instant, between waking and sleep, I was at rest with my father.

When Christina and Linda took me to dinner tonight to The Full Moon, Jennifer and Antonia, to whom I had just been talking in Atlanta and Washington, were there waiting for me. They were specters and they were real.

January 30, 1998, Boulder, Colorado

PS: My nephew Tom (Francis' fifth child) called me tonight for the first time since my mother's funeral, which he had attended from a motel in Denver. He wanted to know about his genealogy and about the heartache of being haunted by his father and the questions of blood, fate, and freedom. He is a Jewish convert and I correspond with his fourteen-year-old son by e-mail. I said that he must settle matters with his father's ghost. I've got to get this manuscript off to Bob Pellegrini and Ted; it was due in San José yesterday.

February 1, 1998, Boulder, Colorado

An hour ago I finished editing the Hungarian version of this paper that I am co-authoring with my brother. This is the second English version. I asked my brother if perhaps we need to write a sentence that confesses some weakness where I am constantly looking for co-incidences to be interpreted as connections.

"Oh, is this *your* buried treasure? The light in the heart."[13]

February 21, 1998, Boulder, Colorado

NOTES

1. I believe that my mother had one Jewish grandparent on the Lieberman side— although this was hushed up during the Hitler era.

2. The name of the Hungarian ultra-Nazi group that took power at the end of the war. These were the people who exported the Jews to the death camps.

3. Yesterday as I drove thirteen-year-old Christina and eleven-year-old Linda to see *Madama Butterfly,* we had an argument about whether there is such a thing as destiny or precognition. I said I thought that in a sense there is. They disagreed. I have the same disagreement with Ted.

4. The theme music of my radio show about the University of Colorado. I'm thinking of changing it to *The Silence of the Lambs.*

5. That is to say, the definition of *Jew* in the German race laws was simply copied from American laws defining *Negro.* Substitute *Jew* for *Negro.* It is said that the Apartheid-era race laws in South Africa were simply copied from American legal definitions and segregation policies. No substitution needed.

6. Genevieve Sarbin's goddaughter.

7. Or at times, "A baby named Pa."

8. Billy. Or Bili. Hungarian for potty. My father's first name was Vilmos—William.

9. Or, according to another story, lung cancer, from smoking too many cigarettes.

10. I wrote a stinging letter of resignation to Lyndon Johnson telling him that the Vietnam War was militarily unwinnable. I am sure that this was decisive in his not seeking a second term.

11. Hungary's would-be Hitler.

12. Marlow—in Conrad's "Heart of Darkness." The storyteller. The narrator is not identified. Joseph Conrad, "Heart of Darkness," in *Youth and Two Other Stories.* New York: McClure, Phillips, 1903.

13. Virginia Woolf, *A Haunted House and Other Short Stories.* New York: Harcourt, Brace and World, 1949.

Chapter 18

My Measure, My Guide, and Still a Mystery

Karl E. Scheibe

When I was fourteen and a freshman in Hillsboro High School, I remember hearing the expression, "Every son must rise above his father." It puzzled me. On one hand, it seemed a pious little formula for guaranteeing the progress of humanity. On the other, it seemed possibly subversive, impracticable, and in my case, confusing. My father had so many dimensions, was such a singularly complicated person, that the precise respect in which I might rise above him was far from clear. Certainly I could aspire to make more money than he and perhaps to attain a higher degree of education. But in certain ways, not all of them admirable, he seemed to me then and seems to me now to be unsurpassable. I could never match him for self-denying discipline, steely determination, mechanical ability, or raw energy. And I hoped never to match him for his temper, the sheer number of his projects, his mobility, and his dreamy otherworldliness.

Even so, I silently accepted the challenge to rise above my father. He would have approved the aspiration, for he was enthusiastic about almost every prospect for human betterment. If I have achieved this goal in any important respect, it is because of the guidance I received from him. I am especially grateful to him for one particular sign of direction, given at a critical moment, to be discussed later in this essay.

SMALL-TOWN PREACHER, IN MOTION

During my high school years, John Henry Scheibe was the Baptist minister in a small Illinois town, married to a woman too attractive for a preacher's wife, the father of four boys (I am the third), hardworking, energetic, multitalented, but always scrabbling to make ends meet. In addition to preaching, he usually worked as a traveling salesman, and we grew much of our own food in large gardens. Hillsboro was our seventh small town of residency in the brief span of my life. One of the ways I hoped to surpass my father was in permanence of dwelling. In this I have succeeded, for I have lived thirty-five years in the same New England town. He was a motile organism, not rooted in place, so I vowed to be sessile. His sort of motility left him in the end with no community he could call his own—a preventable sadness. This is one of the many lessons I learned from my father by way of negative example.

From Germany to Kansas to Illinois

I relate below the basic facts about the formation of the man who provided for me so many standards, positive and negative, in my own development.

Johann Heinrich and most of his mother's family had emigrated from Germany in 1911 when he was a frail boy of nine years, the eldest of four children.[1] His own father did not make the trip, for he was fatally ill with silicosis, had a peg leg, and was given to drink. So my dad was not properly fathered. He was known on the farm where they settled in Kansas as "Krug's Heinrich," after the surname of his mother, Catherine Krug. His uncles provided him with model and instruction. He grew apace on the Kansas plains, became robust, and proved to be *klug* (clever) as well as Krug. He learned English with no trace of an accent and progressed rapidly in the rural Kansas schools.

When he was about fourteen, he had a profound experience of religious conversion while hunting jackrabbits by himself. He attested that the fears that had plagued him since his departure from Germany suddenly left him, and from that moment on he knew no fear and never doubted that he was a Christian. As nearly as I can tell, he did not show fear in his entire life, and there are certainly many times when he was incautious. He also seemed incapable of being bored, finding everything in this world and in the hypothetical next world full of fascination. He was alive to spiritual as well as material realms, and he made it his business for the remainder of his life to be avidly involved in the exploration of both.

As an adult, he was 5'10", 185 pounds, and quite strong. He was hearty, rarely ill, and rarely complained of physical ailments. He became bald while still young, but never complained of this as a handicap and was a handsome man.[2] He wore rimless glasses to correct for astigmatism and nearsightedness. He had long arms and big, farmer's hands—the strong, callused hands of a man who knew honest toil.

To prepare for the ministry, he went to Tabor College in nearby Hillsboro, Kansas, where he took lodging with the family of the owner of the local lumberyard. He fell in love with the youngest and prettiest of the lumberman's daughters, and he and Esther were soon married. After finishing college, he went to Kansas City Seminary— a school of the American Baptist Convention. He assumed his first ministry at the Oak Park Baptist Church in Kansas City, where he was ordained. After several years at Oak Park, he accepted a call to be minister at a small rural church in Highland, Illinois, and from there went to a series of churches in small towns and rural communities throughout Illinois.

The reason for this restlessness had more to do with my mother than my father, truth to tell. This is not the place to detail the strains in the marriage, other than to say that she was as given to fun and frivolity as he was to discipline and earnest, hard work. In these days, they would have divorced after a few years of unhappy quarreling. In those days, for a minister to divorce meant the end of his career, and so they stayed together perforce—quarreling at home openly and constantly. I suppose I owe my existence to this stricture—for I was born thirteen years into the marriage. Even so, the atmosphere at home formed another respect wherein I hoped to rise above my father. I could easily see the futility and gratuitous pain caused by constant bickering. I vowed to remember this lesson. I also learned something about human psychology, though the term "psychology" was not part of my vocabulary. I learned that things are not always what they seem, that rapid changes of mood and posture are to be observed between the kitchen and the pulpit—within minutes—and that anger seems to limit utterly one's ability to see the other person's point of view. I could easily see that anger makes an intelligent man act stupidly. I knew that my father was a good man—I have never doubted this. But I often observed him acting badly.

A Man of Sayings and Voice

Normally, outside the home, Dad's manner was cheerful and open. He loved stories—both the telling and the hearing. He had a prodigious memory for epigram, anecdote, and aphorism, as well as for Scripture. He was a man of sayings, both in English and German. "Time to rise and shine," was his too-cheerful way of rousting us out of bed. *"Morgan Stunde hat Geld im Munde."*[3] He met strangers easily and was naturally trusting. He seemed happiest when in "fellowship"—engaged in animated conversation, trading experiences. Working with him or riding with him in the car, he was rarely quiet. Conversation to him was as natural as breathing. I did not find it tedious. He was a great talker.

When he was young, he learned to play oboe as Mother played violin—and they made a pretty duet. Later, the instruments were abandoned, but both parents had lovely voices—Dad a tenor, Mother a contralto. As a vocal duet, they would often enter amateur competitions, and they won many prizes. At the end of his life, when all of his memory was gone in a version of Alzheimer's disease, he continued to sing, often in German. I could never surpass or come close to matching his voice.

FATHER AS TEACHER AND TASKMASTER

In *Iron John,* the poet Robert Bly makes the observation that fathers in America are commonly unknown to their sons. The life of the father—where he works, what he does—is largely invisible to the curious young son. Bly also suggests that this vacancy of experience becomes translated by the son into a vacancy of soul. Where the father is absent, a hole is formed in the soul of the son, and these empty spaces come to be occupied by demons. As a practical matter, the absent father is not in a position to pass on to the son the skills he has learned. Since the ways of the world are complex, it is a serious handicap not to have your father as a teacher.

In this respect, I have been as fortunate as my own father was unfortunate, for I believe I saw and participated thoroughly in the world of his work and rounds of activities. Indeed, there are times I wish I had been left more alone, for it was often hard work to keep up with him. The parsonage was adjacent to the church, and church members would flow through our house with regularity, often holding meetings in our living room. Also, my brothers and I were early enlisted in work for the church—folding Sunday morning bulletins, tending the grass and furnace, performing odd jobs. Dad would often invite me just to come and stay with him in his office while he counseled people. More commonly, he would take me with him on his interminable pastoral calls, where I learned to be a patient and silent guest, and only after much suffering would I venture a tug on his sleeve. When he went from farm to farm to sell cattle feed, I would often accompany him and be introduced to his customers as his "sidekick." In our basement workshop, I was often required to lend a hand—to hold a wrench or a light, or clean up after a repair job was finished. Our automobiles were constantly in need of repair, and here again the services of me and my brothers were required. I remember slithering underneath the recalcitrant Nash to hold a trouble light, as Dad secured new rod bearings to a crankshaft. Garden work was required, giving palpable meaning to the phrase "You've got a long row to hoe." Construction projects were frequent—involving the installation of plumbing, heating, and electricity in our houses, as well as the more enjoyable tasks of hanging wallpaper and painting, interior and exterior. There was usually a cow to be milked, and sometimes a goat. And chickens were to be cared for, eggs to be gathered, butter to be churned.

The result for me is that I became a person who knows how to do things—how to repair cars, how to plant a garden, how to build and fix things. In the life of a teacher and scholar, such skills are hardly necessary, but I find them a great consolation—for there are times when commerce with ideas seems a dry business.

Around our home, there were always jobs to be done. Mother was counseled, when first she visited the family farm in western Kansas, "Never look idle." She did not take well to this advice, for she loved to take her ease. But Dad would take his ease only on Sunday. After his sermon, after reading us the funnies, after the obligatory fried chicken dinner, he would stretch out on the couch and take an afternoon snooze. But soon it was time to get up to prepare for the Sunday evening service, which we were all obliged to attend. He rose early and worked with a will. He got a lot done, but it usually seemed at the end of the day as if there were even more jobs for the morrow.

I don't know of anything in his work life that remained invisible to me, though parts of it were certainly mysterious. I remember in particular being impressed with the immense waders he used for the total immersion baptisms conducted in our church. These boots seemed to me imbued with magic and were oddly sinister, as if they represented the underside of the divine rite of transformation accomplished by the backward dip into the baptismal pool. Also, I never understood where he got all of the knowledge that he seemed to deploy so effortlessly— whether in the planting of a cornfield, doing a valve job on the Nash, the castrating of pigs, the laying of brick, the roofing of a house, or the singing of lyric ballads with Mother.

Indeed, I don't think I ever understood how he thought, despite all of his talking. I did know that he did not seem like other fathers, or like other people. He was abstemious to a fault. He never drank or smoked and would not even drink coffee. He had a particularly intolerant attitude about smoking, long before it was proved to be unhealthy. In my youth, I did experiment with tobacco, but I would have risked utter castigation had I ever smoked in his presence. I never had the courage. His convictions were unswerving.

Never fearful, never bored, he still had time for hobbies. He learned to fly, and with my brother, Bob, restored and flew a wrecked Taylor Craft two-seater. He taught me how to fish and how to hunt rabbits and pheasants. All of his hobbies were purposeful. You ate your catch.

Despite his evident musical gifts and talent, he had no ear at all for popular music. The rhythms of swing puzzled him entirely. It is as if he had his own strongly built-in cadences and new beats could not displace them. In temper and character and guiding passions he seemed remarkably consistent throughout his life, even if old age did turn down the flame of intensity and erode his memory.

It used to infuriate him to hear of young people just hanging out or "killing time." "Never kill time," he said. "It's the most precious thing in the world." Alas, in his last years, his loss of memory took him quite out of play and vacant time was about all he had.

A CRITICAL PIECE OF ADVICE

It was August of 1955—still in Eisenhower's first term, after Korea, still well before Vietnam. Foreign cars were almost unknown, and by the time I graduated from the high school in Hillsboro just a few months earlier, I had tasted pizza maybe once—on a trip to St. Louis with my brother, Paul. My limited world seemed pretty much in full view—nothing was exotic—and yet I was acutely aware that my horizons were about to undergo a radical extension—but I did not know in what direction. I needed some guidance.

I had been for the last several weeks attending a summer Bible study institute, run by the New Tribes Missionary Society. I had a critical decision to make. In retrospect, it seems ridiculous—a situation of almost comical absurdity. But such was my envelopment in the circumstances of the time that the matter seemed of utmost seriousness—a matter of life or death. I have learned to respect the power of circumstance. Considered abstractly and by the light of my present understandings, my agony makes little sense. At the time, the dilemma was real enough.

I had come to the Bible Institute in response to urgings from my two older brothers, Bob and Paul. They were both in training at the time to become foreign missionaries to Brazil. Bob, the oldest, had joined the New Tribes Missionary Society after a conversion he had experienced while serving in the Air Force. He became so adamant and radical in his Christianity that he seemed to doubt whether his own minister-father was truly a Christian. Dad respected his experience while respectfully disagreeing with his theology. Before his conversion, Bob had been a hellion, dropping out of high school at age sixteen to work at a local airport, then taking to the road to live by his wits in pursuit of women and booze. Dad found his conversion a relief, even if his new self-righteousness was uncomfortable.

Bob witnessed to Paul, who was three years older than I, with such force as to cause him to drop out of Washington University, where he had completed his freshman year, joined a fraternity, made the football team, found a lucrative part-time job, and had a beautiful girlfriend. Now both brothers had "given their lives to Christ." I was mightily impressed, and fearful that I was making a selfish and sinful choice by not joining them in service to the Lord.

I had graduated from Hillsboro High School with a full scholarship to attend Trinity College in Hartford, Connecticut. High school had been a delightfully satisfying and self-indulgent time of my young life. I was popular, successful academically and in athletics, and headed for an exciting educational venture in a traditional and highly respectable school—a long way from the confining prejudices of small-town Illinois. I imagined smoking without guilt.

Immediately after graduation, two friends and I found jobs in Peoria, Illinois. Initially, I worked for the Libby Company, laboring at night on their harvest of sweet peas. Then I obtained a job at the Hiram Walker distillery, where I worked in the tax-pay room, handling barrels of aged whiskey, learning to pull bungs from barrels with a single stroke of a special tool. The idea was to earn some money prior to my departure for Hartford, for while I had a scholarship, I could not depend on my parents for much support for books and spending money.

Such were the outward circumstances of my life. Inwardly, I was in agony—for my eldest brother, Bob, had long since been after me to define myself as a Christian in a way that he could believe. Now he was supported by Paul, who had been my closest brother—someone I looked up to for his intelligence, his many skills, and now for his evident sacrifice of all worldly pleasures in order to answer what seemed to be a divine call.

Halfway through the summer after my high school graduation, I decided to give up my distillery job and spend the rest of the summer at the New Tribes Bible Institute in Milwaukee. I went back to Hillsboro and told my parents of the decision I had made. Mother was in despair. She imagined that she was about to lose her third son to a wacky bunch of religious nuts. Dad was more supportive. He respected my decision, gave me the use of a car to travel to Milwaukee, and pledged to visit me there later in the summer.

At the time of their visit to the Bible Institute in late August, I had been in the program for several weeks. This experience was truly remarkable for me. For the first time, I was living in a community of people who seemed united by common faith, common devotion, and selfless commitment to the cause of spreading the gospel. I took part in street corner preaching in downtown Milwaukee. We went to witness to the down-and-out bums in the missions. We spread gospel tracts from door to door and passed them out on streets. And we studied the Bible in a prolonged and serious way—memorizing passages, discussing, planning, and imagining new ways to spread the Word.

My brothers were already well known in New Tribes as promising new recruits. So the leaders of the Bible Institute in Milwaukee spent some time with me discussing my plans and prospects. The question arose of renouncing plans to attend Trinity College. The prospect placed before me was to join in full-time missionary training, at the society's "boot camp" in California, as my two brothers had done.

I remember being asked to defend my plan to attend Trinity. I was told that Trinity, an Episcopalian school, was not likely to have the faintest contact with fundamental Christianity. When asked what I might study there, I vaguely responded, "psychology"—Paul's intended major at Washington University. I recall being told that psychology was basically the devil's work, and that perhaps the only thing worse would be philosophy. My brother Bob put the strongest arm on me—suggesting that my refusal of the scholarship would be headline news back in Hillsboro, and a most powerful witness for the Lord. I was powerfully confused. These people in Milwaukee had a profound sense of assurance about them, and the authority of the Bible was everywhere. My two brothers had both renounced their worldly and sinful lives. Both were now married to attractive young women, also missionaries in training, and were clearly, in my eyes, doing the Lord's work. Would I have the courage to renounce my worldly ways?

Mom and Dad arrived in Milwaukee to spend a weekend near the end of my stay there, at a time when a decision was to be required of me. The critical scene occurred one evening after dinner. The dinner was communal, as usual, with prayers and Bible reading and the singing of hymns. Afterward I went for a walk with my parents. During the walk, I discussed my anguish over the choice presented to me— my doubts, my hesitation. Mother cried in despair. At the end of our walk she threw herself over the hood of their car and sobbed. Dad was sympathetic with my plight, but his advice was firm. "Karl," he said, "I think you should go to college." And he said more. He did not challenge or negate the power of a call to Christian life, since he himself had dedicated himself to such a calling. Mother put down the New Tribers as a "bunch of nuts," but Dad was not so dismissive. Instead, he argued that the people at the Institute presented just one perspective on Christian service, and that I needed to inform myself of other, less radical possibilities. To this end, he set up a meeting for me with a gentleman who was an official of the American Baptist Convention, with offices in Milwaukee.

I remember that meeting exceedingly well, for the gentleman began our meeting by suggesting that we get down on our knees to pray for God's guidance. In the course of our conversation, he gently suggested that while he was no advocate of the sort of liberal Christianity practiced by Episcopalians, he still felt that I could go to Trinity College and maintain my identity as a Christian—and more, that the education I could receive there would fit me for a much more productive and valuable life than I might be able to achieve by choosing another path.

I didn't keep a journal at the time, and it is difficult for me now to reconstruct what I actually was thinking at the time. I know that I felt divided. On the one side, a life of self-denial and arduous missionary training held little appeal to me. But I was terribly afraid that to choose otherwise was to choose sin and possibly eternal damnation—or to put it another way, to risk being shamed by my brothers. It is possible that I built up the possibility of defection to the missionary camp for dramatic effect. It is hard for me to reconstruct my intentions at the time. But I do know that Dad provided me with what I needed to say NO to the missionaries and YES to a college education. I was unimpressed with Mother's histrionics. In fact, the more she carried on, the more inclined I was to persist with the possibility of defection. My mother was never a moral force for me, but my father certainly was.

SEQUELAE

Who knows what turns and developments my life might have taken had I chosen differently in 1955—had Dad not gone out of his way to counsel me to go to college? I am not so complacent and self-satisfied with my life and career as to claim that things could not have been bettered. But I shudder to think that I came close to taking a path toward darkness rather than toward light.

Both of my brothers did complete their missionary training, and duly went to work on their placements in Brazil. Paul proved adept at languages, and after completing his in-country training in Brazil, began to work with the Nyengatu Indians near Manaus on the transliteration of their language. Bob defected from the New Tribes Missionary Society before going to Brazil, and instead was supported by a more Pentecostal-like group. After his language training in Brazil, he moved to a small town, Lagoa Santa, in the state of Minas Gerais, with the objective of establishing a group of believers in that community.

After three years, Paul left Brazil with his missionary wife, and returned to the United States to complete his undergraduate education at the University of California in Berkeley.[4]

Dad resigned from his last church in 1956, again because of troubles with Mother. Soon thereafter, he moved to St. Louis, where he began to manage a failing sheet-metal business for an old friend. Neither liking nor profiting from this business, he resolved in 1960 to sell out and join Bob in Lagoa Santa in Brazil. This he did. Mother refused to go to Brazil, and went instead to California with my youngest brother, Steve, and my Aunt Julie, so that she could be near at least part of her family.

Dad imagined a variety of ambitious projects for Brazil. He acquired an old sawmill from a friend in California and shipped it to Brazil, only to lose it entirely as the truck carrying the equipment sank with its barge in the Rio São Francisco. He tried single-handedly to establish a hardwood lumbering project in several regions of the Brazilian jungle, in the state of Pará, and also on the island of Marajó. This project came to nothing. He had the idea of introducing macadamia nuts into Brazil, and actually planted thousands of macadamia shoots in the lots and fields of various bemused Brazilian volunteers. He became known as "Joao Macadamia"—sort of a Johnny Appleseed of Brazil.

He was living in the Brazilian jungle, pretty much by himself, with a couple of Brazilian hired hands, when I got a message to him in late 1960 announcing my intention to get married in September 1961, and asking him to perform the marriage. He wrote back to say that he would do it. But I didn't hear anything more from him as plans for the rather large wedding, to be held in my fiancee's town of Needham, Massachusetts, neared completion. We had a contingency minister in reserve at the local church. Finally, the day before the wedding, my father miraculously appeared and performed the wedding in good order. He was in excellent spirits and had no thought of apologizing for having been out of touch and having kept everyone in suspense.

Soon thereafter, Bob moved to a remote region in the deep interior of Minas Gerais, a new town called Montalvania. Dad joined him there and set up a repair shop for machines and tools. Bob was a pilot and spent a fair amount of his time ferrying local people to hospitals and picking up materials for use in the newly settled town. In July 1966, while training one of his friends to pilot the Cessna aircraft he owned, the plane was caught in a windshear upon landing, crashed, and both Bob and his friend were instantly killed. Bob left his wife, Verla, with three children and expecting a fourth.

Dad was devastated, but even as Verla and her children returned to the United States, Dad decided to continue by himself in Brazil—and to do what he could to continue Bob's mission in the remote town of Montalvania. Still, Mother refused to join him, and in fact instituted divorce proceedings from her residence in California. Steve, now nineteen years old, decided to go to Brazil to provide aid and support for Dad. (He had previously spent a year with Bob in Lagoa Santa and had learned Portuguese.)

Paul, the former missionary, now a graduate of the University of California and a well-established businessman, offered help and placement for Verla and her family in California. I had completed my PhD in psychology at Berkeley and had taken a job at Wesleyan University. Since I was eligible for a sabbatical in 1967-1968, I decided after my brother's death to study Portuguese during the 1966-1967 academic year and to spend my first sabbatical in Brazil, so that I, too, could be of help to Dad. Thus it happened that in the summer of 1967, I and my wife, Wendy, and our two small boys, David, age three and Daniel, age six months, moved from Middletown, Connecticut, to Belo Horizonte, capital of the state of Minas Gerais. We rented a home there, with the help of a Brazilian friend, Roberto Bouchardet, who had become our Portuguese tutor during the previous year at Wesleyan. Dad made frequent trips to stay with us during the 1967-1968 year, and we were, in fact, able to provide considerable support for him, as well as for Steve, who lived with us in that year, while teaching English and still making trips to Montalvania to help Dad.

I was able, in that year, to complete the writing of a number of ongoing research projects, including my first book, *Beliefs and Values*. Near the end of my year, I received word from my Chair at Wesleyan that I had been promoted and awarded tenure. In April of that year, my Portuguese was sufficient for me to be able to offer a couple of courses at the newly established Federal University in Brasília. Because of our interest in Brazil and our ability in Portuguese, Wendy and I brought our family back to Brazil—this time to São Paulo, in 1972-1973, where I had been awarded a Fulbright Fellowship at the Catholic University of São Paulo, and we have been back to Brazil frequently over the years. Steve continued to live and work in Brazil, aside from three years he took to finish his undergraduate degree at Wesleyan. Recently, he and his Brazilian family moved back to San Diego.

Paul eventually divorced his wife, remarried, and moved to San Diego, where he has had an adventuresome career as a businessman and raised a second family.

Dad remained in Brazil, off and on, until 1974, living for his last period there with Steve and his wife, Angela. In 1974, Dad returned to the United States, but had difficulty knowing what to do or where to do it. He was, as the Brazilians say, *a toa*—that is, without direction or purpose. Once I asked him, rather absently, whether he had filed his U.S. income tax in recent years. "Well, what would I say?" he asked. "No runs, no hits, no errors, and nobody left on the bases." Quite right.

In his early seventies, his memory began to fade sadly and continuously. He lived for a time with us in Middletown, for a time with Paul in California, and for a time with his sister, Elizabeth, in Kansas City. Finally, his disorientation was so complete that he required around-the-clock care, and in 1977 I placed him in a rest home near Middletown. By now, he had forgotten the names of everyone, his own name, his own history. He was loose in time. Once he told me that he had recently returned from an expedition to Africa, and that later he had visited the moon on a secret expedition with Russian astronauts. All of this was exceedingly sad. Even so, he would continue to sing—as I have said, often in German. The greatest sadness in his life was that he could not manage to hold the woman he loved. He died of congestive heart failure in 1983, and ten years later, Mother died as well, in a home in California. They are buried next to each other in Indian Hill Cemetery in Middletown—a gesture that Dad would have appreciated but that Mother might have found questionable.

EPILOGUE

Dad could make me furious.

He insisted on attending an anthropology class with me while I was a student at Trinity. This was okay. But in the midst of the lecture, he raised his hand and asked the professor a question. I was mortified.

Again: After he attended my graduation ceremony at Trinity in 1959, he accepted an invitation of my roommate to visit their family house in Philadelphia. Later, I learned that he had used the occasion to try to convince my Jewish roommate and his family of the possible value of a Christian conversion.

And again: After the wedding ceremony he performed in 1961, he thought it opportune to hitch a ride with me and my new bride on our honeymoon trip across country—from Massachusetts, where we were married, to California, where I was to resume graduate study. Fortunately, I was able to convince him to disembark in Kansas, to visit with some of his relatives there.

I could list many incidents of this sort.

But then I remember the extraordinary gifts that my father has given me. He was a man of honor, of spirit, of genuine principle. He always cared, in politics, for the little guy—the poor, the dispossessed, the weak. He was generous to a fault, and expected others to be naturally generous as well. He was naive, and yet worldly wise. He was an avid reader and had an inventive and original mind, though he was hardly a scholar. He was a man who could use his hands, and did so with amazing effect.

He once disappointed me by turning down my request to borrow some money so that I could buy a 1952 MG while I was in college. "It's not a practical car," he said, "and you can't afford it." I was less surprised that he turned down my request than that he genuinely regretted doing so—for he would do anything for me if he thought it right. He hated to dampen a dream.

It's amazing how things turn out. Dad told me to go to college rather than train to be a missionary in Brazil. As a result, I was able twelve years later to go to Brazil to help him in his own missionary efforts. And later, when I could afford it, I finally bought an old MG on my own. When I gave him a ride in it, Dad was mighty proud. And so was I.

Dad was a measure for me and was my guide. If I never quite understood him, I learned from him that one might love something without quite knowing what it is that is loved. I suppose this to be a form of faith and the ability to exercise that faith, a grace.

NOTES

1. From the little village of Uengsterode, just east of Kassel, in north-central Germany. The motives for emigration were several—but the chief ones were poverty and the threat of German militarism. My grandmother did not want her sons to be

enlisted in the Kaiser's army. I recently learned that the Scheibe part of the family strongly opposed the emigration and cut off all contact with the defectors thereafter.

2. I found his cheerful acceptance of baldness to be instructive and helpful.

3. The morning hour has money in the mouth.

4. As it happened, I graduated from Trinity just as Paul was returning from Brazil, and was on my way to graduate study in psychology at Berkeley. For my first two years at Berkeley, before my marriage, I lived with Paul and his wife and daughter.

Chapter 19

Farewell to Vienna:
The Authority of Nostalgia

George C. Rosenwald

Dear Bob,

You very kindly invited me to join a group of colleagues, each of whom would tell you a story concerning a critical incident in his life involving his relationship with his father or his son. This should be done, you wrote, in a manner that has wide, even popular, appeal rather than in the form of traditional disciplinary scholarship. Ted Sarbin would then comment on the collection of these stories from his conceptual perspective. I thought this was an attractive division of labor: The contributors all narrate away, as they might sitting around a campfire, and Ted will do the interpretive work.

But as I thought further about your proposal, I realized its difficulty. Can I tell "just the story?" Would that be anything like telling "just the observed facts" and letting theory come later—a notoriously impossible postponement? We know that scientists need theories to inform them as to what will count as a relevant and legitimate observation; theory and fact depend on each other. In similar fashion, it is a person's life history that determines what he or she regards as an incident worth reporting. An incident is not critical as such; it is critical *for* the life. Also let us be clear that when we say "life history," we mean not just the personal relationships and the external events in that life, but also one's abiding perceptions and preoccupations and, finally, one's intellectual and ideological commitments. In my case, this includes prominently my commitment to certain theoretical positions.

Here is the point. The incident I want to relate to you happened more than fifty years ago. I don't remember telling it to anyone else before. Why then, after all this time, do I choose to tell it to you now?

Think of it this way. In addition to the story of the incident, there is also the story of how I come to tell it. This second story would be hard to tell in full and perhaps not very interesting. But a few pieces of it are essential if you and your readers are to grasp what the incident means to me *today*. As it happens, these two histories—the one of the *telling* and the one that is being *told*—are not wholly unconnected. To let the cat all the way out of the bag, the incident I have selected bears on the role of paternal authority. As a story, this brings together two engagements of my life—my engagement with my father and my engagement with theories about authority. I cannot sensibly tell about the one without mentioning the other; my life includes them both. I hope Ted will forgive me if I trespass briefly on his territory.

I may as well start in 1936, when the *Studien über Autorität und Familie* were published in Paris—yes, in Paris—in the German language, written by authors who had fled the Nazis and were teaching at Columbia University in New York (*Institut für Sozialforschung*, 1936). This is a fat and daunting book. I daresay not many people have read it from cover to cover. To read the names in the table of contents is a moving experience. Many of the contributors ended up in the United States and went on to shape American social science during and after the war. When the volume appeared, I myself was three years old and living comfortably with my parents in Vienna. Believe me, my interest in paternal authority was entirely atheoretical at that age.

I did not become acquainted with this book until about thirty years later, and it impressed me deeply. It dealt with the mentality, the morality, and the human relations characteristic of modern Western societies. In particular, it addressed the political disasters of the first part of the twentieth century, asking why so many civilized people had lined up behind some of the vilest authoritarian forces in the annals of history. Since my own life had been marked by these events, I took a special interest in what these authors had to say.

I shall put the central point briefly. Traditionally, human beings have become morally autonomous as they internalized the values and standards of conduct observed in those nearest to them. During the nineteenth century a young male's most significant model was still the father, whose standards, values, and self-regard were most evident to others when he represented his own, his family's, or his group's interests to the world at large. A son could learn what his father stood for, how he managed his fears and ambitions, which values he insisted on and which ones he would compromise—in short, he could learn about his father's morality when he witnessed his role and his decisions within the context of work and in his dealings with institutions and fellow human beings outside the family.

But our own world is not what it was then, the authors argued. Today the autonomy of the individual vis-à-vis the society at large is sharply reduced. Individuals' private concerns are increasingly controlled by corporate organizations and by the state—forces and organizations of enormous influence and neither fully comprehensible nor significantly controllable by individuals. Experts take over our guidance more and more as tradition becomes less and less relevant. Within the family, the father has lost authority in proportion as he has lost self-determination outside it. Fathers who have relatively little say about the most decisive aspects of their own lives—especially their economic and social condition—do not represent a significant *moral* force for their sons to reckon with. This is so because a man who has few opportunities to *act* on his values with significant consequences leaves his sons with few occasions to observe and experience what really matters to him. Thus, sons whose budding vitality, impulses, and desires do not encounter or confront ideals and values that their fathers hold and act upon with conviction cannot internalize standards in the usual sense of the word.

Here is how Max Horkheimer, the senior author of the *Studien,* put this point some years later: "The socially conditioned weakness of the father, which is not disproved by his occasional outbreaks of masculinity, prevents the child's real identification with him. In earlier times a loving imitation of the self-reliant, prudent man, devoted to his duty, was the source of moral autonomy in the individual" (Horkheimer, 1949, p. 365). But now, rather than listening to an inner voice, the sons end up conforming rather easily to the agendas of the corporate state. Their orientation to the society at large is docile rather than critically evaluative. What they fear above all is that they might be left out of the "action." "Where once the agencies of conscience, individual independence, and possible *resistance* against the pressure of social conformity had their place, the only yardstick left is that of success, popularity, and influence, together with the subject's eagerness to succeed through uninhibited identification with anything that exercises authoritarian strength in reality. No *ideal* authority, be it religious, moral, or philosophical, is accepted for its own sake; only what is, is recognized" (Horkheimer, 1949, p. 369, italics added).

The authors then went on to speculate that in our century political and military leaders—and other celebrities—have often managed to usurp the place vacated by the socially enfeebled father and present themselves as powerful models worthy of loyalty and emulation. With this account the authors intended to offer a partial explanation of the rise of mass society and totalitarianism.

This theory of society relates the moral makeup of the individual and his regard for political, moral, and religious authority to changes in the form and function of the family, and it relates the role of the family to historical changes in Western society during the last century and a half. The family is seen as creating precisely the sorts of nimbly adapting individuals required by democratic as well as totalitarian mass societies and corporate states: pliant employees, suggestible and eager consumers, patient citizens.

What appealed to me in this view is that personal development and relationships are seen as specific to contemporary societal conditions. The intimacies of family life are shown to be penetrated and shaped by history writ large. One no longer thinks of the family as the individual's most decisive background. Rather, it is the society in its particular historical form that represents the background of individual *and* family. This seemed important. Not only is man not an island unto himself, but the family, too, is not isolated from the society. You may say that this insight is old hat. But how often do social scientists and even clinicians really take it into account in their scholarship or their interventions? At any rate, other authors soon offered similar views (Marcuse, 1970; Lasch, 1979; Sennett, 1977; Benjamin, 1988).

These ideas have helped me over the years. As a college professor trying to foster critical thinking, I have had the emotional, intellectual, and ethical character of today's students on my mind quite often. But as I try to get clarity about family, authority, and individuation, I want something more, and for this I cannot help consulting my own experience occasionally. Perhaps you agree with me that nothing beats personal narratives when it comes to filling in the gaps in theory. One question interested me in particular about these theories that sought to explain individual lives in terms of large historical forces: How do the facts of social life enter the individual's horizon? How do social forces trickle down into personal life experiences? The story I decided to tell you is meaningful to me and will, I hope, be interesting to you because it is informative about the pathways by which the general becomes particular. In doing so, it brings out an unexpected side of the problem of disfranchised fathers and their sons (and daughters). What I am about to relate does not contradict the theories of Horkheimer and his colleagues, but it adds complicating dimensions.

In 1938, two years after these ideas saw the light of day in Paris, my parents and I left Vienna, masking our escape as an afternoon stroll so as to avoid the suspicions of Nazi spies lurking around street corners. We spent the next ten years as exiles in Switzerland. If you have been attentive to recent exposés, you know that the Swiss did not dispense to refugees the elaborate hospitality they shower on tourists. The citizens of Switzerland wished to be secure against job competition from refugees. Therefore, all of these were denied the right to earn a living and depended for their survival on whatever personal assets they managed to bring with them or on privately organized charity, for instance, by the Swiss Jewish community. You can well imagine that as a result we lived in straitened circumstances. While my father was idled against his will and temperament, my mother, who had had a live-in maid in Vienna, was suddenly thrust into the role of homemaker and had to find ways to make the three of us as comfortable as possible on a skimpy allowance.

Our home in Vienna had been open to friends and visitors, social gatherings, and chamber music soirees. My father had begun his legal career in a firm that counted the Imperial Court among its occasional clients. "Papa, did you ever speak to the Kaiser?" I once asked him. He later developed his own law practice patronized by a distinguished clientele including members of the nobility.

Life in Zurich proved to be quite a change. There were tens of thousands of Jewish refugees living in Switzerland during the war, from many countries and all walks of life. They were not all experiencing the same socioeconomic decline that we were, but they were all idled by decree, demoralized, and in a sort of suspended animation. My family was lucky in one respect. Soon after our arrival we were befriended by a wealthy family of Swiss Jews who became our very close companions and most generous benefactors. The valor of Swiss Jews in supporting the refugees has yet to be fully recorded.

Now that I have set the general stage for you, you will want to know how these circumstances affected me in relation to "paternal

authority and individuation" and what was the encounter that proved
to be important enough to tell you about today. After all, if the theoretical view I have just summarized is valid, then my father's life situation during the years in which I grew up would have had a devastating effect on me. So you would want to know how I saw him. How did
I evaluate him as a model? Let me make clear what I saw him doing
week after week.

He spent some time each day reading the newspapers in cafés,
studying foreign languages—as many as possible: you never knew to
what part of the world you would have to emigrate once the shooting
was done—rehearsing with a Jewish men's amateur chorus, taking
technical skills courses of the kind we associate with community col-
leges today—again, in preparation for a possible career change in
who knows what corner of the world—or speculating with other refugees who were equally at loose ends about the progress and likely end
of the war. Many of these acquaintances attributed great perspicacity
to my father in these matters: "What do you think, Herr Doktor? How
much longer will it go on?" Even his shrugs and evasions were taken
as significant—emblems of a general perplexity.

According to social thinkers who regard a man's occupational engagement as decisive for his overall psychosocial identity, this picture of my father and the conditions of our existence in Zurich might
be deemed injurious to my own development. To see no clear purpose
in one's father's existence, to have no estimate of what his capacities
and limits are in the accomplishment of socially and personally
meaningful tasks, to see no pattern of satisfaction in his pursuits could
cause a son to turn away and look elsewhere for discipline and moral
strength—or, even worse, to fall prey to self-doubt and cynicism.

You can see that this sort of situation challenges many people today. Their parents are kept from realizing their talents and the promise of their education because they have been politically or economically displaced. What confidence in their world and in the worth of
human potential can children absorb from parents who were stopped
from realizing their own futures by economic pressures or by an exo-
dus necessitated by political or ethnic totalitarianism? In fact, a heap
of evidence shows that parents' stressful experiences, such as economic pressures, have deleterious effects on their adolescent children's development and result in aggressive moods and behavior, depression, alcoholism, and the like (e.g., Brownfield, 1987; Ge et al.,

1992). You might suppose that not much good could have come to me from the sense of futility and the social decline experienced by my parents—at least not if our theories are any guide.

However, I can tell you that my experience was different. The theorists, you see, thinking of paternal authority as depending on the visible workaday practice of an occupation and on the visible exercise of a man's values and standards in the pursuit of this occupation, overlooked what you and I know so well, namely that human beings are the makers of stories and indeed the vehicles of their own histories. My father managed to keep his former pride and standards alive through a nostalgia openly practiced. He told tales of his former work, of his clients, of sojourns on the estate of a baron who had summoned him for his advice in a business matter. He spoke to me proudly, even boastfully, of the school grades he received when he was my age. He reminisced about his piano and violin studies, his voice recitals, the social hubbub of Viennese society, the cultural life of the city, and the like. Notwithstanding our outward privations, he feasted— and I through him—on a wealth of stories. And he could still help me with inverse proportions, plane geometry, French irregular verbs, and translations from the Latin. The glory of *his* past was in *my* present. The Royal and Imperial State Court was in session in our shabby little apartment. Take my metaphor literally. My father expected a lot from me—good grades, flawless violin playing, polished shoes, untiring application, and impeccable manners in all my dealings with things and people. In most things he was a model of what he demanded from me.

The effect of his actual idleness on me was, as you can see, precisely the opposite of what the theories would lead one to expect. I was confronted with an authority whose power seemed boundless. I never saw him stumped by a task, never bested by a superior rival. There were no meaningful tasks or rivals. Perhaps opportunities existed, even in his unemployed existence, to take up risky challenges, tasks that might defeat him—perhaps nothing more than a game of chess with a worthy opponent. But I never saw him take up such a challenge. Perhaps he was too discouraged about his fate to take chances on further defeats and simply avoided them. At any rate, there were times when his daunting figure as model and mentor worried and encumbered my own school performance. In short, during my childhood and early youth I saw no limit to his strength—at least for a while.

I suppose what this shows is that a father's way of dealing with his "socially conditioned weakness" is what matters to the son more than the weakness as such. Mine happened to deal with it in a way that magnified his moral relevance. Others may do so in ways that are disspiriting to their sons. Dear Bob, I am afraid you and your readers have lost all patience with me for dwelling so long on the context—first the context of the act of telling about the incident and now the context of my life at the time of the incident. The fact is that the incident itself is far from dramatic, and anyone who approaches it with suspense will almost surely be disappointed. Great events—great loves, great hatreds, great losses, great reunions—these are the bread and butter of much fiction. But lives are often shaped by small events that could not, by themselves, command any reader's interest and that derive their great meaning solely or largely from the context. So, I finally come to the immediate circumstances of the incident.

My parents' intellectual and social polish had opened doors for them to a segment of Zurich's prewar Jewish community—mostly Eastern Europeans who had come there in the first two decades of the century, looking for and often finding a better life than the one they had under the czar. As I said earlier, these people did a great deal to support those of us who had fled Nazism. Although my family associated with these "natives" socially, it was clear all around that we were refugees and thus their beneficiaries. Fund-raising was a constant preoccupation in these circles, and some of it was done in several-times-a-year fancy balls, complete with elegant clothes, home-baked tortes, lotteries, auctions, a dance band, and artistic presentations. The Jewish men's chorus or the Jewish dramatic society might put on a concert or a play; a children's chorus might delight or amuse the parents; a violin-piano duet might play a piece or two. On the occasion I have in mind—this was on a Sunday afternoon and I was eleven or twelve years old—a group of children and adults was about to put on a couple of choreographed Yiddish musical sketches with costumes and scenery. I can't remember the name of the first of these on the program, but the second was called "Die Mashke" ("The Liquor").

I picture it clearly. The musical accompaniment on such occasions has almost always been provided by a chubby, lively man named

Solly, who sits at the piano just below the stage. However, this afternoon it is my father who is slated to accompany the two pageants. This is his debut, and to me it is an extraordinary coup and perhaps the first of many equally exciting opportunities for him to shine in public. I have been at some of the rehearsals and know that he is easily Solly's equal at the keyboard. For him—and therefore also for me—the visible contribution to the life of the community and the approval this will probably bring will surely be very gratifying, given our normal sense of futility and dependency during these years.

A hundred or so people are comfortably chatting over coffee and cake in the social hall this afternoon, all of them used to spending countless such afternoons and evenings together in one another's company. It is a cozy group of people, feeling relatively secure in this seemingly safe little island of a country in the middle of a sea of death.

While the cups and forks are clinking in the hall, there is great excitement on the other side of the velvet curtain. The sets are up, the performers in place—adult actors' nervousness better contained than children's. I am standing in the wings, a privileged position for a non-participant with no other distinction than his pride in being the accompanist's son. The lights have just been dimmed. Solly, today filling the role of stage manager, is hushing the players. There's the signal. Curtain up. Downbeat of the overture at the piano.

But I feel vaguely uneasy as I hear the first few chords. And then: "No, no, that's 'Die Mashke'!" Solly strides diagonally across the open stage toward Papa, his arms outstretched wide in consternation. "That's 'Die Mashke'!" Papa stops playing. Oh my God! Everything stops. Papa has begun the wrong overture. "Die Mashke" is scheduled to be the second piece on the program.

There you have it. This is the image I remember most clearly today—Solly's agitated and indignant emergence from the wings in violation of all theater etiquette, breaking the aesthetic illusion and the audience's suspense, and ruining the whole fairy tale. He might as well have announced that a fire had broken out.

I cringed. I felt the incident as a humiliation. I, who had just been allowed backstage as though the accompanist's qualifications somehow included me, was now mortified by the same inclusion. How could he be so careless as to play the wrong piece?

But it seems the agony was mine alone. Papa appeared unfazed, opened the other score, and played the accompaniment flawlessly. "Die Mashke," too, was a total success, and everyone had a marvelous time.

I mulled over this new wrinkle in the otherwise oh-so-smooth countenance of my father. Yes, he had limits. Yes, his performance, too, not only mine, could on occasion be impaired by nervousness. He, too, was finite, human, fallible.

I hardly dared look at him after the show. I did not wish to make his excruciating lapse an explicit theme between us. Neither could I ignore it; it lay upon me heavily—at least for a while. But he and I soon returned to our old relationship. It was to be understood that his was an inconsequential little mishap and that I was not to take it as license to become careless in my schoolwork.

You may wonder if this experience steered my development in a new direction. Wasn't this exactly what a young boy needed to give him the courage to explore life? Yes, of course. But bear in mind that a turning point is only a point. Anyone who has studied lives knows that an experience such as this becomes part of a sequence. It retroactively transforms what came before, putting it, as we say, in a new light. It also resets the stage for what comes later. New incidents gain meaning that they might not otherwise have had. I cannot guarantee that this was the first time I ever saw shadows cast on the paternal glory. Painful as it was, this event may have done no more than to confirm prior hints of his imperfection. But precisely because it was painful, it became a reference point. It may have helped me to sort out ambiguities in my perception of my father. It may also have desensitized me to the modesty of his employments after we settled in the United States.

I told you this story, Bob, to illustrate that even though the reality of what a man is and does is of undeniable consequence in shaping a son's sense of the world's and his own possibilities, there are often elapsed realities that a man recalls and envisioned futures that he may conjure with. Such reminiscences and vistas of hope as well as the family myths that may preside over several generations—these all can override the factual present, as Erik Erikson has shown so memorably (Erikson, 1968). The *activity* and consequences of storytelling are, if anything, even more neglected in the study of lives than the narrative *method* exhibited in this volume.

I would not want your readers to suppose that I have dismissed Horkheimer's and Marcuse's social-psychological or rather societal-psychological perspective on the development of human individuality. My story suggests only that it has its limitations—just as my late father did. But it is also a perspective whose extraordinary power I hold in high esteem—as I did his.

There you have it, Bob, my story and the story of my story. Small as it is, it is now yours to tell and then your readers'. I like that, and my father, that great raconteur, would have liked it too.

Best wishes to you always, and to Ted.

George

REFERENCES

Benjamin, J. (1988). *The bonds of love: Psychoanalysis, feminism, and the problem of domination.* New York: Pantheon.

Brownfield, D. (1987). Father-son relationships and violent behavior. *Deviant Behavior 8*(1): 65-78.

Erikson, E. H. (1968). Foundations in observation. In *Identity: Youth and crisis.* (pp. 44-90). New York: Norton.

Ge, X., Conger, R. D., Lorenz, F., Elder, G.H. (1992). Linking family economic hardship to adolescent distress. *Journal of Research on Adolescence 2*(4): 351-378.

Horkheimer, M. (1949). Authoritarianism and the family today. In R. Anshen (Ed.), *The family: Its function and destiny.* (pp. 359-374). New York: Harper.

Institut für Sozialforschung (Frankfurt am Main, Germany). (1936). *Studien über Autorität und Familie: Forschungsberichte aus dem Institut für Sozialforschung.* Paris: Alcan.

Lasch, C. (1979). *The culture of narcissism: American life in an age of diminishing expectations.* New York: Warner.

Marcuse, H. (1970). The obsolescence of the Freudian concept of man. In *Five lectures; Psychoanalysis, politics, and utopia.* Boston: Beacon.

Sennett, R. (1977). *The fall of public man.* New York: Knopf.

Epilogue

Theodore R. Sarbin
Robert J. Pellegrini

The commentaries in Chapter 2 attempted to highlight certain features of the seventeen stories. The recognition of the rendered character of personal narratives notwithstanding, the stories told provide support for the notion that we live in a story-shaped world. Even authors' rememberings—the raw materials for the texts—are products of commerce with events that with the aid of imagination have been given form through the process of storytelling. The editors of this collection, after reading and rereading each contribution, are more convinced than ever of the importance of poesis in human affairs. That is to say, the raw material of our socialization, our strivings, our disappointments, are not so much in the movements made or the sounds uttered as in the poetic skills that make possible the joining of movements and sounds into a story form. These particular father-son narratives reflect a wide range of variation in story making. Explicit in many, and implicit in the others, is a *motif*—the longing for continuity. It is quite possible that what makes us human is the ability to create stories that serve to connect the generations.

Although we were able to sort the stories into themes, it is important to note that we did not find it useful to interpret the stories as variations of a single prototype, such as the Oedipus myth as advocated by a generation of Freudian authors, or the hero myth as reflected in the writings of Campbell. The exigencies of social life require a large library of plots to make intelligible human actions. Such a library is necessary to take into account variations in historical time and place and other contexts in which such human actions occur.

The goal here was *not* to write a book about father-son relationships from the standpoint of conventional social-scientific concepts, methodology, and data, with some obligatory practical generalizations about fathering or "soning" derived as inferences based on the content thus presented. Rather, the objective was to explore the heart and soul nature of father-son relationships by means of autobiographical reconstructions of critical incident experiences in men's lives. The richness, depth, and variety of expression characteristic of the essays that resulted from this novel application of the narrative approach are seen as validating (a) the intensity of personal involvement, which can be evoked *as much in the teller* as in those to whom stories are told; and (b) the potential utility and versatility of the narrative as a still largely underrepresented method for investigating psychosocial development.

Index

Order Your Own Copy of
This Important Book for Your Personal Library!

BETWEEN FATHERS AND SONS
Critical Incident Narratives in the Development
of Men's Lives

_____in hardbound at $49.95 (ISBN: 0-7890-1511-0)

_____in softbound at $24.95 (ISBN: 0-7890-1512-9)

COST OF BOOKS_____

OUTSIDE USA/CANADA/
MEXICO: ADD 20%____

POSTAGE & HANDLING_____
(US: $4.00 for first book & $1.50
for each additional book)
Outside US: $5.00 for first book
& $2.00 for each additional book)

SUBTOTAL_____

in Canada: add 7% GST____

STATE TAX____
(NY, OH & MIN residents, please
add appropriate local sales tax)

FINAL TOTAL____
(If paying in Canadian funds,
convert using the current
exchange rate, UNESCO
coupons welcome.)

❑ **BILL ME LATER:** ($5 service charge will be added)
(Bill-me option is good on US/Canada/Mexico orders only;
not good to jobbers, wholesalers, or subscription agencies.)

❑ Check here if billing address is different from
shipping address and attach purchase order and
billing address information.

Signature_____

❑ **PAYMENT ENCLOSED: $_____**

❑ **PLEASE CHARGE TO MY CREDIT CARD.**

❑ Visa ❑ MasterCard ❑ AmEx ❑ Discover
❑ Diner's Club ❑ Eurocard ❑ JCB

Account #_____

Exp. Date_____

Signature_____

Prices in US dollars and subject to change without notice.

NAME_____

INSTITUTION_____

ADDRESS_____

CITY_____

STATE/ZIP_____

COUNTRY_____ COUNTY (NY residents only)_____

TEL_____ FAX_____

E-MAIL_____

May we use your e-mail address for confirmations and other types of information? ❑ Yes ❑ No
We appreciate receiving your e-mail address and fax number. Haworth would like to e-mail or fax special
discount offers to you, as a preferred customer. **We will never share, rent, or exchange your e-mail address
or fax number.** We regard such actions as an invasion of your privacy.

Order From Your Local Bookstore or Directly From
The Haworth Press, Inc.
10 Alice Street, Binghamton, New York 13904-1580 • USA
TELEPHONE: 1-800-HAWORTH (1-800-429-6784) / Outside US/Canada: (607) 722-5857
FAX: 1-800-895-0582 / Outside US/Canada: (607) 722-6362
E-mail: getinfo@haworthpressinc.com
PLEASE PHOTOCOPY THIS FORM FOR YOUR PERSONAL USE.
www.HaworthPress.com

BOF00